500 POPULAR

SHRUBS & TREES

FOR AMERICAN GARDENERS

BARRON'S

First United States of America edition published in 1999
by Barron's Educational Series, Inc.
Adapted from *500 Popular Shrubs & Trees for Australian Gardeners*.
© Copyright 1998 by Random House Australia.
Photo Library © Copyright 1998 by Random House Australia.

Editor   Loretta Barnard

Consultants Geoff Bryant
               Dean Murakami
               Tony Rodd

Page Layout Joy Eckermann

All inquiries should be addressed to:
Barron's Educational Series Inc.
250 Wireless Boulevard
Hauppauge, NY 112788
http://www.barronseduc.com

International Standard Book Number 0-7641-1178-7
Library of Congress Catalog Card Number 99-72098

Printed in Hong Kong by Sing Cheong Printing Co. Ltd
987654321

CONTENTS

Introduction

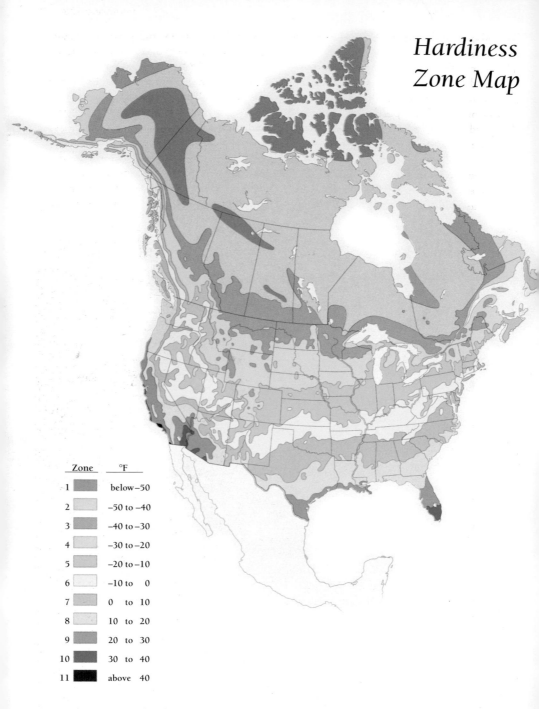

Hardiness Zone Map

Zone	°F
1	below −50
2	−50 to −40
3	−40 to −30
4	−30 to −20
5	−20 to −10
6	−10 to 0
7	0 to 10
8	10 to 20
9	20 to 30
10	30 to 40
11	above 40

Hardiness zones are based on
the average annual minimum
temperature for each zone.

Just about every garden has at least one or two trees, and of course many shrubs. These are fundamental to the structure of a garden. They provide shade, shelter and privacy; and can be used as windbreaks or to define a particular area of the garden; or they can be planted in containers and placed indoors or outside.

The botanical distinction that trees have one main stem, shrubs several is not always helpful horticulturally, so we have followed the usual gardener's rule of thumb that a shrub grows less than about 15 or 18 ft (5 or 6 m) tall. But note that some genera contain both trees and shrubs. 'Subshrubs' have been excluded from this book, so you won't find such well-known garden plants as geraniums and marguerite daisies here.

Even so, the 500 shrubs and trees in this book present the gardener with a wide choice—a choice which is increasing all the time, for the world's trees and

The glorious pink blooms of *Prunus serrulata* make this a truly magnificent spring garden.

Acer species are very effective bird-attracting plants.

shrubs have not yet all been discovered, named and introduced. For example, in the last two decades at least half-a-dozen *Pinus* species, hitherto unknown, have come to light in the mountains of Mexico. South Africa is a rich area for new discoveries, including members of the protea family and *Erica* species, and in China 'new' maples, magnolias and camellias still come to light.

Native or exotic?

When planning your garden, consider the balance of exotic and native species. Two extreme views have developed about native plants. At one extreme is the view that natives are scraggy, sparse plants with specialized growing requirements that do not fit properly into a well-planned suburban garden. At the other extreme is the view that only native plants are appropriate for Ameri-

can gardens and that exotic plants should be regarded as dangerous invaders. But most gardeners are happy to grow both natives and exotics, treating every species on its merits as a garden plant regardless of its origins.

One important factor to remember when planting natives is the risk of fire. Some natives are highly flammable plants and care must be taken not to plant too many of them too close to your house.

Native plants require less maintenance and in particular less watering than exotics, though this depends on selection of species. Many natives are adapted to soils that lack the major plant nutrients such as phosphorus and nitrogen, and so will give good results in poor soil.

Native plants also attract native fauna, especially birds, with the fruit, seeds and nectar they produce. Many smaller native birds are also primarily insectivorous, and these seem to be more plentiful in gardens in which native trees and shrubs predominate.

It is also important to look at the difference in climate between a plant's native region and the places where gardeners want to grow them. Choose natives that are suited to your climate, soils and cultural habits.

There is a long history of plants being introduced for ornament and becoming serious pests, in many cases spreading out from gardens and invading native vegetation. A watch should always be kept on trees and shrubs with small berry-like fruit or fleshy seeds as these are the kinds most readily dispersed by birds.

Another motive for growing some natives is the feeling that one may be helping to save a species from imminent extinction. The Western Australian *Grevillea scapigera* was believed extinct but was then found surviving in an enthusiast's garden and has since been distributed by nurseries.

It would be wrong, however, if in our enthusiasm for native plants, we ignored the advantages of exotics. Natives are not always the best choice of plants. There are many non-native trees and shrubs that are extremely well-suited for various gardening conditions. Many exotics perform well, and can often be a better choice for your landscaping needs and aesthetic vision.

A blend of native and non-native plants works well for most gardens.

Don't feel restricted in your use of native plants. They fit in well in any garden design and are very adaptable with regard to climate, soil type and moisture levels. They can be used in the same ways as their exotic cousins and combine well with them.

Evergreen or deciduous?

Many new gardeners prefer evergreens, thinking that year-round foliage equals year-round interest, but deciduous plants have much to offer. They are no less attractive or more demanding than evergreens and their constantly changing appearance adds vitality and interest.

Often there will be no need for a conscious choice between evergreen and deciduous. If you want rhododendrons, most will be evergreen; hydrangeas, however, will largely be deciduous. When you have a choice, consider how foliage retention will affect that part of your garden. Bulky evergreens take up considerable space and though they have leaves throughout the year they may flower only briefly. Deciduous plants may be just as large and as fleeting in their flowering but they have a more open feel and allow in

The leaves of the silver birch turn a brilliant gold in autumn.

more light in winter. If you need the bulk and foliage as a filler, a windbreak or to disguise something unattractive, opt for the rhododendron or camellia, and don't forget the deciduous alternative, such as a deciduous azalea or a magnolia.

Some evergreen and most deciduous plants offer changing foliage color in autumn. Of course, deciduous plants offer much more striking changes in fall foliage color. Some deciduous plants with the most spectacular fall color include maples, *Enkianthos* and *Liquidamber*.

Not all deciduous plants lose their leaves to cold. Many tropical species become bare during the dry season when there is not enough soil moisture to support foliage on a plant. If you want 'green' trees and shrubs under such conditions, it may be best to select

The bracts of *Euphorbia pulcherrima* are a vibrant red.

evergreen species that will not lose their foliage under drought conditions. This will save you the difficult extra watering efforts of trying to 'work against nature' in order to retain the leaves of those deciduous plants.

Fast-growing or slow-growing?

The question of how fast the species grows can be critical. Why plant a tree which will take 30 years to show its full beauty if we know that we may be moving house in five years?

With fast growers the problem is twofold. On the one hand, they may be short lived, for example acacias and poplars. On the other hand, they may be fast because they are in a hurry to grow big, like willows and honey locusts. Often, this fast growth is supported by rampaging root systems that wreak havoc on any drains or foundations that get in their way. This is fine in a large garden, but think carefully about them in a suburban garden.

Some of the fastest-growing trees
Acacia baileyana
Cupressocyparis × leylandii
Sequoia sempervirens
Schinus molle
Taxodium mucronatum

Some of the fastest-growing shrubs
Callistemon citrintus
Choisya ternata
Escallonia × exoniensis
Grewia occidentalis
Tibouchina urvillea

Flowers, fruit, foliage

While they tend to be the most spectacular feature, do not think in terms of flowers alone. The appeal of a plant rarely lies in just one part of it, rather it is the sum of many aspects and it pays to consider all a plant has to offer when making a selection.

Choosing a plant usually comes down to four main points: climatic suitability, size, color and season. Having decided your size requirements and determined your climatic limitations, think about how plant color varies with the seasons. First there is the bud, then the flower followed by the fruit or seed pods, and finally the seeds. The leaves too are constantly changing: bright fresh growth darkens as it matures then changes color and dries as it ages and falls. Then there are the selected variegated and colored foliage forms that offer a little additional foliage color and contrast.

Some of the most boldly foliaged
Acalypha wilkesiana
Agave americana
Brahea armata
Fatsia japonica
Leucadendron argenteum
Rhododendron sinogrande
Schefflera actinophylla
Tetrapanax papyifer

Growing conditions and plant location affect the amount and intensity of color. Sunny positions yield more flowers and fruit, and brighter foliage colors, especially the yellow and red tones. Shade produces fewer flowers and fruit but larger leaves with the emphasis on lush greens. Why think of roses as just flowers when the brilliant red hips may be just as spectacular? Don't consider crab apples only for their fruit—they have magnificent spring flowers and some offer brilliant autumn foliage. Southern and other warm area gardeners should pay particular attention to choosing their plants to spread the flowers over as long a season as possible.

Some of the best for autumn color
Acer rubrum
Acer saccharum
Cotinus coggygria
Enkianthus campanulatus
Gingko biloba
Larix decidua
Liquidambar styraciflua
Quercus coccinea
Taxodium distichum

Some of the most colorful flowers
Abelia
Buddleia
Camellia
Choisya ternata
Daphne
Escallonia
Hibiscus
Nerium oleander
Weigelia

Some of the best for cut flowers
Calluna
Camellia
Forsythia
Gardenia
Genista
Hydrangea
Paeonia
Photinia
Rhododendron
Viburnum

Sculptural effects
Some plants provide greater design opportunities than others. The bold outlines of yuccas, agaves, saguaro and other large succulents and cacti are truly architectural plants. Palms, billowing shrubs and grasses flex with the wind; their effect is softer, they blend with the garden, respond to the elements and are sculptural rather than architectural. Yet others are tactile and demand to be touched.

Striking flowers and foliage make *Aloe marlothii* a truly stunning architectural plant.

Careful selection of textures and forms can lead to an interesting garden even with just a few varieties. For example conifers offer a huge range of textures and shapes — soft, billowy, stiff, arching, erect.

Shape and texture combined with plant type can create the feeling of a particular location. Cacti and succulents say desert wherever they are planted, while Japan comes to mind when we see moss-covered rocks and evergreen azaleas. The effect is due as much to the plant shapes — angular and sharp for the desert, rounded and soft for the Japanese effect — as any other aspect.

So choose plants with an appearance that appeals to you, but don't forget that they have to blend. This is a key feature that is missing from many urban gardens, which are often a jumble of mismatched shrubs and trees. Combining similar forms appropriately and knowing when to break up the lines brings out the sculptor in any gardener.

Attracting birds

Birds add life and vitality to a garden. While the range of birds that will visit your garden varies greatly from place to place, the strategies used to attract them are much the same anywhere. All birds need water for drinking and bathing. A small pond or a bird bath will guarantee a regular crowd of visitors. Keep the water level very shallow; most bird baths are gradually sloping bowls and birds feel comfortable with them. Ponds, however, can be too deep or move too sharply from shallow water to deep water. Add a few rocks and flat stones to make a shallow bath within the pond, and keep the bathing area clear of foliage as birds will not settle for long if they feel something may be lurking in wait for them.

Garden birds fall into two main categories: solid food feeders such as finches, that are satisfied with bird seed, soft fruits and grain, and nectar feeders like hummingbirds, which are a little more difficult to cater for. Fast-growing plants with plenty of nectar include kowhai *(Sophora tetraptera)*, *Catalpa speciosa*, *Weigela florida*, banksias, buddleias and *Cantua* species.

Providing nesting sites will help to maintain a year-round bird population. Large, densely foliaged shrubs and trees offer plenty of natural nesting opportunities and you could also consider nest boxes or even a dovecote.

Some of the best bird-attracting shrubs and trees

Acer
Berberis
Cotoneaster
Mahonia
Morus

THE CULTIVATION OF SHRUBS & TREES
The importance of climate

Trees and shrubs are usually grown outdoors, and some knowledge of the kind of climate and conditions under which they grow is desirable—both in choosing the appropriate kinds to grow, and in giving an idea how best to deploy them in design. A design that reflects the local ecology is likely to be both easier to look after and to have that indefinable sense of belonging to its place that has always been one of the hallmarks of a fine garden.

Broadly, there are four main climate zones—cold, cool, warm and hot. However, such factors as altitude or the closeness of the ocean or large lake can make a great difference to the climate—bathed by the Gulf stream, the British Isles have a milder climate than parts of the United States which lie much closer to the Equator. The hardiness zone map on page 6 is a very useful guide to what will and will not grow in your area.

Eucalyptus niphophila thrives in cool mountain areas.

Cold climates (Zones 1 to 4)

Cold climates are those where the winters are long and frosty, with the ground frequently covered with snow, and where summer is apt to both arrive and leave quite suddenly. While it is there, it can be surprisingly hot. Such places as Canada, Scandinavia, Central Europe, Russia, the northern parts of China and the New England and Rocky Mountain states, as well as much of the Midwest of the USA have cold climates. Conifers, the hardiest deciduous trees and dwarf shrubs dominate this climate.

Cool climates (Zones 5 to 7)

Cool climates, or 'cool-temperate' zones have frost and maybe snow in winter, but not such intense cold. Spring and autumn are clearly marked, and sum-
mers are longer, though not necessarily hotter, than in the cold zones. Such climates include the British Isles, most of France, the north of Japan, much of China, the Pacific Northwest and the Mideastern states of the USA, and parts of southern Africa and South America. Such mountainous regions as the Himalayas might also be included.

Deciduous shrubs and trees dominate many of the cool regions, and the conifers of the cold regions are also represented. The cool zones are rich in flowering shrubs, most of them deciduous, that now play a leading role in temperate-climate garden design—look at the lilac, forsythia, weigelas, deciduous azaleas and roses.

Warm climates (Zones 8 to 10)

Warm climates, or warm-temperate and subtropical zones, include those of California, the Mediterranean countries, the Deep South and Gulf states of the USA, those of the Middle East and Kashmir; the southern parts of China and Japan; most of Australia and most of southern Africa. Here winters are mild; though there may be occasional

The rainforest floor supports an amazing diversity of species.

Drought-resistant shrubs, like *Cistus*, often bloom over a long season.

frosts, they are rarely severe or prolonged. Summers can be quite hot and long, and spring and autumn often rather short.

Warm climates are a kind of transition zone between those where winter is cold enough to bring the growth of trees to a stop and the hot climates with their year-round summers. Plants tend to keep their leaves all year, and the forests are dominated by evergreen hardwood trees and shrubs. Yet there are some deciduous species too. Surprisingly, the conifers reappear in many places too, but here their problem is drought, and they are as adapted to resist warm dry seasons as they are frigid dry ones.

Some of the most drought-tolerant plants
Brahea
Cistus
Dodonacea
Grevillea
Nerium oleander

Hot climates (Zones 11 to 12)
In hot climates, frost is unknown, and there is sufficient warmth, rainfall permitting, for plants to grow throughout the year. Except for the highest uplands, every country within the tropics is included, though some places outside those boundaries can be considered 'hot' also, including the southern parts of Florida, North Africa, much of Saudi Arabia, central Australia, and parts of southern Africa.

One of the striking things about tropical gardens is the magnificence of the flowering trees. No temperate tree can approach the splendour of the royal poinciana, *Delonix regia* — or *el arbol del fuego*, the tree of fire — or the Indian laburnum *(Cassia fistula)* or the jacaranda: one scarlet, one gold, one blue, each arrayed with myriad flowers in its season.

Palms, which dispense with branches entirely, relying on the enormous size of their leaves to supply them with their crowns, are also favorite garden plants in hot climates.

Within the tropics there is often a sharp division of the year into two seasons, the wet and the dry — a 'monsoon' climate. Here we find deciduous trees again, but this time bare in the dry season; shedding their leaves to conserve moisture. They still put on a dazzling show of flowers; indeed sometimes they flower on bare branches, the leaves following as the flowers fade. The jacaranda is a typical example.

Planning the garden
However you conceive your garden, trees are indispensable. Longest lived of

plants, they will be there to give shape to the garden and shelter to the house long after more ephemeral plants and features, even the house itself, have been replaced. They anchor it in time; a house without its protecting trees may be fine architecture but it is difficult to think of it as home. It is not for nothing that we speak of 'putting down roots'.

A garden needs to be planned carefully. Consider privacy and shelter. Trees and shrubs create the shade and break the wind (cold in winter, drying in summer); they shape the spaces; they block out undesirable views like the neighbors' washing and frame desirable ones, including the view of your house from the street.

There is no need for your plans to be works of art: sheets of butcher's paper and marker pens are all the tools many professionals use to stimulate their thinking. Sketch in color; use dark green circles for evergreens, light green ones for deciduous trees, pink or gray for paving, and so on. Don't rush. Allow yourself to have second thoughts: all designers do.

In your planning, consider any existing trees. If so, take great care. Mature trees hate changes to their environment, especially having the level of the soil around their roots altered. Lower it, and you expose the roots to air and dryness; raise it, and they will suffocate. If the tree is standing higher than the rest of the garden will be, you need to contain the area of its roots (roughly that beneath the spread of its branches) with a retaining wall of some kind, which may become an attractive feature. If you want to raise the level, you can either build a timber deck, so the natural ground level beneath is left unaltered; or you can fill with earth, after placing a conical 'breathing layer'

of stones over the roots. This only needs to be a stone or two deep at the edge of the root system, but at the trunk it must reach to the full depth of the fill and be exposed—the effect is of the tree standing in a collar of stones—so the air can get in. Just how far this will allow you to raise the soil depends on the tree, and you should seek the advice of an expert arboriculturalist before you do anything. Make sure your builder neither drives heavy equipment over the tree's roots nor stockpiles heavy materials there. Either will compact the soil and the roots will suffocate.

Watch what sort of gardening you do beneath your tree. In dry climates, be sure you don't suddenly give your tree an artificial rainfall greater than it has

Vision and patience can turn your garden into a private retreat.

With careful planning, your garden can be colorful for much of the year.

been used to. Many a centuries-old indigenous tree has succumbed to root rot from having a sprinkled lawn created at its feet. (Either pave, or plant groundcovers or shrubs which don't need watering.)

Some of the best for poorly-drained soil
Aronia arbutifolia
Cornus stolonifera
Magnolia grandiflora
Salix babylonica
Thuja occidentalis

5 great coastal plants
Aronia arbutifolia
Coprosma repens
Lagunaria patersonia
Metrosideros excelsa
Pittosporum tobira

Choosing the shrubs & trees
Most trees are not particularly fussy about soil. Poor drainage is the most common problem and laying ground drains can ameliorate this; or you can choose species that like wet feet. Also important is the amount of lime in the soil, that is, whether it is classed as acid or alkaline. Most trees and shrubs can grow in a range of soil pH. However, most do grow best in slightly acidic conditions of about 6.2–6.8. Some

ericaceous plants prefer even more acidic soil conditions to thrive. These plants include warm and cool climate rhododendrons, camellias, azaleas, heathers and the Chilean fire trees (*Embothrium coccineus*).

As climate tolerance is vitally important, choose species that are native to your climate zone or most often planted there. You can try growing species from the climate zones either side of your own. However, if you expect frost each winter, the hot-climate species are not for you. They have evolved no resistance to it, and it will kill them. Equally important is rainfall. You can water a young tree, but its roots may eventually go too deep for the hose.

Shrubs are a little more flexible. You can create a warmer microclimate by planting a tender species against a sunny wall, and you can give it extra assistance with the hose should the rain fail it. Still, it is not wise to make species that need extra care the backbone of your plantings, even if they always seem to be the most beautiful!

The best way to see which species do well in your area is to take a tour of the neighborhood, looking at other people's gardens. Your local nursery will be able to give you good advice. Do your homework and know just what you are looking for. Don't be afraid to ask if a suggested plant has any problems like susceptibility to mildew or greedy roots.

Remember that nurseries only rarely have mature specimens of their selections to show you. The local botanic garden is the place to go for that; though here you may well encounter a specimen planted 100 years ago—and you don't have that much time to wait! Refer to the table at the end of this book for an estimate of how big you can expect each species to be at different ages, given the

A formal hedge such as this one at Sissinghurst Castle in England, requires regular trimming.

sort of growing conditions it likes. Spacing is also important. The usual recommendation is that trees should be spaced so that they only just touch when they reach maturity, so consider the spread as well as the height of large trees.

Don't forget that when you plant a tree you have a legally enforceable duty of care for public safety, and your trees' limbs or aggressive roots should not encroach on neighboring properties. If they do, your neighbors may have the right to trim the trees back to the boundary. Such arbitrary pruning is not good for neighborhood relations; it is far better if you and your neighbors coordinate your tree planting to the benefit of all and the beautification of the area.

THE USES OF SHRUBS & TREES
Shade, shelter & privacy

Trees can help to make a house more pleasant to live in by allowing in the sun in winter and blocking it out in summer. In the northern hemisphere, the sunny side is the south. Most houses are situated so the most important rooms face the sun, with ample glass to allow sunlight to enter. Of course, this is fine in winter, but not in summer. This is where the trees come in. By planting deciduous trees across that side of the house, you admit the winter sun when the trees are bare; in summer their leaves shade you. You can also place deciduous trees east and west, although in warm climates you may prefer to use evergreens to the west; even the winter afternoon sun can be unwelcome. As the sun sets, its rays penetrate beneath a tree's canopy. You need foliage to the ground, and so augment your trees with shrubs.

Privacy is another important consideration. High hedges and screens are one solution, but they require regular trimming and can make a small area dark and shady. Instead, check the potential lines of view. A few strategically placed large shrubs or small trees will be sufficient to shield you from prying eyes.

Trees with dense foliage can make a garden look somewhat gloomy. But there are many species that only cast dappled, lacy shade, and the balance between these and the denser species is usually best and is especially worth considering in hot climates, where year round shade is desirable and there are few deciduous trees anyway. Consider the size of the garden too; choose trees that won't be too big for the available space.

Some great hedges
Berberis
Buxus
Chamaecyparis
Laurus nobilis
Nandina

Windbreaks
In a large garden, a row of trees can be planted as a windbreak. For smaller gardens, a hedge may be more appropriate. Hedges are usually formal, although they need not be — simply plant a row of shrubs of suitable height rather closer than normal, so their branches interlace in a billowing mass of foliage and flowers. You may need to prune occasionally to keep everything bushy.

A formal hedge needs regular clipping, the aim being to shape it so it presents a vertical wall of foliage and an even flat top. This kind of growth does not bear the best flowers, and clipped hedges are usually chosen for their fine textured greenery.

Conifers such as yew and cypresses are favorites, and so are small-leafed shrubs such as privet and box. The choice of species depends on how high you want your hedge. For miniature edgings that enclose flower beds, opt for the dwarf box, *Buxus sempervirens* 'Suffruticosa', lavender or rosemary.

Poplar trees make a handsome and effective windbreak or screen.

Head-high hedges can be made from such tall shrubs as holly, *Camellia sasanqua, Thuja occidentalis, Myrtus communis*, or *Pittosporum tenuifolium*. There is no need to confine yourself to a single species; you can mix a selection chosen for contrasting foliage to make a tapestry hedge. Tall hedges can be clipped from trees also; yew, the leyland cypress (× *Cupressocyparis leylandii*), copper beech, hornbeam, *Ficus hillii*, and the hawthorns all have their admirers. The competition that comes from close spacing — as close as 3 ft (1 m) — and constant clipping keeps them from growing to full size.

GROWING SHRUBS & TREES
Planting
Planting is one of the most satisfying tasks in all gardening. Plants deserve the best start in life, and a tree or shrub will be there for a long time.

The first stage is to carefully prepare the bed. Dig the soil as deep as the spade will go, meticulously getting rid of any

Dig the soil as deep as the spade will go.

When the hole is ready, prepare to lift the plant out carefully.

Place the plant at the same depth it was in the pot.

Fill soil back around the plant and add compost.

A heavy watering will help the plant settle into its new home.

Remove stakes after about 12 months.

weeds. Add lots of old manure compost or planting mix, then dust with a complete or starter fertilizer such as blood and bone. Make the bed at least 3 ft (1 m) in diameter, more if the plant is being planted from a large container.

Planting from a container is easy. First water the plant thoroughly because a dry root ball may not absorb the water after planting. Take the plant out carefully. If it is too big to lift out of the pot, lay it on its side and slide it out. Don't try to pull it up by its stem; you'll leave half the roots behind. Check the roots; if the plant is pot bound and they are going round and round, they may never break out into their new home. Either tease them out gently or, better, make two or three vertical slashes about 1 in (2.5 cm) deep from the top of the root ball to the bottom with a sharp knife. Although you are cutting the roots, new roots will grow straight out from where you cut.

Then, make a hole deep enough so that the plant will finish up at the same depth as it was in the pot: no more, no less. Often this isn't critical, but shallow-rooted plants like camellias resent having their roots buried too deep, and others, like citrus, can suffer the often-fatal condition known as collar rot. If you plan to stake, put the stake in first. That way you can be certain you aren't going to drive it through a delicate root. Place the stake on the sunny side to give a little shade to the tender bark. But don't tie the tree to the stake too rigidly; ensure that the topmost branches wave in the breeze.

The hole can be as wide as you please. The wider the better as the roots will have plenty of nice soft soil to expand into. In clay soil, dig with a fork because a spade can compress the sides of the hole, making a barrier that fine roots

find difficult to cross. Then place the plant, fill the soil back around it, and water heavily to settle it all in.

Planting an 'advanced' tree from a large container is done in just the same way, the problem being that the heavy root will almost certainly need two people to shift it. (Always lift by cradling the root ball: if you simply grab the trunk the weight will certainly tear roots.) Big trees like this are usually grown in plastic bags or wooden boxes, and you can plant bag and all, cutting it away and easing the bottom piece out from under before you fill the soil back in. Add extra compost to the filling soil, to create a transition zone between the fine-grained potting mix and the natural soil. This is especially worth doing in heavy soils. Roots can be lazy, and you don't want them simply going round and round in their original ball of soil. It is best to support a big tree by guying it, flagpole fashion, to three stakes rather than tying it to just one.

If the plant came with its roots bundled up in natural burlap, don't remove it. When the tree is in place, just cut any string and fill in. The burlap will rot quite quickly, and while it does the new roots can push through it.

If the tree has been supplied bare-root, that is with no soil around its roots — such as rose bushes and deciduous fruit trees — then place it in its hole, using the dirt-mark on the stem to judge the depth, and gently fill the soil around the roots. A pointed stick can be a help to ease the soil in between them and make sure there will be no air pockets. Don't leave bare roots exposed to dry out, even for a minute; carefully carry the plant to its new home in a bucket of water.

After planting, spread mulch all over the bed to conserve water and keep weeds down. Weeds are great robbers of water and nutrients, and research has shown that a young tree growing in a patch of bare soil about 3 ft (1 m) wide needs only about a quarter of the water that it would if weeds were allowed to grow. Grass counts as weeds here, and if you are planting a tree in a lawn, keep that 3 ft (1 m) wide clear bed for at least two or three years. Then you can allow the grass to grow back, but take great care not to knock the tree with the lawn-mower or string trimmer. Many a young tree has been crippled by the mower cutting away its bark.

Don't leave stakes in place for more than a year: by that time the tree or shrub will be self-supporting, and the ties can easily strangle the stem as it thickens. Furthermore, a steel stake protruding from the trunk where the tree has grown over it is not only an ugly sight, it is a perpetually open wound inviting rot and fungi to attack the tree.

If you keep them watered in hot weather, you can plant container-grown trees and shrubs at any time of year except when the soil is in the grip of heavy frost; burlapped and bare-root specimens can only be planted in winter or early spring. If you garden in a dry climate, try to plant in the spring and fall or whenever rainfall is more plentiful. Remember that both sun and wind can dry a young plant out. If the plant is small, put three sticks around it and drop a plastic shopping bag with the bottom cut out over them. For a bigger tree, do the same with burlap stretched between three stakes. It need only be kept in place for six months or so.

Watering & feeding

Once planted, trees and shrubs demand very little attention. The first year or two after planting is the most important time, when they are still getting their roots established and building up their branches. Give them attention now, and you will be rewarded by much faster growth and more vigorous plants in the future. Allow them to struggle, and they may never establish properly and grow to their full beauty.

Pull weeds out, and spread a mulch to smother any that try to return. Mulch conserves moisture too, and reduces the amount of watering needed. Water when the weather is dry. Don't just sprinkle; wetting only the surface soil does more harm than good by encouraging the development of roots close to the surface, where they suffer when the soil dries out again. The aim is to encourage the roots to go deep where the soil dries out more slowly. Not often but thoroughly is the rule.

Watering depends on a number of factors. Look at soil types: sandy soils absorb water quickly, but don't hold it tight and so dry out fast, and clay soils absorb it slowly but hold it for longer. Water evaporates from the soil faster on hot days—and on windy ones—than it does in cooler weather. Remember too, that frost dries the soil, and young plants may need to be watered to compensate. Watering in the heat of the day is wasteful, as much of your water will evaporate. Watering in the early morning or evening is preferable. Take care in adjusting your sprinklers so they don't deliver the water faster than the soil can absorb it.

Even in places with abundant rainfall, drought can strike and long-established, deep-rooted trees can suffer. They don't usually wilt, but reduce their rate of transpiration by shedding leaves out of season, and there is a risk that when the rain returns they will make more growth and foliage than their drought-damaged roots can support. They may then suddenly die just when you thought the danger was over. You must get water down deep into the roots by applying it very slowly but for a long time. Leaving a hose to trickle at the base of the tree for at least 24 hours is the best thing to do.

Mulching with compost fertilizes plants as well as stemming moisture loss; this can be boosted with a light dressing of something more concentrated as the regular growing season begins. Artificial fertilizer is fine, but it doesn't maintain the essential humus on which the continued health of the soil depends. For that, organic material is needed. Happily, trees and shrubs supply their own, by dropping their leaves. Leaving these to rot where they fall is one of the few times in life when laziness is rewarded!

An established tree that doesn't seem to be growing well will respond dramatically to being fertilized, but you need to get it down deep where the roots are.

You can buy specially formulated fertilizers, but any general-purpose fertilizer is fine. Starting about 1 ft (30 cm) away from the trunk, topping it off with a mixture of soil and compost, make a number of holes about 3 ft (1 m) apart across the entire spread of the roots (the area covered by the outermost branches). These should be about 2 in (4 cm) wide and at least 20 in (50 cm) deep. Divide the allowance of fertilizer by the number of holes and pour in the calculated amount, watering it in.

Pruning

Pruning is the removal of part of a tree or shrub in order to correct an imbalance of growth or to encourage it to grow the way its owner wants. The sort of mutilations you commonly see, where someone has hacked chunks out of a tree to keep it out of the way of telephone wires or simply lopped off its branches in a (vain) attempt to make it smaller is

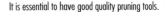
It is essential to have good quality pruning tools.

Even tip pruning promotes bushiness and more profuse flowering.

not pruning, but butchery.

Pruning is not compulsory. Trees and shrubs growing in the wild are not pruned, and most can spend all their lives in cultivation without ever needing it. But a garden, park or street is an artificial environment, and the gardener may want to supplant the tree's natural form by an artificial shape, such as topiary. Or the gardener may want to encourage more flowers and/or fruit; or enhance the plant's natural form. The Japanese are the masters of this: the beautiful, seemingly natural lines of the trees and shrubs in a classical Japanese garden are the result of many years of exquisitely practiced art.

The tools you use are important. For your own comfort, use the smallest tool adequate to the job but don't try to force the tool to do more than it can. Hedge shears are not meant to cut woody branches. Invest in a long-handled pair of lopping shears, which allow you to apply more force. They should handle branches as thick as a man's thumb; bigger than that you need a saw. The best is the traditional curved-bladed, one-sided pruning saw, or rather two, one with coarse blades, one fine. Double-sided saws, coarse on one side, fine on the other, look like a bargain until you find yourself in a tight corner, cutting both the branch you want to keep as well as the one you are removing. Buying a chainsaw is not recommended—if you have to remove branches that big, it is best to call in an experienced tree surgeon. Keep tools sharp. Blunt instruments don't make clean cuts, they tear; and ragged wounds heal slowly if at all.

Pruning trees

Pruning should only be an occasional episode in the life of most ornamental trees: it is only if you want to create an artificial form that you would consider pruning on an annual or semi-annual basis. If you find that you are constantly cutting a tree trying to make it smaller, then you should consider replacing it.

A young tree growing in the forest grows upwards towards the light, concentrates its energy on gaining height, and only spreads its branches when it receives its share of sunshine. A tree in a garden is usually planted in the sun, and it will start to develop its branches at once, so it will grow up with its branches much lower, even sweeping the ground, than it would do in the wild. To get the tree to grow on a suitably long trunk you need to discourage the side shoots, doing with the pruning shears what nature does by depriving these shoots of light. Don't cut off the developing branches altogether. That deprives the tree of the foliage it needs to sustain its growth. Rather, shorten them—merely cutting back their tips once or twice during the growing season will often suffice—but leave the leading shoot untouched. These branches may well respond by shooting leafy twigs, which is fine; the more leaves the better at this stage. But the young tree will take the hint and divert its chief energy into the leader, with the result that it will gain height faster than it would otherwise.

When it has grown sufficiently that the lowest, previously shortened branches can be removed entirely, then do so. Do not remove them before this time. When this will be depends on the species and on your climate, but generally, it will be at least four or five years before your tree reaches this stage.

When the time comes to remove those lowest branches, do not cut them off flush with the trunk. If you look carefully, you will see that where a branch springs from the trunk (or a larger branch) there is a necklace of swollen bark called the 'branch collar'. If you cut right to the trunk, you remove the collar, and that is inviting trouble. The collar is the tree's natural defence against the loss of its branch. It is the cells of the collar that proliferate over the wound and eventually cover it with bark: and if a branch dies, this is where it dies back to, no further. So cut back to the collar, taking care to preserve it. This usually means that the cut is made at a slight angle to the trunk. It may not look quite so neat, but when the scar heals and the trunk thickens it will grow to a smooth line again. Be patient! If the collar remains intact, healing will be quick, and there will be no need to paint the wound with pruning compound to seal it against weather and rot-causing fungi.

Once the young tree is up on its trunk and developing its crown, put your pruning tools away, perhaps forever. But keep an eye on how those branches are developing. You may need to remove a few which are crowding each other or threatening to unbalance the crown. Watch out for weak crotches. The wider the angle at which a branch grows from the trunk, the stronger it will be. While not all trees grow their branches straight out at right-angles, you should prevent narrower-than-normal, V-shaped crotches from developing. They can easily break under the burden of rain-laden and storm-whipped foliage, often many years later. Just cut out the offending branch when you see it.

Removing a branch altogether is invasive surgery, and should never be done while the sap is actively running, that is when the tree is making new growth. The best time is when it is dormant, usually in winter; but you can prune in late summer after growth has stopped. Some cold-climate trees, the maples being the chief example, are exceptions. Cut them about in winter, and they bleed copiously, as anyone who has made maple syrup knows.

Pruning fruit trees

With fruit trees, pruning is not compulsory. Assuming (as always) that it is suited to your climate, it will grow and fruit without pruning. In fact, the evergreen fruit trees of hot and warm climates—mangoes, jack fruits, lychees, avocados, citrus, olives, etc.—are very rarely pruned, except for shape, even by orchardists. They are given the usual guidance in infancy and then left to grow as they please. If the idea of a backyard orchard appeals, arm yourself with a good textbook written by an expert familiar with your own area.

Pruning shrubs

Pruning shrubs is not nearly as big, nor as careful, a job as pruning trees. The general principle is the same: by removing a branch, you encourage new growth elsewhere. To encourage a branch to elongate, trim its side shoots; to encourage the side shoots, shorten it; and if it's dead, remove it altogether. That's all there is to it.

Just how you put the principles into practice depends on the shrub and its role in your garden design. To make a shrub bushier and more compact, shorten the branches to encourage side shoots. If it is too bushy for your taste, thin out the branches, either cutting them right to the ground or to where another strong branch is springing. Most often you will do both, thinning out old twiggy branches and shortening others. When you shorten a branch, always cut it to a point where a new branch is already growing or where there is a dormant bud waiting to grow. This is sometimes difficult to see; but if you cut back to just above a leaf, or where a scar on the bark shows there has been one, you will be cutting to the right place.

Let your eye guide you. By the time a shrub is old enough for pruning, you should be sufficiently familiar with how it grows that the right course of action will suggest itself. You will have noticed how some shrubs flower on their current growth, the way a hybrid tea rose, a hibiscus, or an oleander does. These almost always flower in summer; spring bloomers don't have time to make that much growth after their winter rest and so bloom on the branches they grew last year. Such include the rhododendrons, weigelas, forsythias and lilac. If you prune these in winter, you will be cutting away your flowering wood, so the time to prune is immediately after flowering but before the new growth begins.

Summer-bloomers can wait until winter, as they don't grow again before spring. Dead branches and dead flowers can be removed at any time.

There is, however, a great exception to the prune-after-flowering rule. You may be faced with a great, overgrown shrub full of decrepit branches—an elderly lilac for instance—and decide that the only way to restore it to youth and vigor is to cut it almost to the ground to force it to renew itself entirely. This must only be done while the plant is dormant, even if (as will be the case with the lilac) you thereby sacrifice flowers for a year or two. If that bothers you, you can take the job in stages over three years, cutting out a third of the bush each year so that by the end of the third year you have replaced it entirely. This is a wise course if you are not sure that the species will in fact respond to drastic cutting back. Some evergreen shrubs are badly shocked by the sudden removal of all their foliage.

Turning a shrub into a tree

Usually, a shrub is pruned to make it bushier; but sometimes, you might want to make it more open. This is a matter of thinning. Simply cut the excess branches right out. Thin its main branches a little and remove the lowest side branches, and it will be transformed into a small, multi-stemmed tree under which you can now plant shade-loving flowers. This is usually the best way to treat those kinds on the borderline between tree and shrub, such as the larger-growing cotoneasters and calliandras, pittosporums, and even camellias.

Transplanting or removing trees

Transplanting a mature tree is a big job. Not all adult trees can be transplanted;

some never get over the inevitable damage to their roots. Magnolias, eucalypts and birches, for example, have open, rather sparse root systems and rarely survive transplanting. The best candidates have densely fibrous root systems, like rhododendrons, or those that grow new roots vigorously if the old are cut, like willows, poplars, planes, and palms.

Preparation for transplanting should begin about a year before, with pruning the roots. This reduces the root ball to a manageable size and provokes the growth of a mass of fine new roots to nourish the tree in its new home and, incidentally, to bind the root ball together when it is lifted from the ground. Cut a circular trench about a third of the way out from the trunk to the outer branches and as deep as possible, using sharp spades and pruners if big roots are encountered. Then fill in with fine soil enriched with organic matter watering as you fill. Mark the line of the trench in some way, such as a line of pebbles. Then you know where to dig and won't damage precious new roots.

At transplanting time (mid to late winter in temperate areas, the start of the rainy season in the tropics) dig beneath the root ball, and sever roots that you couldn't get the first time. The majority of a tree's feeder roots are in the upper part of the root system. When you remove it from the ground and transport it, always cradle it from below. If the tree is picked up by its trunk the roots will tear off, and the tender bark will be crushed.

Plant the transported tree into a freshly dug hole where it will end up at precisely the same depth as before. Orient it as before, so the same side will be in the sun. Do not loosen the soil from the roots. If the tree is a big one, the weight of the root ball may be enough to keep it steady once in place; but to be sure, give it three or four guy ropes.

It will be at least two or three years before you can remove the guys and allow the tree to look after itself. In the meantime, water regularly, and fertilize in spring.

Transplanting an established shrub is done in exactly the same way and with the same delicate care. It isn't such a huge job, because the root ball is smaller.

If you have to remove a tree altogether, check with local authorities whether you need permission. Some trees have a preservation order on them.

Pests & diseases

Ornamental trees and shrubs are usually trouble free. A few insect-eaten leaves are normally not much to worry about, and a trip to the nursery with a specimen of the damage will usually bring forth the appropriate remedy, often a chemical spray. Large trees, however, are difficult to spray, and you may have to rely on a visit from an arborist, or perhaps natural controls (if the birds and beneficial insects haven't been driven away by insecticide and other pollutants) to deal with the problem.

Once established, most shrubs and trees are remarkably resilient. Every so often, however, a devastating disease strikes, the most famous being the Dutch elm disease which has almost destroyed the elms of America and Great Britain, though stringent quarantine has kept it out of some other countries so far. It is ironic that the finest specimens of the English elm are now to be seen in Australia and New Zealand. In such cases the wisest solution is usually to cease cultivating the affected plant.

Fruit trees are commonly attacked by such bugs as codling moths and fruit-flies, the species varying from place to place, and they may be attacked by various fungi also. If you are planning to grow your own fruit, you should take the advice of your local government county extension agency or equivalent as to the best types of trees for your area and whether you will be required by law to spray them.

Shrubs & trees in containers

Growing trees or shrubs in containers is easy. Select a suitable container, make sure it has adequate holes for drainage, fill it with a good commercial potting mix, and plant. Then water regularly — never let the plant dry out to the point of wilting — and fertilize regularly, as the

Potted plants add life and color to a courtyard or patio.

constant watering will leach nutrients from the soil very rapidly. A slow release fertilizer is recommended.

The container should be big enough for the root system, so you need quite a large container for an ordinary-sized shrub and an even bigger one for a tree; but even so the plant will eventually outgrow its root space. There are two ways to deal with this — plant into a bigger container (potting up), or remove it and prune the roots before putting it back with some fresh potting mix (re-potting).

Consider the size of the plant. An orange tree is about as big a tree as you can comfortably accommodate in a container; and the best trees and shrubs for container growing are ones with a compact root system that don't mind having their roots disturbed by pruning. By pruning the roots in early spring and replacing at least some of the soil, you get over the problem of long-term deterioration of the soil. Deprived of contact with natural surroundings and all the various microorganisms that constantly renew its quotient of organic matter, the potting soil loses its structure and begins to compact like concrete or a mud pie. The fine feeding roots suffer and the plant starves to death.

If you live in an apartment, remember that a tree in a tub or even a shrub is heavy and you don't want to risk bringing the roof or balcony down, so seek the advice of a structural engineer first. Roofs and balconies are also apt to be windy places — remember that wind dries plants out very efficiently.

Shrubs & trees indoors

If you want to grow plants from warmer climates than your own, you need a greenhouse, or you can grow them indoors. Plants indigenous to evergreen forests are used to constant temperatures and able to put up with low light levels.

Palms have long been fashionable, and have been joined by such trees as the Norfolk Island pine *(Araucaria heterophylla)*, the silky oak *(Grevillea robusta)* and the Moreton Bay chestnut *(Castanospermum australe)*. These eventually outgrow their containers, but do quite well for a few years at least. They don't always branch out and develop a crown. In the same manner as the ubiquitous India-rubber tree *(Ficus elastica)*, they tend to grow up on one or two ceiling-high stems. *Ficus benjamina*, the small-leafed weeping fig, makes an elegant branching tree from its earliest youth.

Indoor plants need good light, humidity and the right amount of water. The light should be strong enough to cast a faint shadow. This means keeping the curtains open during the day. (If privacy is an issue, a light, transparent curtain will block prying eyes but still let in a reasonable amount of light.) Turn the tree around every so often, so that all sides will have their turn in the light. Supplementary lighting (fluorescent or incandescent) will dramatically increase the variety of choices, and will be necessary for some plants.

They need humidity: dry air will cause them to drop their leaves. Air-conditioning and central heating both dry the air out to desert-like levels. The best remedy is to stand the tree on (not in) a tray of pebbles which you dampen every few days; or, simplest of all, place a bowl of water nearby.

Third, they must not be over-watered, especially in winter when growth slows down. More houseplants drown than die of thirst. The soil should be just evenly moist but never wet. The pot should never stand in a saucer of water, or the

The delicate, bell-shaped flowers of *Pieris japonica* 'Variegata' are shown to great effect in this blue pot.

roots will suffocate. The best thing to do is to stand the pot on blocks or stones. You can then leave the water in the saucer to evaporate and raise the humidity.

Any standard commercial potting mix designed for indoor plants is suitable. Fertilize in spring and again in early summer. Re-potting should only be needed every two or three years. However, the pot needs to be big enough so the whole thing isn't top heavy and at risk of being easily knocked over.

Taking cuttings from shrubs & trees

Plants can be propagated by seed, by layering and by grafting, but we are going to concentrate on taking cuttings.

A cutting is simply a piece of branch placed in the soil in the hope that before it dies it will make roots of its own. Many shrubs do this quite readily, others less readily; but many trees are reluctant strikers. Take the cutting from a soft, actively growing shoot, from one which has slowed down but not yet matured (the best times are usually spring and summer), or from mature

Take the cutting from an actively growing shoot.

Trim the cutting with a sharp knife.

Plant several cuttings to the pot.

Enclosing the cuttings in a plastic bag or bottle will keep them moist.

wood, which may indeed have already lost its leaves for the winter. Each can give excellent results, depending on the species. Fuchsias and other fast-growing, warm-climate shrubs are usually grown from soft cuttings, camellias from semi-mature ones, roses from mature ones. Take cuttings from young, vigorously growing plants.

Now trim the cuttings. Re-cut the base with a very sharp knife: if the cut is at all ragged, it won't heal, and it is from the healing callus that the new roots spring. Trim off the lower leaves, then dip the base of the cutting in rooting hormone, which makes a great difference as long as it is fresh, and insert it in a pot of sharp sand or half-sand-half potting mix. Put several cuttings to the pot, and avoid confusion by putting only one variety to each pot. Label it accordingly. Do not tip the pot out to see if the cuttings have struck—you will disturb the incipient roots, which are very delicate. When they have struck, you will see signs of new growth or of roots peeking out though the drainage holes. Then is the time to take your new plants out and pot them into individual pots.

Striking a cutting is a race with time, and you need to do everything you can to help. The ideal is to put pots of cuttings in a greenhouse equipped with a heating system that will keep the soil in the pots just a little warmer than the air ('bottom heat') and a watering system that surrounds their tops in a constant, gentle fog. These 'mist systems' are widely used commercially and have made it possible to grow such formerly intractable things as rhododendrons from cuttings. You can buy small mist-propagating units; although the initial outlay for these is quite high, in terms of what they can produce they are extremely cost-effective. You can, however, create your own version by enclosing your cuttings, pot and all, in a clear plastic bag or bottle which will keep them moist. Keep it in a warm but shaded place.

An explanation of plant names

The shrubs and trees featured in this book are arranged alphabetically by their scientific names. Because these names are in Latin, they may not be familiar to every gardener, but there are many difficulties associated with with using plants' common names.

The cherub in the pond provides a focal point for this charming old-fashioned garden.

It's hard to beat rhododendrons for spectacular color and performance.

One major problem is that many plants share the same common name—for example, 'cedar' refers to quite unrelated trees in Asia, North America, South Africa and Australia. A plant may have more than one common name, even in the one language, not to mention common names that it may have in different languages. As well, a large proportion of the world's plants have never received a common name, on account of being too rare, hard to distinguish, or found only in wilderness areas.

Scientific names are in Latin because when the systematic description of plants began to receive attention in the Renaissance period, the common language of European scholarship was Latin. The Swedish naturalist Carolus Linnaeus identified plants by two names, following a similar principle to people's names, though with the surname and the given name reversed. So *Quercus alba* and *Quercus rubra* are both members of the same 'family'. The second part of the name, for instance *rubra* can be the given name in unrelated families. Thus there is an *Ulnus rubra* and a *Morus rubra* as well as a *Quercus rubra*.

The first part of the botanical name is the *genus* name, which can stand on its own; thus *Quercus* is the genus of oaks and no other plant genus can share the name. Each genus may consist of several or many *species*, each designated by a

Shrubs and trees are the main creators of form and structure in a garden.

two-part name as described, so the name of the white oak species is *Quercus alba*, not just *alba*, the latter word being referred to by botanists as the 'specific epithet'.

Species may also include *subspecies*, for example the European *Pinus negra* is now treated as consisting of three (sometimes more) subspecies: subsp. *nigra* is the Austrian pine, subsp. *laricio* is the Corsican pine, and subsp. *pallasiana* is the Crimean pine.

Variant forms that have been created or perpetuated by gardeners are now named as *cultivars*, and are given names in modern languages rather than Latin.

We are familiar with the cultivar names of roses ('Olympiad') and camellias ('Nuccio's Gem'). Cultivar names are always in a different typeface from the botanical name and are usually in single quotes.

Because botanists the world over use the same system of plant nomenclature and follow its conventions, plants from all parts of the world can be identified and described without confusion. For gardeners, knowing the names of plants and how they relate to each other can help in understanding the conditions in which they flourish.

ABELIA
Caprifoliaceae

A genus of both deciduous and ever-green shrubs, abelias are valued for their elegant growth and abundant production of small tubular or trumpet-shaped flowers over a prolonged summer–early autumn season. They have dark green foliage on arching canes and can withstand heavy pruning, for example when used for low hedges, though poor flowering results if the long canes are constantly cut back.

Cultivation

Species vary from moderately cold-hardy to somewhat tender. The hardy species are trouble-free plants, capable of surviving harsh conditions: even if cut back by frosts, they sprout again from the base. They prefer sun or light shade, and need regular water in summer. Abelias are easily propagated from cuttings.

Abelia × grandiflora

This hybrid between *Abelia chinensis* and *A. uniflora* grows to 6–8 ft (2–3 m) tall and wide, with arching reddish brown canes and small, glossy, dark green leaves. The pale mauve and white

Abelia × grandiflora 'Francis Mason'

flowers are profuse in early summer, often with a second flush at summer's end. The dull pink calyces of the flowers persist into winter, in contrast with the leaves which turn purplish bronze. The cultivar 'Frances Mason' has yellow-edged leaves on vigorous shoots, but they have a tendency to revert to plain green. *Zones 7–10.*

ABIES
Pinaceae
Fir

The true firs, sometimes known as silver firs to distinguish them from *Picea* (from which they differ in their upright, not pendent, cones), comprise 40-odd species. These have regular spire-like shapes and richly textured, aromatic foliage. Most *Abies* come from cool- to cold-climate mountain areas of the northern hemisphere. Because of their narrow shape and slow growth, many species fit comfortably into a larger suburban garden, but they don't tolerate urban pollution and prefer a moist climate without extremes of heat or dryness.

Cultivation

Soils should be deep, with adequate drainage and moisture retention. Propagation is from seed. Grafting is used for selected clones but takes time, and a compatible seedling fir as root-stock. Remove the twin leading shoots when they appear.

Abies balsamea
Balsam fir

The 'balsam' is a clear, thin resin in the bark which once was used for varnishes and pharmaceuticals; the resin has the same refractive index as glass and is used to glue compact lenses for tele-scopes, etc. The balsam fir is the most widespread North American species. A short-lived, spindly tree, it is seen in gardens mainly as dwarf cultivars, the most popular being 'Hudsonia', a compact miniature shrub up to 24 in (60 cm) high. *Zones 3–8.*

Abies pinsapo
Spanish fir

A column-shaped tree reaching 100 ft (30 m), often with multiple leaders and densely crowded branches, this fir adapts to a wide range of soils and climates. The short, rigid needles which appear on all sides of the thick, stiff twigs are less flattened than in most firs, and have fine bluish white stripes. Small purple pollen cones on the lower branch tips appear in spring. The purplish seed cones are produced near the top of the tree as in most firs. Seedlings are selected for bluish foliage, collectively referred to under the cultivar name 'Glauca'. *Zones 5–9.*

Abies pinsapo

Abies balsamea 'Hudsonia'

ABUTILON
Malvaceae
Chinese lantern, flowering maple

This genus of mainly evergreen shrubs comes from mostly warmer climates of South America; additional species are found in Australia. The flowers are pendent and lantern-shaped in most cultivated species. Although the name 'Chinese lantern' is applied to other abutilons, it can hardly apply to these in view of their more saucer-shaped flowers.

Cultivation

They need full sun or part-shade and well-drained soil. In cooler climates they can be grown in containers in sheltered, sunny spots or in greenhouses. They need good watering. Propagate from softwood cuttings in late summer. Watch for flea-beetles, aphids and caterpillars.

Abutilon × hybridum
Chinese lantern

Abutilon × hybridum is a collective name for the cultivars derived from hybridizing some South American species, principally *A. striatum* and *A. darwinii*. The lantern-like flowers, borne from

Abutilon × hybridum 'Orange King'

Acacia baileyana

spring to autumn, come in yellow, white, orange, pink, mauve and scarlet. Named cultivars include 'Golden Fleece', with rich golden yellow flowers; 'Orange King'; 'Ruby Glow'; and 'Souvenir de Bonn', with variegated foliage and red-veined orange flowers. In warm climates they will grow up to 8 ft (2.5 m). They can be grown indoors. *Zones 9–11.*

ACACIA
Mimosaceae
Wattle

This large genus contains over 1,200 species of trees and shrubs. Over 700 are indigenous to Australia. They are also common in tropical and subtropical Africa. Most African species are characterized by vicious spines and referred to as 'thorn trees'. Australian species range from low-growing shrubs to tall trees. Those described here are evergreen. Plants have either bipinnate leaves or their leaves are replaced by flattened leaf-stalks (phyllodes), which are used for photosynthesis. The tiny flowers range from deep golden yellow to cream or white, and are crowded into globular heads or cylindrical spikes.

Cultivation

Many species are fast growing but short lived (10–15 years) and in their native regions often disfigured by insect or fungus attack. They do best in full sun and well-drained soil.

Acacia baileyana
Cootamundra wattle

A fast-growing, small, spreading tree to 20 ft (7 m), the Cootamundra wattle has a short trunk and arching branches, silver, finely divided, feathery leaves and fragrant, golden yellow flower clusters in late winter. It is widely used in warm-temperate gardens as a feature tree. *Zones 8–10.*

ACALYPHA
Euphorbiaceae

This genus of hot-climate, evergreen shrubs includes many species in tropical Asia and the Pacific. Some have decorative spikes of tiny massed female flowers (males are on different plants), and one species has variegated foliage.

Cultivation

They need a sunny to semi-shaded position, well-drained light soil with

Acalypha wilkesiana cultivar

than the inconspicuous flowers. The bark is commonly smooth, gray or greenish; in the 'snakebark maples' it has longitudinal gray or brown stripes and in others, including *A. griseum*, it is flaky or papery. North America has 9 native maples, including the sugar maple *(A. saccharum)* famous for maple syrup and its lumber, and the box-elder maple *(A. negundo)*. Maples suit cool to cold climates and are deciduous, but there are evergreen and semi-evergreen species, including the rainforest tree *A. laurinum*.

Cultivation
Propagation is generally from seed for the species, by grafting for cultivars. Cuttings are difficult to root, but layering of low branches is successful for some species. Seed is easily germinated and can be aided by overwintering in damp litter, or refrigeration.

plenty of water during summer and protection from wind. Plants are killed or damaged by frosts. Prune lightly to shape in late winter, followed by additional feeding and watering. Propagate from cuttings in summer.

Acalypha wilkesiana
Fijian fire plant
Originating in Fiji and other Pacific Islands, this species grows to a height and spread of 10 ft (3 m), forming an irregularly rounded bush with erect stems branching from the base. It has large, serrated, oval leaves in a very wide color range, depending on cultivar, from mid-green to reddish bronze, some with contrasting margins. Inconspicuous tassel-like catkins of reddish bronze flowers appear in summer and autumn. It prefers a warm, sheltered position and the foliage colors best in full sun. 'Macafeeana' has deep bronze leaves splashed with coppery red. *Zones 10–11.*

ACER
Aceraceae
Maple
Maples have distinctive 2-winged fruits (samaras) which are more noticeable

Acer griseum
Paperbark maple
The chief glory of this species is the bark, rich chestnut brown peppered with paler corky dots, which it sheds each year in wide curling strips. The foliage is also attractive, dark green and

Acer griseum

small-leafed, and autumn color is deep scarlet. It makes a narrow-crowned tree to 30 ft (10 m). Under moist, sheltered conditions in good soil, growth can be rapid. In cultivation it produces plenty of seed but most of these are infertile, so it is not easy to find in a nursery. *Zones 5–9.*

Acer negundo
Box-elder maple, box elder

Occasionally reaching 50 ft (15 m), this maple has a thick trunk and upright branching habit. American farmers regard it as a 'weed tree' and its free-seeding habits have made it a minor nuisance in other countries. It is fast growing and tolerates poor conditions, but its branches break easily in high winds. The cultivars 'Variegatum' and 'Aureo-marginatum' have leaves attractively edged white or gold respectively; 'Flamingo' has strongly flushed pink leaves on new growth. 'Violaceum' is a male clone with purplish new shoots and twigs; the male flower tassels are also pale purple. *Zones 4–10.*

Acer palmatum
Japanese maple

The Japanese maple is compact, with delicate ferny foliage and brilliant autumn coloring. Cultivated for centu-

Acer palmatum

ries in Japan, and since 1830 in the West, there are now over 300 cultivars, from rock garden miniatures to vigorous small trees. The usual mature height is 12–15 ft (4–5 m). Though easily grown and more tolerant of warmer climates than most maples, without some shade and shelter the leaves may shrivel in late summer. A popular cultivar is 'Atropurpureum', with dark purple spring foliage. In the Dissectum group, the primary leaf lobes have a deeply cut filigree pattern; their drooping twigs grow down rather than upward, so they are grafted onto a standard. The best for landscaping are 'Dissectum' and 'Dissectum Atropurpureum'. *Zone 5–10.*

Acer platanoides
Norway maple

This fine European tree makes a large, round-headed tree and thrives in a wide range of soils and situations, but not in warm climates. Yellow flowers appear before the leaves; autumn color is gold to reddish orange. 'Drummondii' has variegated leaves. Named cultivars with deep purplish foliage include 'Schwedleri', 'Faasen's Black' and 'Crimson King', between which there is

Acer negundo 'Variegatum'

Acer saccharum

Acer rubrum

Acer platanoides 'Crimson King'

much confusion. All are quite slow growing, so suit smaller gardens. *Zones 4–9.*

Acer rubrum
Red maple

This large maple from eastern North America displays brilliant autumn tones of deep red with striking blue-white undersides. It grows up to 100 ft (30 m) in the richest forests on deep alluvial soil. As a planted tree it makes rapid growth, with a straight trunk and narrow crown at first, but spreading broadly with age. The timber is prized for furniture. *Zones 4–9.*

Acer saccharum
Sugar maple

Commercially important for its sap (maple syrup) and durable timber, this maple ranges across eastern North America from Newfoundland and Manitoba in the north to Florida in the south, and west to Utah. In the south

and west, regional subspecies occur, including *Acer saccharum* subspp. *floridanum, grandidentatum, leucoderme* and *nigrum*: all have been treated as distinct species by some botanists. Its leaf adorns the Canadian flag. Often slow growing in the first 10 years, in the garden it makes a low-branching, broad-crowned tree of 40–50 ft (12–15 m), though it will grow much taller in forests. Autumn color varies from tree to tree, with yellow, orange, scarlet and crimson all common. *Zones 4–9.*

Aesculus × *carnea* 'Briotii'

Aesculus hippocastanum

AESCULUS
Hippocastanaceae
Horse-chestnut, buckeye

These deciduous trees and shrubs have a finger-like arrangement of leaflets in their compound leaves, and eye-catching spikes of cream to reddish flowers at branch ends in spring or summer. The large, nut-like seeds, released from round capsules, resemble chestnuts but are bitter and inedible. At least half of the 20 or so species occur in North America, the remainder in temperate Asia and Europe. They are primarily trees of valley floors, growing in sheltered positions in deep, moist soil.

Cultivation
Although most are frost-hardy, they perform best in cool climates where seasons are sharply demarcated and summers are warm. Propagate from seed; propagate selected clones and hybrids by bud-grafting.

Aesculus × carnea
Red horse-chestnut

This hybrid tree, thought to have originated by chance in Germany early last century, grows to about 30 ft (10 m) and often comes true from seed. It gets the reddish pink of its flowers from one parent, *Aesculus pavia*; the other parent is *A. hippocastanum*. A hardy and free-flowering tree, it adapts to slightly warmer and drier climates than *A. hippocastanum*. The cultivar 'Briotii' has larger spikes of brighter pink flowers. *Zones 6–9.*

Aesculus hippocastanum
Horse-chestnut

The common horse-chestnut can reach 100 ft (30 m), though half that is its usual mature size. In full blossom it is one of the most beautiful of all flowering trees for cool climates, with white 'candles' of bloom held above the dense crown of dark green foliage. The individual flowers have crumpled white petals with a yellow basal patch which ages to dull red. Fruits, ripening through summer, have a leathery case covered with short prickles and in autumn release large seeds. Autumn color is yellow-brown. *Zones 6–9.*

AGAVE
Agavaceae

Occurring naturally in the Caribbean region including southern USA, Mexico and the West Indies, these perennial succulents are grown for their dramatic, sword-shaped, often sharply toothed

Agave americana 'Marginata'

leaves and tall flowering stems. The small species flower only after 5 to 10 years; taller species may take up to 40 years to flower. All flower only once in their lifetime and then the flowering shoot dies, in most species leaving offsets which continue the plant's growth. They are tough, drought-resistant plants and are popular in landscape design.

Cultivation
Frost-hardiness varies depending on species. Plant in a well-drained, gritty soil in full sun. Propagate from seed.

Agave americana
Century plant, American aloe
This species consists of large, stemless rosettes of stiff, dull gray leaves with needle-like tips and fierce marginal teeth. Each rosette grows to a height and spread of 6 ft (2 m) but an old clump may be 30 ft (9 m) or more across. The rosette flowers when about 10 years old, the branched flower stem rising to about 20 ft (7 m) and bearing masses of yellow flowers. 'Marginata' is a popular cultivar with yellow-edged leaves. In Mexico the sap of the flowering stems is tapped and fermented into pulque, a highly alcoholic drink. Tequila is the export version. *Zones 9–11.*

AGONIS
Myrtaceae
This is a small genus of warm-climate evergreen trees and shrubs indigenous to Western Australia, with narrow, thick-textured leaves and attractive small white flowers.

Cultivation
They do best in full sun and sandy soil that is well drained but preferably enriched with organic matter for moisture retention. They are frost-tender, but tolerate droughts when established. Propagation is from seed in spring or cuttings in summer. Plants sometimes self-propagate from seed contained in their small woody fruit capsules.

Agonis flexuosa
Willow-myrtle, peppermint tree
The willow-myrtle is a tree to about 30 ft (10 m), broad-crowned with a spread eventually equalling its height, and rapidly developing a brown-barked trunk of quite surprising thickness, sometimes as much as 3 ft (1 m). It has attractive pendulous branches, rather like a small weeping willow. The long narrow leaves are quite aromatic when crushed and in late spring small, pretty

Agonis flexuosa

Albizia julibrissin

white flowers are strung along the branches. *Zones 9–10*.

ALBIZIA
Mimosaceae

Albizia species for the most part are quick-growing tropical trees and shrubs with globular clusters of long-stamened flowers, rather like those of many *Mimosa* and *Acacia* species but larger. They have feathery leaves and densely clustered small flowers in which the stamens are far longer and more conspicuous than the petals. In nature they are often rather weedy small trees, springing up quickly from seed and frequently short lived, but they can be quite ornamental.

Cultivation
Cultivation requirements are summer warmth and moisture and a reasonably sheltered site.

Albizia julibrissin
Silk tree

Occurring from Iran east across temperate and subtropical Asia to China, this deciduous tree is named for the long, silky stamens, creamy white to deep pink, which are the visible part of the flower heads and stand above the leaves.

Often staying under 6 ft (2 m) tall, though flowering freely, in ideal conditions it becomes a flat-crowned tree of 20–25 ft (7–8 m) with luxuriant feathery foliage. In colder climates it is sometimes used as a summer bedding or terrace plant. *Zones 8–10*.

ALNUS
Betulaceae
Alder

Alders come mainly from cool to cold climates of the northern hemisphere where they form thickets on glacial moraines, landslides and floodplains of rivers. They are fast growing, light-loving trees, which can die if they are overtopped and shaded out by other trees. Female catkins are egg-shaped, hanging in groups at branch tips; in the seeding stage they become hard and woody. Alders from cool-temperate regions are deciduous. A few species from subtropical mountain areas are evergreen or semi-evergreen. Alder bark was used in tanning; its charcoal was used to make gunpowder.

Cultivation
They like permanently moist soil. Propagate from seed.

Alnus glutinosa

Aloysia triphylla

Alnus glutinosa
Black alder, common alder
The common alder is valued for its timber, and in cold, bleak climates and on poor, boggy soils it is sometimes the only tree apart from certain willows that will thrive. It reaches heights of 60 ft (18 m) in the wild but planted trees are seldom more than half that. The dark brown bark becomes deeply furrowed and checkered as the trunk increases in girth, and the high crown of the tree is often irregular and rather open. *Zones 4–9.*

ALOYSIA
Verbenaceae
This genus of evergreen shrubs from subtropical and temperate South America has aromatic foliage. The branches are soft and cane-like with leaves arranged in opposite pairs or in whorls of three. Tiny flowers are borne in panicles terminating the branches.

Cultivation
They prefer a well-drained, loamy or light-textured soil and plenty of summer watering. Tolerant of only mild frosts, they do best in sunny positions in warm, coastal environments. Remove dead wood in early summer and prune well in late winter to encourage the flowers. Propagate by semi-hardwood cuttings in summer or soft-tip cuttings in spring.

Aloysia triphylla
Lemon-scented verbena
Grown for its heavily lemon-scented, crinkly pale to mid-green leaves, this shrub has an open, rather straggling habit and reaches a height and spread of 10 ft (3 m). Racemes of dainty lavender-purple flowers appear in summer and autumn. Oil of verbena is produced from the leaves. *Zones 8–11.*

ALYOGYNE
Malvaceae
These hibiscus-like shrubs come from the drier regions of southern and western Australia. The better known of the two species, *A. huegelii* (sometimes still listed as *Hibiscus huegelii*), has large flowers in the lilac-blue range and deeply lobed leaves. Alyogynes are fast growing, erect, leggy plants about 6–10 ft (2–3 m) tall. In the garden they can be improved by regular tip pruning after they have finished flowering.

Cultivation
They suit any frost-free warm climate and need full sun, shelter from strong winds and moderately fertile, well-drained soil. Propagate from seed or cuttings in summer.

Alyogyne huegelii

Alyogyne huegelii

The most commonly grown species, this
is distinguishable from *A. hakeifolia* by its
deeply lobed leaves and usually larger
flowers. It has a wide natural range
across southern Western Australia and
into South Australia. A spreading shrub
of open habit and 4–8 ft (1.2–2.5 m)
high, it can be pruned into a more
compact, bush shape if desired. The lilac
(or sometimes pinkish) flowers are up to
6 in (15 cm) across and open in succession from early spring through to late
summer. *Zones 10–11.*

AMELANCHIER
Serviceberry, snowy mespilus, juneberry

These shrubs and small trees, mostly
native to cool climates of North
America, belong to the pome-fruit group
of trees and shrubs in the rose family,
which includes apples, pears and quinces
as well as many 'berry' shrubs. Most are
deciduous, with simple oval leaves,
clusters of white flowers, frequently with
long narrow petals, and small rounded
fruit ripening to purple or black and
often sweet and edible. Some species
make attractive, graceful trees, valued
for the display of snowy white flowers in
spring and for their autumn coloring.

Amelanchier arborea

Cultivation

They do best in moist, fertile, acid soil in
full sun or light shade. They make good
understory trees for the edges of
woodlands. Propagate from seed or by
layering.

Amelanchier arborea
syn. *Amelanchier canadensis* of gardens
Downy serviceberry

Occurring naturally in the eastern USA,
this easily grown tree reaches about 20 ft
(6 m) in gardens, usually with a
narrowish crown and drooping lower
branches. The finely toothed, pointed
leaves are covered with white down as
they emerge in spring. Profuse flowers,
in short upright sprays, are followed in
early summer by small fleshy fruit. In
autumn the foliage turns red, orange or
yellow. *Zones 4–9.*

ANDROMEDA
Ericaceae
Bog rosemary

Only two species of low evergreen
shrubs make up this genus from the
colder parts of the northern hemisphere.
They have tough short branches that
root along the ground and small oblong
leathery leaves. The small flowers, in
short terminal sprays, are urn-shaped
with a narrow aperture.

Cultivation

Best grown in a shaded rock garden,
they prefer moist yet well-drained
conditions. They will tolerate any frosts
and prefer a cold climate. Propagate
from seed or small tip cuttings.

Andromeda polifolia

This tough little evergreen shrub comes
from the cool-temperate and near-arctic
regions of northern Europe, Asia and
North America. It grows to about 24 in
(60 cm) high and wide, and has narrow,

Andromeda polifolia

Anisodontea × hypomadarum

deep green 1 in (2 cm) long leaves with pale undersides. The tiny white to pink flowers appear in sprays in spring. *Zones 2–9.*

ANISODONTEA

This genus of shrubby mallows from southern Africa has tough, wiry stems and small flowers like miniature hibiscus, carried on slender stalks from short lateral shoots near the tips of the branches. The leaves are small and irregularly lobed. In recent years they have been rediscovered and popularized as free-blooming indoor plants, or in warm-temperate climates as garden shrubs. If grown indoors these plants must receive some sun or very strong reflected light.

Cultivation

They need frequent watering in the warmer half of the year, little in the cooler. Light pruning after flowers finish produces a more compact plant and encourages subsequent flowering. Propagate from summer cuttings, which strike readily. Grow them in a cold frame.

Anisodontea × hypomadarum

This evergreen bushy shrub has an erect habit, and can reach a height of 6 ft (1.8 m). Bowl-shaped, mid-pink flowers up to 1½ in (35 mm) across with darker

veins are borne from spring to autumn. Although regarded as a probable hybrid, its true parentage is unknown. *Zones 9–11.*

ARALIA

This genus of around 40 species of evergreen and deciduous shrubs and small trees and a few herbaceous perennials has a wide distribution in eastern and tropical Asia and the Americas. They have prickly stems, large, compound leaves consisting of numerous leaflets, and large, terminal panicles of densely packed, small cream flowers. Younger plants often make single, unbranched trunks with the leaves confined to the top, but as they age lateral branches develop and multiply to give a broad-headed small tree.

Cultivation

They need shelter from strong, drying winds and tolerate full sun or part-shade beneath taller trees. While a moist, fertile soil suits them well, poorer soils are said to produce hardier, longer-lived specimens. Propagate from seed in autumn or suckers in spring.

Aralia chinensis
Chinese aralia

As a young tree of up to about 10 ft (3 m), this species is usually single-stemmed with an irregular, umbrella-like crown of dark green leaves each about 4 ft (1.2 m) long, consisting of large, oval leaflets with closely toothed margins. It flowers in early autumn, producing large panicles of creamy yellow umbels that droop over the foliage. With age it branches into smaller crowns, with smaller leaves and flower sprays, and may reach as much as 30 ft (9 m) in height. The leaves turn yellowish in fall. *Zones 7–10.*

ARAUCARIA
Araucariaceae
Araucaria, monkey puzzle pine
This ancient genus of evergreen conifers is confined in the wild to South America,

Aralia chinensis

Araucaria araucana

Australia, Norfolk Island, New Guinea and New Caledonia. Most have massive straight trunks and crowded shorter lateral branches. The leathery leaves are incurved and densely overlapping in some species, flatter and spreading in others; male and female cones are on the same tree.

Cultivation
They prefer deep, moist, well-drained soil and full sun. Propagate from seed.

Araucaria araucana
Monkey puzzle pine
The remark that 'it would puzzle a monkey to climb it' gave it its common name. Specimens 80 ft (25 m) tall and 4 ft (1.2 m) in trunk diameter are known. Vigorous young trees have a domelike shape with interwoven branches, but with age the crown retreats to high above the ground, becoming progressively shallower. Leaves are glossy, rigid and prickly, and remain on the branch for many years. Globular cones are carried high on mature trees. *Zones 8–9.*

Araucaria heterophylla

Arbutus menziesii

Arbutus unedo

Araucaria heterophylla
Norfolk Island pine

Fast growing to 100 ft (30 m) or more, this conifer is widely planted along Australian coasts, although in recent years some near cities have suffered because of polluting detergents breaking down the waxy cuticle that makes them salt-tolerant. They are also wind-tolerant and able to thrive in deep coastal sands. They need reliable water when young, but can tolerate dry spells once established. The upright and regular branching pattern and its conical form make it very distinctive. It is widely grown as a shade-tolerant house plant. *Zones 10–11.*

ARBUTUS
Ericaceae
Strawberry tree, madrone

These spreading evergreen trees have thick trunks and sinuous limbs. Thick-textured leaves are finely toothed and flowers are small white or pinkish bells in compact clusters at branch ends. A few flowers develop into fleshy but hard globular fruit often with wrinkled surfaces, which take almost a year to ripen. The 'strawberry' refers to the hard, edible, reddish yellow fruit.

Cultivation

They prefer cool, humid climates, but tolerate summer droughts; climates with extreme heat and cold do not suit them. They adapt equally to peaty acid soils and limestone soils. Propagation is normally from seed.

Arbutus 'Marina'

Found as a chance seedling in a San Francisco garden, this presumed hybrid—showy, tough and relatively quick growing—is a large shrub that can be trained into a small tree of 20 ft (6 m) or more. The dark leaves serve as a backdrop for the soft pink flowers in large clusters in autumn; these are followed by fruit like those of *Arbutus menziesii* but larger. *Zones 9–10.*

Arbutus menziesii
Madrone

The madrone is the giant of the genus, reaching 100 ft (30 m) in height and 6 ft (2 m) in trunk diameter. It grows mostly in humid areas among tall conifers such as redwoods. The madrone has completely smooth orange-brown bark and smooth-edged glossy green leaves with whitish undersides, and produces large clusters of pure white flowers, and profuse small, orange-red fruits. *Zones 7–9.*

Arbutus unedo
Arbutus, strawberry tree

This bushy-crowned tree can attain 30 ft (10 m), though 10–15 ft (3–5 m) is more usual. The bark is dark gray-brown, but the smaller branches and twigs have an attractive reddish hue. In autumn the white or pinkish flower clusters, along with the orange fruits from the previous year, contrast with the dark evergreen foliage. 'Compacta' is a smaller cultivar. *Zones 7–10.*

ARCHONTOPHOENIX
Arecaceae

These fine subtropical palms have tall, solitary trunks topped by a green 'crown-shaft' from which long, arching fronds radiate. Old fronds fall cleanly from the trunk, leaving ringed scars. Large panicles of tiny, fragrant flowers burst one at a time from massive green buds.

Cultivation

They are not frost-hardy, and prefer fertile soils. Propagate from seed.

Archontophoenix alexandrae
Alexandra palm

This species has a straight trunk up to 50 ft (15 m) tall and arching fronds 9–12 ft (3–4 m) long. Distinguishing features are the silver-gray undersurface of the fronds, and the cream flowers on a spreading panicle which appear mostly in autumn. *Zones 10–11.*

Archontophoenix cunninghamiana
Bangalow palm, piccabeen palm

Similar in appearance and requirements to the Alexandra palm, this species

Archontophoenix alexandrae

Archontophoenix cunninghamiana

differs in the green undersides of the fronds, the rusty scurf coating the crownshaft, and the longer, vertically pendulous panicles of pale lilac flowers. From the subtropical Australian east coast, it prefers slightly cooler climates and is quite shade tolerant. *Zones 9–11.*

ARCTOSTAPHYLOS
Bearberry, manzanita

This genus of around 50 species of evergreen shrubs or, rarely, small trees includes 2 species widely distributed through cool climates of the northern hemisphere; all others are native to western North America or Mexico. They are tough plants with woody stems, smallish, leathery leaves and small clusters of white or pink, bell-shaped flowers. Some Californian species from the 'chaparral' evergreen scrub of the coastal ranges can survive the fires that periodically ravage it. The purple, red or orange bark peels in thin shreds or flakes.

Cultivation

They need full sun or part-shade and moist but well-drained, fertile, lime-free soil. The seed, enclosed in a small fleshy fruit, is difficult to germinate. Manzanitas are propagated from tip cuttings hardened off in winter; treatment with smoke may assist germination.

Arctostaphylos 'Emerald Carpet'

A ground-covering form thought to be a hybrid of two coastal Californian species, this plant grows to a height of 12 in (30 cm) although it may spread 6 ft (1.8 m) or more. The pale pink flowers are relatively inconspicuous. It prefers a little shade in hotter regions and is an excellent bank cover. *Zones 8–10.*

Arctostaphylos 'Emerald Carpet'

Arctostaphylos uva-ursi

Arctostaphylos manzanita
Common manzanita

Native to California, this plant reaches 8 ft (2.4 m) or more in height and spread. A slow-growing, stiff, woody shrub, it has thick, oval leaves coated in a whitish scurf when young; the striking, reddish brown bark is sometimes hidden by peeling strips of duller, older bark. Tight clusters of small, urn-shaped, deep pink flowers in early spring are followed by red-brown berries. *Zones 7–10.*

Arctostaphylos uva-ursi
Bearberry, kinnikinnick

Found in the wild in the colder regions of the northern hemisphere, this species is best known as a completely prostrate form that can cascade over walls or embankments to form curtains of neat, dark green foliage that develops intense red tones in autumn and winter. In late spring it bears small clusters of dull pink, almost globular flowers, followed by green berries that ripen to red. 'Vancouver Jade' is an exceptionally vigorous and disease-resistant selection. 'Point Reyes' is tolerant of coastal conditions. *Zones 3–9.*

Arctostaphylos manzanita

ARDISIA
Marlberry

This is a large genus consisting of over 250 species of evergreen trees and shrubs, widely distributed in tropical and subtropical regions of Asia and the Americas. The leathery leaves are mostly toothed in wavy margins. The smallish flowers are star-like, mostly white or pinkish, and the fruit are small, one-seeded berries (drupes), sometimes profuse and decorative.

Cultivation

When grown outdoors they prefer a moist, part-shaded position in well-drained, slightly acid soil with a high humus

Ardisia crenata

Ardisia crenata

Aucuba japonica 'Crotonifolia'

content. Some smaller-growing ardisias are suited to container culture. Propagate from cuttings, or by division.

Ardisia crenata
syn. *Ardisia crenulata*
Coral berry

Growing up to 6 ft (1.8 m) but more often seen half that height or smaller, this shrub species has a wide distribution in Southeast Asia extending to eastern China and southern Japan. Its leathery leaves have attractively wavy margins and are densely massed above a short, single trunk. Small, white flowers emerge laterally in sprays during summer and are followed by densely clustered, bright red berries. 'Alba' has white berries; 'Variegata' has a narrow margin, red on new leaves but turning white as they mature. *Zones 8–11.*

AUCUBA
Cornaceae
Aucuba, spotted laurel

This is a small East Asian genus of shrubs, valued for their tolerance of heavy shade and large, often colorful, evergreen leaves. Clusters of large red berries appear in autumn but, with flowers of different sexes on different plants, it is only the females that fruit.

Cultivation

This tough, resilient plant tolerates neglect and pollution but responds to better treatment with more luxuriant growth.

Aucuba japonica

Usually seen as a shrub of 4–6 ft (1.2–2 m), this aucuba spreads by basal sprouting and self-layering of its soft-wooded stems; as it thickens up, the mass of stems supports each other, allowing an ultimate height of about 10 ft (3 m). 'Crotonifolia' (male) is among the best of many other cultivars with leaves more heavily splashed with yellow. *Zones 7–10.*

BAMBUSA
Bamboo

This genus of around 120 species of clump-forming bamboos is found in tropical and subtropical Asia. Many are very large, up to 80 ft (24 m) tall or more, with strong, woody, hollow stems. In their native lands they are put to all sorts of uses, especially in construction, including scaffolding, and for piping and fencing. The upper parts of the stems are often arching, and branch at the nodes into wiry branchlets with masses of grass-like leaves. The flowers are insignificant, often half-hidden among the foliage on slender, arching panicles which are usually produced intermittently. *Bambusa* species have the advantage over some other bamboos of having short rather than long-running rhizomes and so are much less invasive.

Cultivation

They thrive in warm-temperate to tropical climates with humid conditions and deep, humus-rich soil. Plant in part-shade. Select growing sites with care, as many can become invasive. Propagate by division in spring.

Bambusa multiplex 'Alphonse Karr'

Bambusa multiplex
syn. *Bambusa glaucescens*
Hedge bamboo

A native of southern China, this variable species has gracefully arching stems usually 10–30 ft (3–9 m) tall and 1–2 in (25–50 mm) in diameter topped with plumes of narrow, 6 in (15 cm) long leaves with silvery undersides. One of the more cold-tolerant *Bambusa* species, it is mostly represented in gardens by yellow-leafed and variegated cultivars. 'Alphonse Karr' has yellow-striped stems, tinted pink when young. *Zones 9–11.*

BAUERA
Baueraceae

This small, Australian genus of evergreen shrubs bears star-shaped pink or white flowers. Branches are thin and wiry, and the small leaves are in whorls of 6 at each node, from which the flowers arise on very fine stalks.

Cultivation

They are moderately frost-hardy and grow best in moist, sandy or peaty soil in a sunny or part-shaded position. Propagate from cuttings.

Bauera sessiliflora
Grampians bauera

This species is the most colorful in flower, its long, scrambling branches strung with tight clusters of bright rose-magenta flowers that appear in late spring and early summer. When supported by other shrubs, it often scrambles to a height of 6 ft (1.8 m) or more, but can be kept trimmed if a neat bush is desired. Paler pink and white forms are also known. *Zones 9–10.*

BAUHINIA
Caesalpiniaceae

This variable genus of evergreen and dry-season-deciduous trees, shrubs and climbers comes from warm parts of Asia, the Americas, Africa and Australia. All have characteristic 2-lobed leaves but are grown for their beautiful flowers whose likeness to orchids or butterflies has given rise to the common names of several species. Flattened brown seed pods follow and often persist on the branches for months.

Cultivation

Bauhinias do best in tropical and subtropical areas and need protection from frost and cold winds. Full sun and light, fertile, well-drained soil suit them best. Propagate from seed.

Bauhinia × *blakeana*
Hong Kong orchid tree

Bauhinia × *blakeana* is a presumed hybrid between *B. variegata* and the rather similar *B. purpurea*. It was first found in China in 1908, and was later adopted as Hong Kong's floral emblem. It resembles *B. variegata* but makes a taller, more densely foliaged and ever-green tree, with broader leaves. The slightly fragrant flowers, up to 6 in (15 cm) across on a healthy specimen, are a purplish red except for darker streaks on

the inner petals, and are borne from late autumn through winter. It sets few seed pods. *Zones 10–11.*

Bauhinia variegata
Orchid tree, mountain ebony

This small tree bears abundant, fragrant, large orchid-like flowers in spring and intermittently in summer. These vary from tree to tree, from near-white to rose-pink, but always with a deeper shade on the upper petal. It grows to

Bauhinia × *blakeana*

Bauera sessiliflora

Bauhinia variegata

Beaucarnea recurvata

Berberis darwinii

15–25 ft (5–8 m), larger in the tropics, with a short trunk and spreading branches, and is half-hardy. In tropical climates the orchid tree is semi-evergreen, in cooler locations almost deciduous. *Zones 9–11*.

BEAUCARNEA

This genus consists of 20 or more species of evergreen trees and shrubs from semi-desert regions of Mexico and far southern USA. Related to yuccas, they have remarkable thickened stems and long, thin, grass-like leaves. The numerous small white flowers are borne in large panicles arising from the centers of the leaf rosettes, though only on plants with trunks more than 3 ft (1 m) or so high, which are generally at least 10 years old. The plant usually remains single stemmed until at least this height, but if the top is cut off it will sprout many new shoots.

Cultivation

They can be grown outdoors in mild to warm climates, in full sun and well-drained, fertile soil. Water well while growing, but sparingly in winter. Propagate from seed in spring or from suckers.

Beaucarnea recurvata
syns *Nolina recurvata, N. tuberculata*
Ponytail palm

This slow-growing, evergreen tree is commonly sold in pots for the novel appearance of its swollen stem base; this tapers upward to a palm-like trunk bearing at its apex a dense crown of strap-like, downward-curving leaves up to 3 ft (1 m) long. Mature plants bear large feathery panicles of cream flowers in spring, followed by pinkish 3-winged fruit. Old specimens can achieve massive dimensions, the swollen base reaching up to 12 ft (3.5 m) wide, with multiple trunks 15–20 ft (4.5–6 m) tall. *Zones 9–11*.

BERBERIS
Berberidaceae
Barberry

The barberries are a large group of mostly very hardy shrubs, both evergreen and deciduous, with densely massed canes and weak spines where the small leaves join the stems. Small yellow, cream, orange or reddish flowers are followed by elongated, fleshy fruits.

Cultivation

Barberries are easy to grow and thrive in most soil types; they withstand hard

Berberis wilsoniae

Berberis thunbergii 'Atropurpurea Nana'

pruning. Full sun suits them best. Propagate from seeds or cuttings.

Berberis darwinii
Darwin barberry
A showy evergreen species from Chile and Argentina, *B. darwinii* has small dark green, glossy leaves with holly-like toothing and short, dense clusters of small bright yellow flowers in late winter and spring. It makes a shrub 6 ft (2 m) high and wide. It has been crossed with *B. empetrifolia* to produce *B. × stenophylla*, with several named clones including the dwarf 'Corallina Compacta' and the tall and floriferous 'Crawley Gem'. *Zones 7–10.*

Berberis thunbergii
Thunberg barberry, Japanese barberry
Native to Japan, this low-growing deciduous shrub (almost evergreen in warmer climates), only 5 ft (1.5 m) high, has densely massed stems and small, neatly rounded leaves. Small, bell-shaped flowers appear in spring and are greenish yellow with dull red stripes. 'Atropurpurea' has deep purplish brown foliage turning a metallic bronze-black in fall. 'Atropurpurea Nana' ('Little

Favorite') is a dwarf, bun-shaped plant only 12–18 in (30–45 cm) high with similar toning. *Zones 4–10.*

Berberis wilsoniae
Wilson barberry
Deciduous, or almost evergreen in warmer climates, this species has small, narrow, toothless leaves with rounded tips and a densely bushy habit. It grows about 5 ft (1.5 m) high. Inconspicuous yellow flowers from late spring to early summer are followed by abundant pink fruit, turning deeper red at the same time as the foliage takes on tints of yellow, orange and red. *Zones 5–10.*

BETULA
Betulaceae
Birch
Trees of the far northern regions of the globe, birches are admired as landscape subjects. Their appeal lies in the white to pinkish brown trunks, combined with vivid green spring foliage and delicate tracery of winter twigs. The broad serrated leaves turn gold in autumn. Their fast early growth yet fairly modest final height make them ideal for gardens or streets.

Cultivation

Birches need a cool climate with occasional winter snowfall. Propagation is normally from seed, produced in millions from the cylindrical female catkins. They grow best in deep, well-drained soils but some adapt to poorer, shallower soils.

Betula papyrifera
Paper birch, canoe birch

Famed for its tough papery bark, once used by Native Americans for their light but strong canoes, the paper birch is one of the most wide-ranging North American species and is extremely cold hardy. It reaches 60 ft (18 m) in cultivation, and has a sparse crown. The largish leaves are broadly heart-shaped or egg-shaped. The white or cream bark peels off in thin, curling layers, exposing new bark of a pale orange-brown. From southern Alaska is a smaller-growing tree, *B. papyrifera* var. *kenaica* — up to 40 ft (12 m) with slightly smaller leaves and fissured bark at the base of older trees. *Zones 2–7.*

Betula pendula
Silver birch, white birch

The silver birch has smooth gray-white bark and fine arching branchlets. It is quite trouble-free in terms of pests and diseases. Its height is around 30–50 ft (10–15 m) in temperate climates. However, in Scandinavia it can reach 65–80 ft (20–25 m) and is an important timber tree there. Cultivars include 'Dalecarlica', with deeply incised leaves and strongly weeping branches, and 'Youngii', with growth like a weeping willow. *Zones 2–9.*

Betula pendula

Betula papyrifera

Betula utilis var. jacquemontii

Betula utilis
Himalayan birch

These medium to large trees have pale, smooth, peeling bark and broadly domed crowns. The leaves, dark green with paler undersides and irregularly toothed, are up to 3 in (8 cm) long. The most widely grown is var. *jacquemontii*, with white or cream bark that peels off in horizontal bands. Several clones of this variety have outstanding bark qualities. Forms with darker orange-brown barks have also been introduced. *Zones 7–9.*

BORONIA
Rutaceae

Indigenous to Australia, this genus of small to medium-sized evergreen shrubs bears pretty pink flowers (white, cream, brown or red in a minority of species) and aromatic foliage. Many flower prolifically in the wild but do not adapt well to cultivation and are often short lived.

Cultivation

They do best in sheltered positions in sun or part-shade, in moist, well-drained, acid soil. Propagation is best achieved using semi-hardened tip cuttings.

Boronia heterophylla
Red boronia, kalgan boronia

This erect, compact shrub to 5 ft (1.5 m) tall has finely divided bright green leaves.

Masses of rose-red, bell-shaped flowers are borne in late winter to early spring. A popular commercial cut flower, it prefers a cooler climate than some other boronias, and soil with added organic matter to ensure adequate moisture and provide a cool root run. *Zones 9–10.*

Boronia megastigma
Brown boronia

The perfume of this species is its main attraction. The hanging cup-shaped flowers that appear in late winter and spring are brownish purple to yellow-green outside and yellow-green inside. It grows to 3 ft (1 m) and tolerates light frost, but is short lived. There are a number of varieties with different flower coloration, but they often lack the fragrance of the typical species. 'Lutea' has yellow flowers and yellow-green leaves. 'Harlequin' is a brownish pink and white candy-striped variety. *Zones 9–10.*

BOUVARDIA
Rubiaceae

A small genus of soft-wooded shrubs from Mexico and Central America, these frost-tender plants are grown for their attractive tubular flowers.

Cultivation

They require a warm, sunny position, sheltered from wind. The soil needs to be fertile and well drained. Water well

Boronia megastigma 'Harlequin'

Boronia heterophylla

Brachychiton acerifolius

Bouvardia longiflora

and feed regularly during the growing period. Cut back stems by half after flowering to maintain shape. Propagate from softwood or root cuttings. They are susceptible to attack by sap-sucking insects such as whitefly and mealybug.

Bouvardia longiflora
Scented bouvardia

Previously known as *Bouvardia* 'Humboldtii', this tender, weak-stemmed evergreen grows to a height and spread of 3 ft (1 m) or more. It is easily damaged by strong winds. The strongly perfumed, snow-white flowers are about 1 in (2.5 cm) wide and are borne in terminal clusters in autumn and winter. The dark green leaves are small and lance-shaped. *Zones 10–11.*

BRACHYCHITON
Sterculiaceae

This variable genus consists of warm-climate, evergreen or dry-season-deciduous trees. Some occur naturally in tropical and subtropical rainforests and others in semi-arid areas where their edible leaves and bark are used as fodder in dry seasons. Some of the arid-climate species have massive, swollen, water-storing trunks.

Cultivation

They need light, well-drained soils. Propagate from fresh seed.

Brachychiton acerifolius
Illawarra flame-tree, flame kurrajong

The flame-tree can reach 35–50 ft (11–15 m) in cultivation. Profuse foamy sprays of bright scarlet flowers are borne in spring or early summer on the leafless crown, or on individual branches that shed their leaves before flowering. Flowering is erratic from year to year and seems best following a dry, mild winter. Seedling trees may take years to first flower; grafted plants should flower in 5 to 8 years. It needs shelter from salty winds and from frost. *Zones 9–11.*

Brachychiton populneus
syns *Brachychiton diversifolius, Sterculia diversifolia*
Widely distributed on rocky hillsides, this bushy headed evergreen tree is grown chiefly for shade, or on farms for its fodder value in times of scarcity. During summer it produces among the foliage masses of greenish cream bell-shaped

Brugmansia × candida

Brachychiton populneus

flowers, spotted inside with purple or yellow to attract bees. It will tolerate limestone soils. *Zones 8–11.*

BRAHEA
Arecaceae

This genus of fan-leafed palms range from low-growing plants with no trunk developing, to tall, solitary-trunked palms with compact crowns. Tiny flowers are borne on panicles that may exceed the fronds in length and, as the date-like fruits develop, hang below the crown.

Cultivation

Some tolerate moderately severe frosts when established. Propagate from seed; seedling growth is slow.

Brahea armata

This species is known for the pale blue-gray color of its stiff fronds. It grows to a height of 20 ft (7 m). Arching stems, up to 15 ft (5 m) long, extend well beyond the foliage canopy. *Zones 9–11.*

BRUGMANSIA
Solanaceae
Angel's trumpet

This genus consists of evergreen or semi-evergreen trees and shrubs with

Brahea armata

large, fragrant, pendent trumpet flowers. Leaves are large and soft, and all parts of the plant are narcotic and poisonous.

Cultivation

Frost-tender to half-hardy, they prefer a warm to hot climate, and a light, fertile, well-drained soil. Whitefly, red spider mite and snails can cause problems. Propagate from soft-tip cuttings.

Brugmansia × candida

This tree, 10–15 ft (3–5 m) high, has angel's trumpet branches from a short trunk and long, oval, velvety leaves confined to the branch tips. The pendulous white flowers, strongly scented at night, are about 12 in (30 cm) long and have a widely flared mouth. 'Plena' has an extra frill of petals inside the main trumpet; 'Apricot' (sometimes known as *B. versicolor*) has pale apricot-pink flowers. *Zones 10–11.*

Brugmansia suaveolens
This many-branched spreading evergreen shrub to 15 ft (5 m) has downy oval leaves up to 12 in (30 cm) long. The pendulous flowers are slightly narrow and their tubes are heavily striped with green and may appear in profuse flushes through summer and autumn. 'Plena' has semi-double blooms. *Zones 10–11.*

BRUNFELSIA
Solanaceae
These evergreen shrubs bear fragrant, tubular flowers with 5 flat petals; these change color from their first day of opening through successive days, with flowers of different ages sprinkling the bush. *B. americana* has white flowers which turn cream and pale golden as they age. Most progress through purples, blues and white.

Brunfelsia pauciflora

Cultivation
They need a frost-free site, in full sun and fertile, well-drained soil with adequate water. Propagate from soft-tip cuttings. They may all contain poisonous alkaloids, particularly in their fruits.

Brunfelsia pauciflora
syn. *B. calycina, B. eximia*
This small, slow growing deciduous or semi-evergreen shrub grows to about 5 ft (1.5 m) tall and wide. Large, abundant flowers open to a rich purple, fading to mauve and white over successive days, all through spring and early summer. *Zones 10–11.*

BUDDLEIA
Loganiaceae
Leaves are large, pointed and often crepe-textured, usually in opposite pairs. The fragrant flowers are small and tubular, in dense spikes at branch tips or sometimes in smaller clusters along the branches. They range through pinks, mauves, reddish purples, oranges and yellows.

Cultivation
Propagate from semi-ripe cuttings.

Buddleia alternifolia
In full bloom in late spring and early summer, this tall deciduous shrub from

Brugmansia suaveolens

northwestern China is transformed into a fountain of fragrant, mauve-pink blossoms, the small individual flowers strung in clusters along its arching branches. It looks best trained to a single trunk so the branches can weep effectively from above, and should not be pruned back hard as it flowers on the previous summer's wood. *Zones 5–9.*

Buddleia davidii
Butterfly bush

The butterfly bush is a deciduous shrub of about 12 ft (4 m). In late summer and early autumn its arching canes bear at their tips long narrow cones of densely packed flowers which are mauve with an orange eye. Prune hard in late winter. Cultivars include 'White Bouquet' (cream with an orange eye), 'Royal Red' (magenta) and 'Black Knight' (dark purple). *Zones 5–10*

Buddleia globosa
Orange ball tree

This species has deep golden orange balls of tiny flowers, hanging from the branch tips in late spring and summer.

Buddleia alternifolia

Buddleia davidii 'Royal Red'

Buddleia globosa

The strongly veined leaves are covered in white 'fur', as are the twigs and flower-stalks. It is a tall shrub of 10–15 ft (3–5 m) or so, making fast growth under sheltered conditions but short lived. *Zones 7–10.*

BUTIA
Arecaceae

This genus of moderately frost-hardy palms comes from central South America. They have short thick trunks and thick-textured, recurved fronds, and are adaptable to a range of climates and conditions. They periodically produce among the fronds large panicles of scented small cream flowers (reddish in bud), followed by abundant fruits with juicy but fibrous flesh enclosing a hard stone with 3 'eyes' like a miniature coconut.

Cultivation

Propagate from seed in spring.

Butia capitata
Butia palm, jelly palm

Variable in shape, this becomes a small, graceful palm of around 10 ft (3 m) after 15 years. It has long, gray-green feather-shaped fronds which are arching and recurved. The orange-yellow fruits have edible pulp, used for jellies, or fermented to make wine. *Zones 8–11.*

BUXUS
Buxaceae
Box

Traditional evergreens of cool climates, boxes have small, neat, leathery leaves and a dense growth habit. Though regarded as shrubs, they are capable (except for some dwarf cultivars) of growing into small trees. Creamy yellow box wood was once used for woodcut blocks for printing. Boxes withstand regular close clipping, so are ideal for

Buxus microphylla var. japonica

Butia capitata

topiary, formal hedges and mazes. Flowers are greenish yellow.

Cultivation

They thrive in most soils and in sun or shade, and adapt well to warmer climates. Propagate from cuttings.

Buxus microphylla
Japanese box

This east Asian box, long grown in Japan but unknown in the wild, first came to Western gardens as a dwarf cultivar with distorted leaves. Later, wild forms were discovered in Japan, Korea and China and named as varieties: *Buxus microphylla* var. *japonica* (syn. *B. japonica*), *B. m.* var. *koreana* and *B. m.* var. *sinica* respectively. They are all similar to the European box but the leaves are slightly glossier and more rounded at the tip, with the broadest part somewhat above the middle. The leaves turn a pale yellow-brown in frosty winters. In North America *B. m.* var. *koreana* is popular for its compact, low-growing habit and cold hardiness. *Zones 6–10.*

Buxus sempervirens
European box, common box

The common box has grown as tall as 30 ft (10 m) with a trunk 12 in (30 cm) thick, but as a garden shrub it is commonly only 3–6 ft (1–2 m) high. There is a huge range of forms and cultivars, including variegated clones. 'Suffruticosa' has a very dense, bushy habit. *Zones 5–10.*

Buxus sempervirens 'Suffruticosa'

C

Caesalpinia gilliesii

Caesalpinia pulcherrima

CAESALPINIA
Caesalpiniaceae

This diverse genus is found in warmer regions around the world and includes trees, shrubs and scrambling climbers. The leaves of all caesalpinias are bipinnate; the flowers are in spikes from upper leaf axils, mostly in shades of red, yellow or cream, with separate petals and often conspicuous stamens.

Cultivation

Most species appreciate a sheltered sunny spot and deep sandy soil. Propagation is from seed, which may need treatment such as abrading and hot-water soaking to aid germination.

Caesalpinia gilliesii
Dwarf poinciana, bird of paradise bush

Previously known as *Poinciana gilliesii*; in warm climates this attractive plant with fern-like foliage can grow to a small tree, but in cultivation it seldom exceeds 10 ft (3 m). It is native to subtropical Argentina and Uruguay. Heads of yellow on cream flowers with prominent scarlet stamens are produced in summer. Shelter from strong wind and frosts is essential. Although evergreen in warm wet climates, it is elsewhere semi-deciduous or deciduous. *Zones 9–11.*

Caesalpinia pulcherrima
syn. *Poinciana pulcherrima*
Peacock flower, Barbados pride, red bird of paradise

Mostly seen as a shrub of about 8 ft (2.4 m), this tropical American species can grow to 15–20 ft (4.5–6 m). Short lived and fast growing, it has an open, moderately spreading habit with coarse, prickly leaves and branches with a whitish waxy bloom, which terminate from spring to autumn in tall, upright sprays of vivid, usually scarlet and gold blossom. *Zones 10–11.*

CALCEOLARIA
Scrophulariaceae

Most members of this quite large South American genus are herbaceous perennials or annuals, but a few are shrubs. Their chief attraction is the curiously shaped flower, the petals fused together and inflated into a pouch-like structure, mostly in shades of yellow, orange or red.

Cultivation

They are moderately cold-hardy, but like a sheltered sunny position and ample soil moisture. Propagate from cuttings.

Calceolaria integrifolia

Native to Chile, this is a spreading shrub of loose and untidy habit, kept in shape

Calceolaria integrifolia

Calliandra tweedii

by pruning, and reaching a height of 4 ft (1.2 m). It has closely veined leaves with a fine 'seersucker' texture but is prone to insect damage. From late spring to early autumn a succession of bright yellow or bronze-yellow flowers appear in long-stalked clusters from the branch tips. *Zones 8–10.*

CALLIANDRA
Mimosaceae

A few species of this large genus of evergreen shrubs and small trees from the American tropics and subtropics are cultivated as ornamentals, valued for their showy flower heads with numerous long stamens. Leaves are bipinnate but vary greatly in both number and size of leaflets; in most species the leaves 'sleep' at night or in dull, stormy weather, the leaflets folding together. Many are tough, long-lived plants, thriving in most soils and positions.

Cultivation

Cold-hardiness varies; some can withstand a little frost as long as this is compensated for by hot summers. Propagation is from seed or cuttings.

Calliandra haematocephala
Blood-red tassel-flower, pink or red powderpuff

A native of tropical South America, this species produces large flowerheads around 3 in (8 cm) in diameter. The flowers appear almost year round but are most numerous in autumn and

Calliandra haematocephala

winter. It makes a large, broadly spreading shrub to a height of 12 ft (4 m) and an even greater spread with age. The leaves consist of rather few oblong leaflets about 2 in (5 cm) long, pink-flushed when first unfolding. It will grow and flower well in warm-temperate climates if sheltered from frost. *Zones 10–11.*

Calliandra tweedii
Red tassel-flower

Native to subtropical South America, this evergreen shrub has a height and spread of around 6 ft (2 m). Its fern-like bipinnate leaves consist of numerous tiny leaflets and crimson pompon flowers appear among the foliage through spring and summer. It prefers full sun, a light, well-drained soil and copious summer water. Prune after flowering to promote bushiness. *Zones 9–11.*

CALLISTEMON
Myrtaceae
Bottlebrush

These evergreen Australian shrubs or small trees bear spikes of long-stamened flowers that resemble a bottle brush, hence the common name. Many species are weeping in habit and attract birds. New leaves grow from the tips of the flower-spikes, leaving long-lasting woody seed capsules behind. Prune after flowering to promote bushiness and flowering.

Callistemon viminalis

Callistemon salignus

Cultivation

They are easily grown and adaptable to a variety of conditions and climates, but generally they are only marginally frost tolerant and prefer full sun and moist soil. Propagate species from seed, cultivars from tip cuttings.

Callistemon citrinus
Scarlet bottlebrush

This tough, vigorous plant grows quite rapidly to 6–8 ft (2–2.5 m), with a short basal trunk and many low branches. *Citrinus* refers to the lemon smell of the crushed foliage. The fine scarlet to crimson bottlebrush flowers are about 5 in (12 cm) long and held rather erect, appearing in late spring and summer. Cultivars include 'Burgundy', with clustered wine-colored brushes and pinkish red leaves when young; 'Mauve Mist', with abundant brushes that start mauve and age deeper magenta; and 'Splendens' ('Endeavour'), with bright scarlet brushes. *Zones 8–11.*

Callistemon salignus
White bottlebrush, pink-tips, willow bottlebrush

This dense, erect tree from coastal eastern Australia grows to 15–30 ft (5–10 m). Bark is thick and papery and the leaves are narrow and pointed. The new growth flushes are pinkish. The

Callistemon citrinus 'Burgundy'

long spikes of flowers that appear in spring and summer are normally pale greenish yellow, though red-flowered plants are also in cultivation. A hardy bottlebrush, it tolerates very wet or very dry conditions, salt and wind. *Zones 9–11.*

Callistemon viminalis
Weeping bottlebrush

This tree reaches up to 25 ft (8 m) with a domed crown of gracefully weeping branches. Foliage is aromatic when crushed and the flowers have scarlet or crimson stamens. Often planted as a street tree or used for screening, this species is less cold-hardy but more damp loving than others. 'Captain Cook' is a dwarf seedling variation which forms a tree-like shrub to about 8 ft (2.5 m). *Zones 9–11.*

CALLUNA
Ericaceae
Heather, ling

Heather is the dominant moorland plant of the colder parts of the British Isles and northern Europe; it is closely related to the heath genus *Erica*. In winter the plants turn brownish or dull purple. The numerous cultivars, selected for dwarf and compact growth, flower color or foliage color, are mostly grown.

Cultivation

They are extremely hardy plants, thriving in exposed situations and often performing poorly under kinder conditions. Soils should be acidic and gritty, and of low fertility. Where summers are humid they are prone to root and stem rot. Propagate from tip cuttings.

Calluna vulgaris

Common heather makes a spreading subshrub 12–24 in (30–60 cm) high, rooting from the branches. Flowers are pale pink to a strong purplish pink, occasionally white. Some flower through summer, others from mid-summer to early autumn, others entirely in autumn, such as the pink double-flowered 'H. E. Beale'. 'Mair's Variety' has pure white flowers. 'Orange Queen' is a very compact plant grown for its foliage, golden yellow in summer changing to deep burnt-orange in winter. *Zones 4–9.*

CALOCEDRUS
Cupressaceae

Included in the cypress family *(Cupressaceae)* are several widely scattered small genera that have their branchlets arranged in strongly flattened sprays, each branchlet with small scale-leaves that alternate between large (lateral) and small (facial) pairs. These genera have a characteristic cone structure; in *Calocedrus* the cones have only 4 seed-bearing scales, lying parallel in 2 opposite pairs, each scale with only 2 winged seeds. *Calocedrus* means 'beautiful cedar'.

Cultivation

They do best in cool, moist mountain areas and in deep, moderately fertile soils, but may survive under poorer conditions as small, bushy trees.

Calluna vulgaris 'Orange Queen'

Calycanthus floridus

Calocedrus decurrens

Calycanthus occidentalis

Calocedrus decurrens
Incense cedar

Native to forests of the Californian Sierras and adjacent Oregon, this species is a large, conical tree in the wild, often broad at the base but tapering to a spire-like crown, with dense, aromatic, rich green foliage. The reddish brown bark has thick, spongy ridges separated by deep fissures on the lower trunk. The cones ripen to pale golden brown. The timber is soft, durable and aromatic, and is valued for cabinet-making. It is not very drought-hardy. *Zones 5–9.*

CALYCANTHUS
Calycanthaceae
Allspice

The leaves, bark and wood of these deciduous cool-climate shrubs from North America have a spicy aroma when cut or bruised. Undemanding shrubs, they flower best in a sunny but sheltered position. They have curiously colored flowers, which appear singly among the leaves in late spring or summer and have narrow petals that are deep red-brown or dull reddish purple; the flowers make interesting indoor decorations.

Cultivation

Propagation is usually by layering branches, or from the seeds which are contained in soft, fig-like fruits.

Calycanthus floridus
Carolina allspice

A shrub from southeastern USA, the Carolina allspice grows to about 6–8 ft (2–2.5 m) and has broad, glossy pale green leaves with downy undersides. Flowers consist of many petals that are dull brownish red, often with paler tips. It flowers in early summer. *Zones 6–10.*

Calycanthus occidentalis
Spice bush, Californian allspice

This species, from the ranges of northern California, makes a shrub of rather irregular growth up to 12 ft (3.5 m) tall.

The leaves are larger than those of *C. floridus* and their undersides are not downy. The flowers are also larger, sometimes 3 in (8 cm) across. *Zones 6–10.*

CAMELLIA
Theaceae
There are tens of thousands of cultivars; most are descended from *C. japonica*. Forming evergreen woody shrubs or small trees, camellias have glossy, deep green leaves and abundant blooms over a long period. Flowers are single, semi-double, anemone-form, peony-form (sometimes called informal-double), double and formal-double, and range in size from miniature to over 5 in (13 cm).

Cultivation
Camellias prefer warm-temperate climates and well-drained, slightly acid soil enriched with organic matter; they like semi-shade. Good drainage prevents phytophthora root rot. Many are suited to container culture. Propagate from seed.

Camellia japonica
The original species formed a small scraggly tree 20–30 ft (7–10 m) tall in its natural habitats, but there is now so much variation in shape, size, and in flower form and coloration that no single description suffices. Flowering time varies between winter and spring. Popular cultivars include 'C. M. Hovey', with medium-sized, formal-double, carmine flowers; 'Debutante', with large, full, informal-double, soft pink flowers; 'Hana Fuki' with large, semi-double, cup-shaped, soft pink flowers sometimes splashed white. 'Nuccio's Gem' has large formal-double white blooms with up to 10 tiers of rounded petals. *Zones 5–10.*

Camellia reticulata hybrids
Camellia reticulata and its hybrids have large, leathery leaves and produce

Camellia reticulata 'Dr. Clifford Parks'

Camellia japonica 'Nuccio's Gem'

magnificent single and double saucer-shaped flowers often as large as 8 in (20 cm) across with ruffled, fluted petals. 'Captain Rawes', the original type plant introduced in 1820, is still available, but many cultivars and hybrids are now superior garden subjects, bushier and easier to grow. Flower colors range from red ('Dr. Clifford Parks') through pink ('Pavlova'); some are variegated with white but none is entirely white. *Zones 8–10.*

Camellia sasanqua
The sasanquas are densely leafed plants with small, shiny, dark green leaves and small, fragrant, mostly single flowers in a variety of colors, profusely produced but individually short lived. Sasanquas are faster growing and hardier than most other camellias and more sun tolerant,

performing better in temperate than in cold climates. Among superior cultivars are 'Hiryu', a bushy and upright plant, with bright to deep rosy red flowers; 'Jennifer Susan' with clear pink semi-double flowers; and 'Plantation Pink' with large saucer-shaped single soft pink flowers. *Zones 9–11.*

Camellia sinensis
Tea

All the world's tea comes from this species, grown mainly in plantations in the highlands of tropical Asia but also in southern China (its original home) and Japan, and more recently in other parts of the world where the climate is suitably mild and humid. The tender

Camellia sasanqua 'Plantation Pink'

Camellia × williamsii 'Donation'

new shoots are plucked, fermented and dried in different ways to give black or green tea. It normally makes a shrub of 6–10 ft (1.8–3 m) tall with thin, serrated leaves and insignificant, white to cream with a hint of lemon flowers borne on recurved stalks from the leaf axils; when grown for tea the plants are kept trimmed to about chest height and flowers are rarely seen. *C. sinensis* var. *assamica* is the Assam tea now grown universally in India and Sri Lanka, with larger leaves and more vigorous growth. *Zones 9–11.*

Camellia × williamsii

This hybrid camellia and its many cultivars are tall, relatively fast-growing shrubs that flower prolifically over a long period in winter and spring. They are more tolerant of alkaline soil and low summer humidity than *C. japonica*. They tend to have mainly semi-double, pink flowers. Typical flower forms include 'Caerhays' with medium-sized lilac-rose flowers; and 'Donation' with large orchid pink semi-double flowers, regarded as one of the finest camellias. *Zones 7–10.*

Camellia sinensis

Carpenteria californica

Carissa macrocarpa

CARPENTERIA
Hydrangeaceae
Tree anemone

Only one species from California belongs to this genus, an evergreen shrub with pure white flowers with 5 to 7 petals and a conspicuous cluster of golden stamens. The leaves are narrow, deep green above, paler and felty beneath, arranged in opposite pairs on soft-wooded branches. Although requiring a fairly cool climate, it only flowers well in regions with warm dry summers, and needs ample sunshine and a well-drained, gritty soil.

Cultivation
Propagation is from cuttings, which do not root easily. Do not confuse it with the Australian palm *Carpentaria*.

Carpenteria californica
In the wild this shrub is known from a small area of central California near Fresno, on dry mountain slopes. It can grow to 20 ft (7 m) tall but in gardens is usually 6–8 ft (2–2.5 m) tall and of bushy habit. The flowers, solitary or in small groups, are normally 2–2½ in (5–6 cm) wide but in the best forms may be up to 4 in (10 cm) wide with broadly overlapping petals. *Zones 7–9.*

CARISSA
This genus is made up of 20 species of attractive evergreen, spiny shrubs that occur in eastern and southern Africa, Asia and Australia. They are grown as hedges and container plants in warm-climate areas, valued for their masses of sweet-scented flowers, mostly snow white, and for their neat appearance. All species bear edible fruits. The glossy green leaves are thick and tough; the leaves and stems exude a milky sap when cut or broken.

Cultivation
They prefer warm summers and moderate rainfall, and require full sun and well-drained soil. Plants in pots need moderate water in the growing season, less in winter. Propagate from seed when ripe in autumn or from cuttings.

Carissa macrocarpa
syn. *Carissa grandiflora*
Natal plum
Occurring naturally on margins of evergreen forest on the east coast of southern Africa, this dense shrub grows quickly to a height of 10 ft (3 m) and a spread of 15 ft (4.5 m). The small, rounded leaves have long, sharp spines among them. The white flowers appear from spring to summer. The fruits that follow are red, fleshy and oval; they can be made into a delicious jelly. *Carissa macrocarpa* tolerates salt-laden winds. 'Horizontalis' is a dense, trailing cultivar with bright red fruit. 'Emerald Carpet' grows to about 24 in (60 cm). *Zones 9–11.*

CARPINUS
Hornbeam

The subtle beauty of hornbeams lies in their usually smoothly fluted trunks and limbs, their neatly veined, small, simple leaves that color attractively in autumn, and their bunches of dry, winged fruit. *Carpinus* is a small genus of catkin-bearing, deciduous trees scattered across cool-climate areas of the northern hemisphere. In foliage and fruits there is not a huge variation between species, though overall size and growth habit are distinct for each. Most yield strong, hard and close grained timber that is often used in the mechanism of pianos.

Cultivation

These grow best in well-drained, moderately fertile soil in a sunny or part-shaded position. Propagate from seed; certain named clones must be grafted.

Carpinus betulus
Common hornbeam, European hornbeam

Ranging from Asia Minor across Europe to eastern England, this species can grow to 80 ft (24 m) although 30 ft (9 m) is an average garden height. It has a broad, rounded crown and pale gray bark, fairly smooth and often fluted. The ovate leaves are ribbed and serrated, downy when young, and change from dark green in summer to yellow in autumn. Inconspicuous flowers in early spring are followed by clusters of pale yellow winged fruit. It likes cool, moist conditions. 'Columnaris' is a compact grower to 30 ft (9 m) high and 20 ft (6 m) wide; 'Fastigiata' (syn. 'Pyramidalis') develops into a taller, broadly conical tree. *Zones 5–9.*

Carpinus caroliniana
American hornbeam, blue beech

Often shrubby in habit and rarely reaching 40 ft (12 m), this tree is capable of rapid growth—in fact farmers and foresters consider it a weed. It is widely distributed in eastern North America but rarely cultivated. The bark is pale gray, the leaves large and pointed, turning deep orange or red in autumn. The small catkins appear in mid-spring, lengthening in fruit to 6 in (15 cm). *Zones 3–9.*

CARYA
Juglandaceae
Hickory, pecan

These deciduous trees have tough wood and edible nuts. They have large pinnate leaves which turn yellow or orange in autumn. The bark of most species is rough textured, giving the trunks a shaggy appearance. Male flowers appear in slender catkins at the base of the new year's growth, female flowers in smaller

Carpinus caroliniana

Carpinus betulus

Caryopteris × clandonensis 'Ferndown'

Carya illinoinensis

clusters at its tip. The fruit is an oval nut enclosed in a leathery husk which divides neatly into 4 segments to open.

Cultivation
Grow from seed, or plant out as very young seedlings before the taproot reaches the bottom of the container. Cold-hardy and fast growing, they prefer sheltered, fertile sites with deep, moist soil.

Carya illinoinensis
Pecan

The pecan is one the world's most popular edible nuts. The tree grows to 100 ft (30 m) tall in the wild. In cultivation it makes fast growth, becoming an open-crowned tree of about 30 ft (10 m) within 10 to 15 years. Although frost-hardy, it needs long hot summers to set fruit. Leaves are long, with many narrow, glossy gray-green leaflets. The elongated nuts, in clusters, are enclosed in ridged, leathery husks and are gathered after falling. *Zones 6–11.*

CARYOPTERIS
Bluebeard

This is a genus of 6 species of deciduous, erect subshrubs or woody perennials in the verbena family, all native to eastern Asia. They have slender, cane-like stems with thin, toothed leaves arranged in opposite pairs, and bear small blue or purple flowers in dense stalked clusters in the leaf axils. Only 2 species have been grown much in gardens and even these are now largely replaced by the hybrid between them, represented by a number of cultivars.

Cultivation
They need to be placed in a full sun position, in well-drained, humus-rich soil. Cut well back in early spring to ensure a good framework for the new season's growth and consequent late summer to autumn flowering. Propagate from seed; for many cultivars it is necessary to take soft-tip or semi-ripe cuttings.

Caryopteris × clandonensis
Hybrid bluebeard, blue-mist shrub

This subshrub, a cross between *Caryopteris incana* and *C. mongolica*, is prized for its masses of delicate, purple-blue flowers borne from late summer to autumn. It grows to a height and spread of 3 ft (1 m), and the oval leaves are gray-green and irregularly serrated. 'Ferndown' is a popular choice among the many cultivars; it has dark violet-blue flowers, while 'Heavenly Blue' has blooms of deep blue. *Zones 5–9.*

Caryopteris incana
syn. *Caryopteris mastacanthus*
Bluebeard

This soft-stemmed shrub from China and Japan is often treated as a perennial in gardens. It reaches around 5 ft (1.5 m) in height with upright, leafy stems. The leaves are soft grayish, coarsely serrated and the clusters of bluish purple flowers display prominent stamen filaments, prompting the common name. *Zones 7–10.*

CASTANEA
Fagaceae
Chestnut, chinquapin

These cool-climate deciduous trees bear edible nuts in a prickly burr-like husk. Leaves are elliptical with regularly toothed margins and a feather-like arrangement of veins. In spring or early summer they produce showy clusters of stiff catkins of male flowers at the branch tips; the less conspicuous small groups of female flowers on the same tree develop into the nuts.

Cultivation

Hot dry summers suit them well as long as ample soil moisture is available in winter and spring. In cool climates chestnuts are easily grown in deep, fertile soil. Propagate from fresh seed. Seedlings should be planted out early to avoid disturbing the taproot.

Castanea sativa

Castanea sativa
Sweet chestnut, Spanish chestnut

Vigorous young trees have a pyramidal crown with an erect leading shoot, but with age lower limbs become massive and spreading. It makes a dense shade tree, spoiled only by the prickly burrs strewing the ground beneath at summer's end. These contain the nuts, normally with 3 squashed into a prickly husk. When planting for nuts buy grafted named varieties from a source certified free of disease. *Zones 5–9.*

CASTANOSPERMUM
Queensland black bean, Moreton Bay chestnut

This genus consists of one species from the rainforests of northeastern Australia, valued for its beautiful chocolate brown timber. It is a slow-growing tree with a stout trunk and a dense, domed crown. The leaves are pinnate with glossy dark green, oblong leaflets, sometimes semi-deciduous in late winter. In summer it produces large orange and yellow pea-flowers in stiff panicles. These are followed in autumn by huge hanging pods, deep green ripening to brown, each containing 2 to 5 brown seeds.

Cultivation

This tree needs a frost-free climate, well-drained, fertile soil enriched with organic matter and regular watering. Pruning is rarely necessary. Propagate from seed in spring.

Caryopteris incana

Castanospermum australe

Casuarina cunninghamiana

Castanospermum australe
This tree, widely planted in streets and for shade in parks and gardens, commonly reaches a height of around 40 ft (12 m). The chestnut-like seeds are poisonous. *Zones 10–11.*

CASUARINA
Casuarinaceae
She-oak
Members of this genus of 6 species of evergreen trees are sometimes known as 'Australian pines' because of their conifer-like appearance. Despite bearing only inconspicuous (male and female) flowers they are graceful, fast growing, hardy and adaptable, often to very dry conditions, some to coastal headlands (*C. equisetifolia*), freshwater river banks (*C. cunninghamiana*), saltwater swamps (*C. glauca*), and heavy black inland soils (*C. cristata*). Casuarina wood makes excellent firewood. Different species have particular requirements.

Cultivation
Propagate from seed.

Casuarina cunninghamiana
River oak, river she-oak
The largest casuarina, growing 65–100 ft (20–30 m), this species is valued for its ability to stabilize river banks, its spreading roots helping to prevent erosion. It is also grown for shade and shelter and, because of its rapid early growth with foliage persistent to ground level, it is useful for windbreaks. The tree requires adequate summer water; it tolerates quite heavy frosts but growth will be slower and stunted in colder districts. *Zones 8–11.*

CATALPA
Bignoniaceae
Catalpa, Indian bean tree
Fast-growing deciduous trees, catalpas have large ovate leaves in opposite pairs, panicles of showy bell-shaped flowers terminating the branches, and long, thin fruits which open to release quantities of very light winged seeds that float away on the breeze. They are beautiful trees with a dense canopy of luxuriant foliage dotted with flower sprays, and are capable of very fast growth. Some species yield valuable timber.

Cultivation
They do not like exposure to cold or dry winds or poor soil.

Catalpa bignonioides
Indian bean tree, southern catalpa
This species comes from warm southeast USA, where it grows along river banks and swamps. It grows to 25–50 ft (8–15 m) with a rounded, irregularly

Catalpa bignonioides

Catalpa speciosa

shaped crown. The tapered heart-shaped leaves have downy undersides, and turn black before falling in autumn. Sprays of 2 in (5 cm) white flowers with frilled edges appear in summer, with orange blotches and purple spots on their lower lips. The pendulous seed pods are up to 18 in (45 cm) long. 'Aurea' has lime-yellow leaves. *Zones 5–10.*

Catalpa speciosa
Northern catalpa, western catalpa

This handsome, fast-growing tree reaches over 100 ft (30 m) in its home region, the central Mississippi basin between Arkansas and Indiana, where it grows in forests in rich, moist soil in valley bottoms and on lower slopes. The leaves are larger than those of *Catalpa bignonioides* but the flowers, borne in mid-summer, are similar though individually slightly larger. Northern catalpa is usually regarded as less decorative overall than the southern species. *Zones 4–10.*

CEANOTHUS
Rhamnaceae
Californian lilac

Brilliant displays of blue or violet flowers are the feature of many species of these evergreen and deciduous shrubs from North America. Some coastal species develop dense, prostrate forms highly resistant to salt spray. Leaves are small to medium sized, blunt tipped and usually toothed. The flowers, individually tiny with threadlike stalks, are massed in dense clusters at branch ends. They are often short lived, especially prone to sudden death in climates with warm wet summers.

Cultivation

They require full sun and prefer exposed positions, in well-drained soil. Propagate from seed, or from cuttings.

Ceanothus griseus

A spreading bushy shrub from California, this evergreen species grows to 10 ft (3 m) with rounded, hardly toothed leaves that are downy on the undersides. In early spring, it produces abundant, pale violet-blue flower-clusters. Var. *horizontalis* is a low-growing, densely spreading form from coastal cliffs, which makes a fine rock garden or ground cover plant for exposed sites. *Zones 8–10.*

Ceanothus impressus

This shrub is a free-flowering, small-leafed evergreen species of dense, spreading habit. The leaves are thick, with the veins deeply impressed into the upper surface. In spring it produces a profuse display of small clusters of deep blue, almost purple, flowers. From 3–6 ft (1–2 m), it prefers tough, exposed conditions. *Zones 8–10.*

CEDRUS
Pinaceae
Cedar
A renowned genus of conifers belonging to the pine family. The pollen cones, shaped like small bananas, release large clouds of pollen in early spring. The seed cones are broadly egg shaped or barrel shaped, pale bluish or brownish; they shatter to release seeds with papery wings. In appropriate climatic conditions they are long lived and trouble free, growing massive with age.

Cultivation
Propagation is normally from seed, though cuttings, layering and grafting are used for certain cultivars.

Cedrus atlantica
Atlas cedar
Atlantica refers to the Atlas Mountains of Morocco and Algeria where this tree is endemic, mostly at altitudes above 3,000 ft (1,000 m). In cultivation it makes a pyramidal tree with stiffly ascending branches, but with age it spreads into a broadly flat-topped tree with massive limbs. The bark is dark and scaly, the cones barrel shaped. The densely clustered needles vary from dark green to bluish. The cultivar name 'Glauca' is used for selected seedling plants with bluish foliage. *Zones 6–9.*

Cedrus deodara
Deodar, deodar cedar
The deodar occurs in the western Himalaya, reaching 250 ft (80 m) in the wild, but is now almost extinct over much of its former range. The long leading shoots nod slightly, and smaller branches are pendulous. Foliage is dark, slightly grayish green. It does best in milder, humid climates, in deep soil, making luxuriant growth and reaching 30 ft (10 m) in about 10 years. The most popular cultivar is 'Aurea', with golden branch tips. *Zones 7–10.*

Cedrus atlantica

Ceanothus griseus

Ceanothus impressus

Cedrus libani
Cedar of Lebanon, Lebanon cedar

This magnificent tree has been all but wiped out in Lebanon, with only a few small groves surviving on Mount Lebanon; larger populations survive in Turkey. It was introduced to western Europe centuries ago, and trees in England are up to 120 ft (36 m) in height and 8 ft (2.5 m) in trunk diameter. As a young tree it has a narrow, erect habit but with age adopts a flat-topped shape with massive spreading limbs. The dark green needles are up to 1½ in (35 mm) long. It prefers a moist, cool climate and sunny conditions. It does not tolerate shade. 'Aurea-Prostrata' is a dwarf form with golden foliage; 'Nana' is a very dwarf, slow-growing cultivar of semi-prostrate habit suited to rock gardens; 'Pendula' is a weeping form, usually grafted onto a standard. *C. libani* subsp. *stenocoma* is the geographical race from mountains of southwestern Turkey; it has a more narrowly conical or columnar growth habit. *Zones 5–8.*

CELTIS
Nettle tree, hackberry

This large genus of 70 species includes many evergreens, occurring mainly in the tropics, but the cool-climate, deciduous species from North America, Europe and Asia are the ones mostly cultivated. They are medium to fairly large trees with smooth or slightly rough bark. The leaves are smallish, oval and pointed at the tip, with few or many marginal teeth. Insignificant flowers appear with the new leaves, and the fruits are small, hard drupes carried singly in the leaf axils. Birds eat the fruits and disperse the seeds, and some species self-seed and can become a nuisance. *Celtis* species are planted mainly as shade trees on streets and in parks, where they make shapely, long-lived and trouble-free specimens.

Cultivation

In cooler climates, these fully frost-hardy trees like dry soil and full sun; in warmer areas they prefer rich, moist, well-drained soil and part-shade. Propagate from seed in autumn.

Celtis australis
Southern nettle tree, European hackberry

This deciduous, small to medium-sized tree grows to 50 ft (15 m) in height and

Celtis occidentalis

Cedrus libani

Cephalotaxus fortunei

Cephalotaxus harringtonia 'Fastigiata'

originates in southern Europe, North Africa and Asia Minor. It has broadly lance-shaped, serrated-edged leaves that are mid to dark green and rough to touch on the upper surface, paler green and downy on the underside. *Zones 8–10.*

Celtis occidentalis
American hackberry

This species comes from the east of the USA, the Mississippi Basin and eastern Canada. In its preferred habitat of forests in deep, rich, alluvial soils it can reach a very large size, but when planted in the open it makes a shapely, spreading tree of 40–60 ft (12–18 m). The bark, smooth on saplings, becomes rough as the tree matures. The foliage turns pale yellow in autumn; it can become a pest along riverbanks and channels in some countries. *Zones 2–10.*

CEPHALOTAXUS
Cephalotaxaceae
Plum-yew

This genus of conifers has attractive deep green leathery foliage. All originate

in eastern Asia. The fleshy fruits, which are more like olives than plums, ripen reddish brown. Male pollen sacs are found in small globular clusters on separate trees.

Cultivation

They do best in cool, fairly humid climates in sheltered positions.

Cephalotaxus fortunei
Chinese plum yew

This species from northeastern China makes a spreading shrub or small tree to 20 ft (6 m) with brown bark peeling off in flakes. It was introduced to England in 1849 by Robert Fortune, the man who first brought the tea plant from China to India. The linear leaves, up to 4 in (10 cm) long, have fine sharp points. The oval fruit are about 1 in (25 mm) long. *Zones 6–10.*

Cephalotaxus harringtonia
Japanese plum-yew

The typical form of this species is a spreading bushy shrub 6–10 ft (2–3 m)

tall. The most attractive form is
'Fastigiata': very erect, it sends up a
dense mass of long straight branches
from the base, each with radiating
whorls of leathery, recurving dark
brownish green leaves. It forms a tight
column about 6 ft (2 m) high. *Zones 6–10.*

CERATONIA
Caesalpiniaceae
Carob, St. John's bread

The single species in this genus comes
from the eastern Mediterranean where it
forms a round-headed tree to 40 ft
(13 m). It is usually smaller in cultivation. The bean-like pods, about 6 in
(15 cm) long, are roasted and powdered
as a chocolate substitute. The seeds are a
uniform size and were once used by
jewelers as standard weights—hence the
term 'carat', from the Greek for carob
bean.

Cultivation

It needs hot summers to perform well,
but will survive in warm sheltered
positions in cooler climates. Marginally
frost-hardy, carobs do best in full sun
although they will tolerate light shade
and are also drought tolerant; a moderately fertile, well-drained soil suits them.
Propagate from seed.

Ceratonia siliqua

A long-lived evergreen tree, the carob is
used as a shade tree for streets, parks

Ceratonia siliqua

Ceratostigma willmottianum

and large gardens, and as a farm shelter
and fodder tree. It has glossy pinnate
leaves and clustered spikes of small
greenish flowers in spring and autumn.
As some plants bear only male or female
flowers, interplanting of clonal material
may be needed for production of the
pods. *Zones 9–11.*

CERATOSTIGMA
Plumbaginaceae

The garden species are small deciduous
shrubs and from spring to autumn they
produce loose heads of blue phlox-like
flowers. The small leaves are deep green,
turning to bronze or crimson in autumn
before falling.

Cultivation

They grow in any moist, well-drained
soil in sun or part-shade. Propagate from
seed or semi-ripe cuttings, or by division. In cold climates they will reshoot
from the roots even though the top
growth may freeze to ground level.

Ceratostigma willmottianum
Chinese plumbago

This 24–36 in (60–90 cm) deciduous
shrub from western Sichuan, China, has
small heads of bright blue phlox-like
flowers that open from late summer to
autumn. The leaves are deep green and
roughly diamond shaped. In autumn the

Cercis canadensis

foliage develops bronze or crimson tones before falling. It grows in any moist, well-drained soil in sun or part-shade, and survives heavy frosts with some stem dieback. *Zones 6–10.*

CERCIS
Caesalpiniaceae
Judas tree, redbud

This genus is made up of small deciduous trees or shrubs from North America, Asia and southern Europe. Their profuse clusters of pea-like flowers, bright rose-pink to crimson, line the bare branches in spring; the neat, pointed buds, deeper in color, also make an elegant display. The heart-shaped to almost circular leaves follow, along with flat seed pods up to 4 in (10 cm) long.

Cultivation
They resent disturbance to their roots, especially transplanting. A sunny position suits them best and they thrive in hot dry summer weather, as long as the soil moisture is adequate in winter and spring. Propagate from seed. Growth is usually slow.

Cercis canadensis
Eastern redbud

This tree can reach 40 ft (13 m) in the wild and is strikingly beautiful in flower. In gardens it rarely exceeds 12 ft (4 m), branching close to the ground. The buds are deep rose, and the paler rose flowers

Cercis siliquastrum

are profuse and showy; flowering may continue into early summer. The leaf undersides of subsp. *texensis* have a waxy bluish coating. *Zones 5–9.*

Cercis siliquastrum
Judas tree

Although this tree can grow to 40 ft (13 m), it seldom exceeds 25 ft (8 m). The leaves are slightly bluish green with rounded tips, and the late spring flowers, larger and deeper pink than other species, arise in clusters on previous years' growth. It is the most reliable ornamental species in regions with mild winters. Distinct flower coloration occur in the white 'Alba' and the deeper reddish 'Rubra'. *Zones 7–9.*

CESTRUM
Solanaceae
Jessamine

This genus consists of over 200 shrubs, mostly from the Americas, best suited to tropical and subtropical gardens and grown for their decorative tubular flowers, night-scented in some species.

Flowers are followed by small round berries and all parts of the plants are poisonous. They can be pruned hard to shape. Some (especially *C. parqui*) are free-seeding and invasive, especially in warmer climates.

Cultivation

They grow fast in full sun and moderately fertile, well-drained soil with plentiful water in summer and regular fertilizing. Many self-seed and also grow readily from soft tip cuttings.

Cestrum nocturnum
Night-scented jessamine, lady of the night

An easily grown evergreen shrub 10 ft (3 m) tall and almost as wide, this species has long, slender, arching branches growing from the base. Clusters of pale green flowers appear in late summer and are perfumed at night but scentless during the day. Berries are green at first but whitish when ripe in early winter. *Zones 10–11*.

CHAENOMELES
Rosaceae
Flowering quince

Related to the edible quince *(Cydonia)*, these many-stemmed shrubs display red,

Cestrum nocturnum

Chaenomeles speciosa 'Nivalis'

pink or white flowers on bare branches in late winter or early spring. They are extremely cold-hardy and adapt to a wide range of conditions. The tough, springy branches are often spiny on vigorous shoots; leaves are simple and finely toothed. Flowers appear in stalkless clusters on the previous year's wood, followed in summer by yellow-green fruits with waxy, perfumed skin, good for jams and jellies.

Cultivation

They prefer a sunny spot in well-drained but not too rich soil. Propagate from hardwood cuttings.

Chaenomeles speciosa
Chinese flowering quince, japonica

This species and its hybrids are the only flowering quinces usually grown. Shrubs of 5–10 ft (1.5–3 m) high, they spread by basal suckers to form dense thickets of stems. Flowers are scarlet to deep red in the original species. Several older cultivars are widely grown, including 'Nivalis' (white), 'Moerloosii' (white flushed and blotched pink and carmine) and 'Rubra Grandiflora' (crimson). Most hybrid cultivars belong to *C.* × *superba* and are lower growing, the flowers predominantly in rich oranges, scarlets and deep reds. *Zones 6–10*.

Chaenomeles × superba

This hybrid between *Chaenomeles japonica* and *C. speciosa* has given rise to some first rate cultivars like 'Knap Hill Scarlet' with bright orange-scarlet flowers; 'Crimson and Gold' with deep crimson petals and gold anthers; 'Nicoline' which has a rather sprawling habit and scarlet flowers; 'Pink Lady' with large, bright rose pink flowers; and 'Rowallane' with blood crimson flowers. *Zones 6–10.*

CHAMAECYPARIS

Cupressaceae
False cypress

These stately trees used to be classified as *Cupressus* (true cypresses), and the differences between the *Cupressus* and *Chamaecyparis* are slight. Nearly all *Chamaecyparis* species occur in cooler, moister regions of North America and east Asia. There are a vast number of cultivars which feature colored foliage, usually gold, bluish or bronze; and they have a narrow columnar or dwarf habit.

Cultivation

They prefer a cool, moist climate, deep, rich, well-drained soils and a sheltered position. Propagate from cuttings.

Chamaecyparis lawsoniana
Lawson cypress

This conifer can grow to 120 ft (38 m) tall with narrowly conical trunks with pendulous side branches covered in bluish green to deep green foliage. Over 180 cultivars species are available. 'Erecta' is plain green with erect, narrow sprays of foliage tightly crowded together; it can reach 30 ft (10 m). 'Lane' makes a narrower column with lemony yellow foliage changing to bronze-gold in winter. 'Winston Churchill' has a conical growth-habit and golden yellow foliage. *Zones 4–9.*

Chamaecyparis obtusa
Hinoki cypress

Usually represented by its dwarf or colored cultivars, this valuable timber tree grows to to 60 ft (18 m) in cultivation. 'Crippsii' makes a broad golden pyramid with a vigorous leading shoot; usually about 10–15 ft (3–5 m) tall. 'Tetragona' and 'Tetragona Aurea' are similar, but narrower and more irregularly branched. The best known dwarf cultivar is 'Nana Gracilis' and its

Chamaecyparis lawsoniana 'Lane'

Chaenomeles × *superba*

Chamaecyparis pisifera 'Plumosa'

Chamelaucium uncinatum

Chamaecyparis obtusa 'Crippsii'

numerous variants, little bun-shaped
plants normally 12–24 in (30–60 cm)
high. *Zones 5–10.*

Chamaecyparis pisifera
Sawara cypress
Growing to 150 ft (46 m) in the wild, the
lower sides of the branchlets of this broad
conical tree are marked bluish white
with tiny, prickly scale-leaves on juvenile
growth. Cultivars fall into 3 groups,
Squarrosa, Plumosa and Filifera.
'Squarrosa' is a small tree about 10 ft (3 m)
tall, with pale bluish gray juvenile foliage
that turns dull purple in winter. 'Boulevard' is narrowly conical, about 6 ft (2 m)
tall. Plumosa is the largest group of
cultivars, many of them dwarf. The best
known Filifera is 'Filifera Aurea', a
broadly pyramidal shrub 6–8 ft (2–3 m)
tall with gold and green foliage. *Zones 5–10.*

CHAMELAUCIUM
Myrtaceae
Geraldton wax flowers are well known
commercial cut flowers. Named hybrids

and cultivars have flowers ranging from
white through pale and dark pink to
mauve, rose-purple and carmine. They
are long-lasting in the vase, but the
shrubs with their large, airy sprays of
flowers are difficult to grow, as they do
not tolerate cold winters, wet summers
or high humidity.

Cultivation
Plant in full sun and slightly alkaline,
gravelly soil and prune after flowering.
Propagate from cuttings.

Chamelaucium uncinatum
Geraldton wax
This is the most common species and the
chief parent of most recently bred
cultivars; it grows to 10 ft (3 m) tall and
almost as wide. In its natural habitat it is
a brittle, spreading shrub with fine needle-
like foliage and white, mauve or pink
waxy flowers in late winter and through

spring. New cultivars appear regularly but all seem prone to root-rot in wet soil. Avoid root disturbance. *Zones 10–11.*

CHIMONANTHUS
Calycanthaceae
Wintersweet
This small genus of deciduous shrubs from China has simple, thin-textured leaves, clustered at ends of the stiff branches. Smallish flowers are clustered below the branch tips; they are multi-petalled and cup-shaped, with a translucent waxy texture, and are followed by strangely shaped leathery-skinned seeds.

Cultivation
Seeds germinate readily, or the multiple stems can be layered by mounding with soil; cuttings are difficult to strike. It is frost-hardy but does best against a warm wall in cold climates. Prune weaker stems and shorten larger stems after flowering.

Chimonanthus praecox
The wintersweet makes a thicket of stiff, angular stems 6–8 ft (2–2.5 m) high and wide, with harsh-textured dark green leaves. Flowers appear in abundance on bare winter branches or, in milder climates, among the last autumn leaves; petals are pale yellow to off-white with a dull pink or red basal zone on the inside. The fruits are yellowish brown when ripe. 'Luteus' has late blooming, buttercup yellow flowers. *Zones 6–10.*

CHIONANTHUS
Oleaceae
Fringe tree
In late spring the tree crowns are sprinkled with clusters of delicate white flowers; each with 4 narrow, diverging white petals. The summer fruits are like small olives (they belong to the olive family). They can take 10 years to flower.

Chionanthus retusus

Chimonanthus praecox

Cultivation
A sunny but sheltered position with good soil and drainage suits them best.

Chionanthus retusus
Chinese fringe tree
This tree can reach 30 ft (10 m), developing a broad, umbrella-like crown with age, but in gardens it is often a large shrub. The shiny leaves are variable in shape and size on the one tree. The flowers form profuse small upright clusters which stand above the foliage in late spring or early summer. *Zones 6–10.*

CHOISYA
Rutaceae
This genus consists of several evergreen shrubs from Mexico and the far south of USA, one species of which is widely grown in warm to temperate climates. It is an excellent hedging plant and an attractive addition to a shrubby border.

Cultivation

It grows best in full sun, and preferably a slightly acid, humus-rich, well-drained soil. It tolerates dry soil and light frosts. Propagate from tip cuttings in autumn.

Choisya ternata
Mexican orange blossom

Related to citrus, with spring flowers that have the perfume of orange blossom, this species makes a compact rounded bush to 6 ft (2 m). Its deep green glossy leaves are aromatic when crushed. The clusters of small white perfumed starry flowers appear in spring, sometimes again in late summer. *Zones 7–11.*

CINNAMOMUM
Lauraceae

This small genus consists of evergreen trees from tropical and subtropical Asia

Cinnamomum camphora

Choisya ternata

and Australasia. Aromatic compounds are present in leaves, twigs and bark. Flowers are small and white or cream in delicate sprays and are followed by small fleshy berries containing a single seed. The genus includes *C. zeylanicum*, the bark of which yields cinnamon; and *C. cassia*, which provides the spice cassia.

Cultivation

Half-hardy, it is adaptable to a variety of climates and is best in full sun or dappled shade on light loamy or sandy free-draining soil with plentiful water in summer. Propagate from seed.

Cinnamomum camphora
Camphor laurel

Originating in China, Japan and Taiwan, this tree is known to reach 110 ft (35 m) in height with a rounded crown spreading to 50 ft (15 m) wide. The short, solid trunk has scaly gray bark. Widely grown as a shade tree in parks and gardens, it self-seeds freely and grows so readily, especially in warm climates, that it can become an invasive weed. The roots reputedly release a compound which inhibits growth of other plants beneath the tree's canopy. *Zones 9–11.*

CISTUS
Cistaceae
Rock rose

The flowers of these evergreen shrubs have crinkled petals in shades of pink, purple or white and a central boss of golden stamens, like a single rose. In the wild they occur mainly in coastal scrubs often on shallow rocky soil, in areas with a hot dry summer and cool wet winter. They are drought resistant and adapted to withstand scrub fires.

Cultivation

They are easily grown in a warm sunny position and well-drained, dry soil; they

Cistus ladanifer 'Albiflorus'

Cistus × purpureus 'Brilliancy'

prefer being among large rocks, where their roots can seek out deep moisture. Propagate from cuttings; seeds are readily germinated.

Cistus ladanifer

This *Cistus* is coated with a shiny resin which in the day's heat becomes semi-liquid and aromatic. The Romans knew it as *ladanum* and valued it as an incense and perfume base, as well as for medicinal purposes. Growing to 5–6 ft (1.5–2 m), it becomes sparse and leggy in only a few years but does not take well to pruning. Leaves are narrow and the large flowers have pure white petals with a reddish chocolate blotch at the base of each petal. 'Albiflorus' has pure white petals. *Zones 8–10.*

Cistus × purpureus

This hybrid between *C. ladanifer* and *C. creticus* has deep pink flowers. The flower-coloration and growth habit come mainly from *C. creticus* but the petals have prominent dark reddish chocolate blotches as in *C. ladanifer.* It is hardy and free flowering. Several clones have been named including 'Brilliancy' with clear pink petals, and 'Betty Taudevin', a deeper reddish pink. *Zones 8–10.*

CLERODENDRUM
Verbenaceae

This genus contains trees, shrubs, climbers and herbaceous plants, both

Clerodendrum trichotomum

deciduous and evergreen. Uniting features are leaves in opposite pairs; tubular flowers, usually flared or bowl-shaped at the mouth and with 4 long stamens and a style protruding well beyond the tube; and fruit, a shiny berry at the center of the calyx, which usually becomes larger and thicker after flowering. They vary in their cold-hardiness, and only a few are suited to cool climates.

Cultivation

They prefer a sunny position sheltered from the wind and deep, moist, fertile soil. Propagate from cuttings; but many sucker from the roots and a large root cutting can produce quicker results.

Clerodendrum trichotomum

Native to Japan and China, this frost-hardy species is a small deciduous tree to

Coleonema pulchellum 'Sunset Gold'

Convolvulus cneorum

15–20 ft (5–6 m) in height, of erect growth and sparse branching habit. The lower branches droop with thin, downy leaves. In late summer it produces gracefully drooping panicles of slightly upturned, sweet-scented flowers, white aging pale mauve with large dull pinkish sharply ribbed calyces. The small blue fruits, cupped in enlarged red calyces, make quite a display. *Zones 7–10.*

COLEONEMA

Rutaceae

Diosma, breath of heaven

These small evergreen shrubs from South Africa are often confused with *Diosma* species. They have short needle-like leaves on very fine, wiry twigs and tiny starry flowers in spring or spring through summer. The foliage is aromatic.

Cultivation

Plant in light but moist well-drained soil in full sun. Propagate from semi-ripe cuttings.

Coleonema pulchellum

Formerly known as *Coleonema pulchrum*, this widely grown species is a 5 ft (1.5 m) high shrub with soft foliage and pink flowers in spring and summer. Several forms are cultivated with white or deeper pink flowers. 'Sunset Gold' is a popular form with bright yellow foliage and light pink flowers in spring. It is more compact than the species and usually grows as a low, flat-topped bush or ground cover. *Zones 9–10.*

CONVOLVULUS

Convolvulaceae

Found in temperate regions, this genus consists mainly of slender twining creepers (the bindweeds) and small herbaceous plants. Only a few species are shrubby, and even these are soft stemmed and renewed by shooting from the base. They have simple, thin-textured, usually narrow leaves and the flowers are like morning glories, with a strongly flared tube that opens by unfurling 'pleats'. They usually open in succession over a long season.

Cultivation

They adapt to most soils, and exposed as well as sheltered positions, but prefer full sun. Propagate from cuttings.

Convolvulus cneorum

This shrub from Mediterranean Europe has crowded, weak, upcurving stems sprouting from the base to a height of 12–24 in (30–60 cm). The leaves, in tufts along the stems, have a coating of silky hairs giving them a silvery sheen. The stems terminate in dense clusters of silky buds, each producing a long succession of flowers through spring and summer, flesh-pink in bud but opening pure white with a small yellow 'eye'. It suits a warm dry spot in the rock garden. *Zones 8–10.*

COPROSMA
Rubiaceae

Most of the evergreen shrubs and some trees which make up this genus are native to New Zealand. Grown largely for their great tolerance of salt-laden winds, they are commonly seen as coastal hedging and shelter planting. They have tough, decorative foliage and small fruits, separate male and female plants being needed to obtain fruits.

Cultivation

They do best in full sun on light, well-drained soil and are fast growing and easily maintained. Pruning will maintain leafiness. Propagate from seed in spring and semi-ripe cuttings.

Coprosma repens
Taupata, mirror bush, looking glass plant

This species is most commonly planted to withstand coastal winds, growing where little else will survive. Usually shaped to a mounded bush 3–6 ft (1–2 m), it will grow taller if left unpruned. It has glossy, leathery, deep green leaves. Insignificant flowers are followed on female plants by small orange-red fruits in late summer and autumn. 'Marble Queen' is a variegated form with paler green and cream leaves often producing pure cream growths. *Zones 9–11*.

Coprosma repens

CORDYLINE
Asteliaceae
Cabbage tree, ti

Centered in the southwest Pacific region, most species of this genus of palm-like shrubs and small trees are tropical or subtropical, but a few New Zealand species are moderately frost-hardy. Most cordylines can be kept in pots or tubs for many years. A peculiarity is their underground rhizome-like stem that grows downward, sometimes emerging through the drainage holes of a pot; its main function appears to be food storage. Cordylines somewhat resemble yuccas in habit and foliage but the flowers are small and starry in branched spikes.

Cultivation

Propagate from stem cuttings or seed.

Cordyline australis
New Zealand cabbage tree, ti kouka

This evergreen tree looks tropical but occurs even in New Zealand's coldest regions. At 6–8 ft (2–3 m) tall, the first large panicle of small white sweet-scented flowers terminates the stem, which then branches into several leaf rosettes. Old plants may be 20 ft (7 m) tall with a thick trunk and numerous erect branches.

Cordyline australis

'Purpurea' with bronze-purplish leaves is a popular cultivar. 'Albertii' has striped cream leaves. *Zones 8–11.*

CORNUS
Cornaceae
Dogwood, cornel

Most of these cool-climate shrubs and small trees are deciduous. Flowers are small, mostly white, cream, greenish or yellowish, arranged in clusters on short twigs. Some appear to have large

Cornus florida 'Rubra'

Cornus alba

'flowers', but these are bracts which surround tight heads of tiny flowers. The fruits are small drupes, sometimes fused into a larger compound fruit. Most are easily grown in a cool climate.

Cultivation
Propagate from seed, or semi-ripe cuttings or layers in late spring.

Cornus alba
Red-barked dogwood
Shiny red branches and twigs are the feature of this east Asian shrub. It makes a dense thicket of slender stems 6 ft (2 m) high and often twice that in spread, with lower branches suckering or taking root on the ground. In late spring and summer it bears clusters of creamy yellow flowers, followed in autumn by pea-sized white or blue-tinted fruits. The red-barked dogwood thrives in damp ground. *Zones 4–9.*

Cornus florida
Flowering dogwood
Early explorers in eastern North America declared this the most beautiful of native trees. Usually 10–20 ft (3–4 m) tall with a single crooked trunk, in mid-spring it bears profuse flower heads, each with 4 large white or rose-pink bracts. In late summer the scattered red fruits make a fine showing and the autumn foliage is a mixture of scarlet and deep purple, with a whitish bloom on the leaf undersides. It prefers a warm summer. 'Rubra' has dark rose bracts that are paler at the base next to the cluster of small greenish flowers. *Zones 5–9.*

Cornus kousa
Japanese flowering dogwood
Occurring in the wild in Japan, China and Korea, *C. kousa* can reach 20 ft (7 m) or more at maturity, with dense, deep green foliage and tiered lower branches.

Cornus kousa

Correa pulchella

At the start of summer when the leaves have fully expanded, the flower heads with large, pure white bracts appear, each bract tapering to an acute point. At least as popular in gardens as the typical Japanese race is var. *chinensis*, with slightly larger 'flowers' and of more vigorous growth. *Zones 6–9*.

Cornus nuttallii
Pacific dogwood
In the wild this is a slender tree to 50 ft (15 m), but in gardens it is often only a tall shrub. The large flower heads have 4 to 7 pure white bracts, aging slightly pinkish, and the small flower-cluster at the center is dull purple. Flowering occurs from mid-spring to early summer, and may start at a fairly early age, a partial compensation for its short-lived habit. Autumn foliage is a mixture of yellow and red. It is frost-tender, but thrives in a cool, rainy climate, in a part-shaded position. *Zones 7–9*.

CORREA
Rutaceae
This small Australian genus is made up of irregularly shaped, downy, densely leafed evergreen shrubs, some semi-prostrate. They bear mostly bell-shaped or tubular flowers with protruding stamens, over a long period through winter and spring. Correas grow naturally in cool, shaded spots often near streams and under trees, and are attractive to birds. They are not fussy, adapting to most non-tropical climates.

Cultivation
They do best in part-shade in moderately fertile, free-draining but moist soil. Tip prune to promote a densely leafed bush. Propagate from semi-ripe cuttings taken between spring and autumn.

Correa pulchella
This species occurs naturally on better soils in sheltered places along creek margins in southern Australia. It is a compact shrub growing to less than 3 ft (1 m) and bears masses of attractive tubular flowers in shades of salmon, orange, pink and red through winter and spring. *Zones 9–10*.

CORYLUS
Corylaceae
Hazel, filbert
These deciduous large shrubs and small to medium-sized trees, best known for their edible nuts, have massed stems springing from ground level. Leaves are broad, somewhat heart-shaped and strongly veined. Male and female flowers are on the same plant, the male in slender pendulous catkins which shed their pollen before the leaves expand, the female in inconspicuous small greenish clusters at the branch tips. These develop into the distinctive nuts, each enclosed in a fringed green husk and ripening in summer.

Cultivation

Propagation is often possible by detaching suckers, or by fresh nuts. For fruit there is a cold requirement during winter of around 1,000 hours below 45°F (about 7°C); cool moist summers also assist nut production.

Corylus avellana
Hazel

The common hazel typically makes a broad mass of stems about 12–15 ft (4–5 m) high. In winter the bare twigs are draped with the developing male catkins. The ripening nut is enclosed in a green fringed tube that leaves the end of the nut showing. The ornamental cultivar 'Contorta' has branches that

Corylus avellana

Cotinus coggygria

wander and wriggle in all directions; when leafless they are cut for sale by florists. *Zones 4–9.*

COTINUS
Anacardiaceae
Smoke bush, smoke tree

Two species comprise this genus of cool-climate deciduous shrubs or small trees. Both have simple, oval, untoothed leaves. The delicate inflorescences have many branches; few of these fine threadlike stems carry flowers, but they resemble fine puffs of smoke scattered over the foliage. Flowers and fruit are inconspicuous.

Cultivation

Smoke bushes adapt to a range of temperate climates but prefer moderately warm, dry summers. Propagate from softwood cuttings in summer or from seed in autumn.

Cotinus coggygria
Smoke bush, Venetian sumac

A bushy shrub about 10–12 ft (3–4 m) in height and spread, this has oval, long-stalked leaves. The fuzzy, tiny, plumelike inflorescences appear in early summer, pale pinkish bronze, aging to a duller purple-gray. Some flowers produce small, dry, flattened fruits in late summer. 'Purpureus' has rich purplish spring foliage becoming greener in summer and glowing orange mixed with purple in autumn, but it doesn't flower very freely. *Zones 6–10.*

COTONEASTER
Rosaceae

This temperate Eurasian genus of shrubs (rarely small trees) includes deciduous and evergreen species. The name *Cotoneaster* dates from Roman times, and means something like 'useless quince'. The hardy lower-growing shrub species

Cotoneaster horizontalis

Cotoneaster dammeri

are popular in temperate gardens for their dense, spreading habit and display of red fruit. Excellent for rock gardens, embankments and foundation plantings, some species are also used for hedges and espaliers. The evergreen species provide fine displays of berries.

Cultivation
They do best in full sun, and are prone to fireblight. Propagate from seed or cuttings.

Cotoneaster dammeri
A fully prostrate cotoneaster, the relatively large, round-tipped leaves have veins deeply impressed into their upper surfaces; the scattered starry white flowers are followed by solitary scarlet fruits which last well into winter, when the leaves turn bronze. The varietal name 'Radicans' is often added, but there is confusion as to which form of the species it belongs. *Zones 5–10.*

Cotoneaster horizontalis
Popular in cooler areas where its fine foliage takes on bronze-purple, orange and reddish autumn hues, this semi-prostrate shrub has horizontal, flattened sprays of branches building up in stiff tiers with age to 3 ft (1 m) high and up to 8 ft (2.5 m) wide. The small flesh-pink flowers are dotted along the twigs in early summer, followed by deep red fruit. *Zones 5–10.*

CRATAEGUS
Rosaceae
Thorn, hawthorn, may
Most *Crataegus* species have long sharp thorns among the summer growth, leaves that are either toothed or lobed, and the white or rarely pink flowers cluster into circular umbels in late spring. They are followed in autumn by fruit in shades of red or yellow. Hawthorns are hardy deciduous trees, compact enough for small gardens. They are sun-lovers and not fussy about soil type or drainage. Some species sucker from the base.

Cultivation
Some hawthorns are prone to fireblight, controlled only by prompt removal and burning of affected branches. Foliage may also be disfigured by the 'pear and cherry slug' (sawfly larva); spray severe attacks with insecticide. Propagation is from seed with cold stratification, or by grafting for named clones.

Crataegus laevigata
Midland hawthorn
This small, shrubby tree reaches 15–20 ft (5–7 m) in height and spread. Native to Europe, North Africa and the British

Isles, it has dark green, glossy leaves and produces few thorns. The cultivar 'Paul's Scarlet' has bright red double flowers opening in late spring. *Zones 4–9.*

Crataegus phaenopyrum
Washington thorn

From southeastern USA, this thorny tree reaches 20–30 ft (7–10 m), forming a round-headed, densely branched tree with sharp thorns. The leaves have 3 to 5 sharply toothed lobes, and are dark glossy green. Dense clusters of fragrant white flowers in mid-summer are followed in autumn by the shiny orange-

Crataegus laevigata

Crataegus phaenopyrum

red berries. It is often sold under an old name, *Crataegus cordata. Zones 4–10.*

CRYPTOMERIA
Taxodiaceae
Japanese cedar, sugi

Only one species is generally accepted in this conifer genus from China and Japan, though many variations have been named. A fast-growing evergreen, its branches are clothed in short leathery needle-leaves that are densely overlapping and curve inward slightly. Male (pollen) and female (seed) cones are on the same tree, the former in profuse clusters and releasing clouds of pollen in spring, the latter in sparser groups behind the branch tips. It is suitable for windbreaks, hedges and avenues. In Japan it is venerated in historic groves.

Cultivation

Rainfall must be adequate, and dry or shallow soils are unsuitable. Propagate from seed or from cuttings.

Cryptomeria japonica

This species grows rapidly, to 20–25 ft (7–8 m) in 10 years. Trees are conical in shape with a long, pointed leader. The Japanese race has thicker branchlets

Cryptomeria japonica 'Globosa Nana'

and stiffer habit than the Chinese (var. *sinensis*) one. There are at least 50 cultivars, most dwarf but a few approaching the wild types in size. 'Araucarioides' has a tangle of long rat's-tail branches, and reaches 10 ft (3 m). 'Globosa Nana' makes a dense ball with intricate branching; it is plain green, with paler green new growth in spring and summer. While listed as a dwarf, in good soil it may grow to 10 ft (3 m) across in only 15 years! The tiny 'Vilmoriniana' grows to about 12 in (30 cm) high. *Zones 7–10.*

CUPHEA
Lythraceae
From Central and South America, these small evergreen shrubs seldom exceed 30 in (75 cm) high and wide; they have weak stems and tubular red, pink or yellow flowers. Most are frost-tender but as they are fast growing they are often treated as annuals. The large number of species differ quite considerably in appearance. They bloom throughout the year.

Cultivation
Cupheas prefer moist, well-drained soil in sun or very light shade. Propagation is usually from small tip cuttings, though they are also easily raised from seed, which often self-sows.

Cuphea micropetala
The leaves of this Mexican species are bright green and elliptical with a prominent midrib. The tubular flowers occur in rows at the branch tips and are orange-red with golden-yellow tones, tipped with greenish yellow. Tougher than most, this species will withstand occasional light frosts. Although in the wild it occurs on streamsides, *Cuphea micropetala* grows well in normal garden soils. *Zones 9–11.*

Cuphea micropetala

× *Cupressocyparis leylandii*

× CUPRESSOCYPARIS
Cupressaceae
Leyland cypress
The '×' in front of the name indicates that this is a bi-generic hybrid, that is, a hybrid between two different genera, in this case *Cupressus* and *Chamaecyparis*. First raised in England in 1888 as a chance hybrid, it combines rapid growth with reasonable frost-hardiness, and adapts as well to poorly drained soil and very windy sites (but not arid climate). It is planted for fast-growing hedges.

Cultivation
Propagation is from cuttings, which strike readily under nursery conditions.

× Cupressocyparis leylandii
This name encompasses a number of seedling clones, some of which have

been named as cultivars. They make vigorous upright trees with a long open leading shoot and slightly irregular outline. Foliage is deep green or slightly grayish. In good soil it will reach 30 ft (10 m) in 10 years. 'Naylor's Blue' has more strongly bluish gray foliage and is more columnar in habit. *Zones 5–10.*

CUPRESSUS
Cupressaceae
Cypress

These conifers have a limited cold tolerance. They come in many foliage hues; and range from tall to dwarf, from columnar or high-crowned and spreading to weeping. Their dense foliage and rapid growth makes them good screens and windbreaks. Some are drought tolerant, others need moist conditions.

Cultivation

Propagate from seed. Cultivars can be raised from cuttings. However, some cypress species suffer from the disease cypress canker which disfigures the trees and finally kills them.

Cupressus arizonica
Arizona cypress, rough-barked Arizona cypress

This pyramidal species originated in Arizona, and grows to 50 ft (15 m).

Cupressus arizonica

Its mature foliage is gray-green and does not display the white spots of the smooth Arizona cypress. It has short-stalked, large, round cones, and a brown, stringy and furrowed bark. It is popular both as a specimen tree and as a hedge. *Zones 7–10.*

Cupressus sempervirens
Mediterranean cypress, funereal cypress

This species has fine, dark grayish green foliage with tiny scale-leaves in slightly flattened sprays, and large, slightly elongated, pale brown cones. The form usually cultivated, 'Stricta', is narrowly columnar, but a proportion of its seedlings grow into trees with side branches at a wide angle to the trunk, the form known as 'Horizontalis'. Drought tolerant and slow growing, it makes vigorous growth under good conditions in a warm climate. The 'Stricta' form can reach 15–20 ft (5–7 m) in 10 years, often as a slim column, but old trees of 30–40 ft (10–13 m) are usually much broader. The foliage of 'Swane's Golden' is flecked golden-yellow with deeper gold tips. *Zones 8–10.*

Cupressus sempervirens 'Swane's Golden'

Cycas revoluta

CYCAS
Cycadaceae
Sago cycads

Fossils show that cycads have been on earth for about 300 million years! They have long pinnate fronds arising from the top of a thick trunk packed with starchy tissue; male and female organs are on different plants, the male in long narrow cones terminating the stem, the female on the margins of furry, leaf-like organs that ring the trunk apex, enlarging after fertilization to make hard oval seeds that hang in a 'skirt' below the trunk apex. Most *Cycas* species do not thrive outdoors except in tropical and warmer subtropical areas.

Cultivation

They like sunny positions, with some shade when young, and deep, well-drained soil. Propagation is from seed, detached offsets, or by cutting off a whole trunk and plunging the base in a trench filled with gravel and organic matter.

Cycas revoluta
Japanese sago cycad

From the islands of southern Japan, this palm-like species grows on short single or multiple trunks to 10 ft (3 m) with a wide, flat rosette of stiff, pinnate leaves which have crowded spine-tipped leaflets. The most widely cultivated cycad in the world, it is a popular landscape subject, especially suited to courtyards and plazas. Slow growing, plants live for 50 to 100 years or more and are readily transplanted. *Zones 5–11*.

Cytisus × praecox 'Allgold'

CYTISUS
Fabaceae
Broom

A diverse group of usually yellow-flowered leguminous shrubs, *Cytisus* is a large and variable genus, in habit ranging from erect to prostrate, some species having well-developed leaves, while others are almost leafless with all photosynthesis performed by the green angular branchlets. All have pea-like flowers, mostly in shades of yellow, in profuse small clusters along the current season's growths in mid to late spring. Generally easy garden subjects, they can be relied upon for a display of color under most conditions except deep shade.

Cultivation

They tolerate both dry and boggy soils, and fertile or highly infertile soils. Some smaller species demand warm, dry positions in pockets of well-drained soil. They can be propagated from seeds or cuttings or by grafting.

Cytisus × praecox
Warminster broom

This hybrid between the very tall species *C. multiflorus* and the lower *C. purgans* includes several popular cultivars which make free-flowering shrubs of 3–4 ft (1–1.2 m) with massed slender branchlets arising at ground level and spreading gracefully. The original hybrid has cream and yellow flowers with a heavy, perhaps overpowering, fragrance borne in mid to late spring. 'Allgold' has cascading sprays of soft golden-yellow blossoms. *Zones 5–9.*

Daboecia cantabrica 'Alba'

DABOECIA
Ericaceae
St. Dabeoc's heath

This genus of small-leafed, evergreen shrubs is commonly grouped with the heaths and heathers *(Erica* and *Calluna)*. They have conspicuous white to purple urn-shaped flowers, which contract to a small mouth, on nodding stalks spaced along bare, ascending flowering branches. The petal tube falls after flowering. They are suited to exposed situations in a rock garden or on retaining walls.

Cultivation

They require soil that is permanently moist and acid. Named varieties normally require propagation from cuttings, but they still produce fertile seed which may breed true to type.

Daboecia cantabrica

This species becomes a straggling shrub of up to 24 in (60 cm) high if not pruned to a lower height. The flowers, borne throughout summer and autumn, vary from white through pink to deep crimson-purple; clones representing these extremes are 'Alba' and 'Atropurpurea' respectively. It has also been crossed with *D. azorica* to give the hybrid *D.* × *scotica*, of which the best known clone is 'William Buchanan' with deep rosy-red flowers. *Zones 7–9.*

DAPHNE
Thymelaeaceae
Daphne

The daphnes belong to a large genus which includes both deciduous and evergreen species. They have simple, leathery leaves and small, mostly fragrant flowers clustered at the shoot tips or in the leaf axils. The flower parts are not differentiated into true petals and sepals, of which there are always 4, characteristically pointed and recurving with a fleshy texture.

Cultivation

They prefer cool, well-aerated, gritty soil with high humus content. They are intolerant of root disturbance. Propagation is normally from cuttings or layers; seeds germinate readily enough but many fail to fruit.

Daphne × burkwoodii

This hybrid between *D. cneorum* and *D. caucasica* was raised early in the 20th century by the Burkwood brothers, well-known English nurserymen, and has been a popular daphne ever since. Semi-evergreen, it is a low, rounded shrub to about 3 ft (1 m) tall with profusely clustered, pale pink flowers, darker in bud. The main flowering is mid- to late spring but flowers may continue through summer. It flowers best in full sun but will also thrive in semi-shade. *Zones 5–9.*

Daphne × *burkwoodii*

Daphne cneorum
Garland flower

This evergreen shrub from southern Europe has a loose, semi-prostrate habit with the main shoots trailing but producing dense clusters of lateral branches with small, dark green leaves and profuse clusters of sweet-scented rose-pink flowers in mid-spring. It is a sun-loving plant but requires its soil to remain moist though perfectly drained. *Zones 4–9.*

Daphne odora

Its perfume has made *Daphne odora* the most popular daphne in temperate southern hemisphere countries. Although capable of reaching almost 6 ft

Daphne odora

Davidia involucrata

(2 m) in height, it is normally seen as a spreading, twiggy shrub of about 24 in (60 cm) with leathery, dark green leaves. From late autumn through to mid-spring it produces a succession of clusters of waxy flowers, typically rose-purple on the outside of the buds opening to almost pure white. *Zones 8–10.*

DAVIDIA
Davidiaceae
Dove tree, handkerchief tree

'Like huge butterflies hovering' is how the plant explorer E. H. Wilson described the long-stalked flower heads of this tree in western China, each nestled between 2 large, drooping white or cream bracts. In full flower it is a very striking deciduous tree. The genus contains one species, though sometimes a variety is distinguished within it. The large, toothed leaves have a soft texture with the surface deeply creased by veins.

Cultivation

The tree is always raised from the large seeds, enclosed in a plum-like fruit. Cold treatment assists germination.

Davidia involucrata

In its native China this graceful tree reaches heights of over 60 ft (18 m) with

Daphne cneorum

a rounded crown and thick trunk. In cultivation it can grow rapidly to 15–20 ft (5–7 m) in moist, friable soil and a sheltered situation, and in a few decades it may double that height. Flowering rarely begins before the tree is 10 years old. A common cultivated form is var. *vilmoriniana*, with paler and less downy leaf undersides. *Zones 7–9.*

DEUTZIA
Hydrangeaceae
Wedding bells

Summer-flowering deciduous shrubs from East Asia and the Himalayas, deutzias have long, straight, cane-like stems springing from ground level, developing a pale flaky bark if allowed to thicken. Leaves are in opposite pairs. The flower sprays terminate short lateral shoots from the previous year's growth, so hard pruning will delay flowering for a year; best results are obtained by selectively thinning out canes and shortening some of the thickest old stems.

Cultivation

Propagate from cuttings. Deutzias like sheltered positions in moist, fertile soil, and plenty of sun.

Deutzia × elegantissima

Deutzia × elegantissima

Including some of the finest and largest-flowered pinks among its clones, this hybrid between the west Chinese *D. purpurascens* and the Japanese *D. sieboldiana* makes a shrub of 4–6 ft (1.2–2 m) with purplish red twigs and flower-stalks. The 2 original cultivars were 'Elegantissima' with flowers near-white inside and rose-pink outside, and 'Fasciculata' with a slightly deeper rose flush. These were followed by the Irish hybrid 'Rosealind' with still deeper flesh-pink flowers. *Zones 5–9.*

Deutzia × rosea

This was one of the earliest crosses, involving *D. gracilis* and *D. purpurascens*. It has the low, spreading habit of the former species and the pink coloration of the second. The original clone has flowers of the palest pink, in shorter, broader sprays than in *D. gracilis*. 'Carminea' has larger panicles of pink flowers with a stronger carmine-pink on the back. *Zones 5–9.*

Deutzia × rosea 'Carminea'

Dodonaea viscosa 'Purpurea'

Deutzia scabra 'Pride of Rochester'

Deutzia scabra

This longest established of the *Deutzia* species in Western gardens is also the most robust, with tall, thick canes to about 10 ft (3 m) high, and one of the most cold-hardy. 'Scabra' means 'rough' or 'harsh' and refers to the rasp-like feel of the leaves. The bell-shaped flowers are white, produced in large panicles terminating all the upper branches from mid-spring to early summer. 'Pride of Rochester' is a double form with large flowers faintly tinted mauve outside, very vigorous and floriferous. *Zones 5–10.*

DODONAEA
Sapindaceae
Hopbush

This is a widespread and almost entirely Australian genus of evergreen trees and woody shrubs. Its common name, hopbush, refers to the abundant, winged, capsular, hop-like fruits which were used for brewing beer in the early days of European settlement. In many species, male and female flowers appear on separate plants. The flowers are small and insignificant.

Cultivation

Hopbushes grow in full sun or partial shade and prefer moderately fertile, light, free-draining soil. They tolerate a wide range of climates and coastal salty winds. Light pruning in early spring restricts height and maintains shape. Propagate from seed cuttings.

Dodonaea viscosa
Hopbush

This very variable species grows throughout Australia and New Zealand, with glossy, slightly sticky, light green foliage and decorative fruits in summer that are green turning to light brown. Dense and fast growing, it is best pruned to an upright shrub form around 10 ft (3 m) tall. It is useful for screening and hedging. 'Purpurea', a bronze-leafed cultivar from New Zealand, has purplish red fruit capsules. *Zones 9–11.*

DRACAENA
Agavaceae

This genus consists of evergreen trees and shrubs, many originating from equatorial regions of Africa and Asia, which are grown for their foliage, many as greenhouse or indoor potted plants.

Dracaena draco

Duranta erecta

Those grown indoors are sometimes confused with species of *Cordyline* and are often termed 'false palms' because of their cane-like stems and crown of strappy leaves.

Cultivation
Dracaenas need warm-temperate to subtropical conditions, full sun or partial shade and well-drained soil.

Dracaena draco
Dragon's-blood tree, dragon tree
This slow-growing, curious tree is said to live to a very great age. A mature specimen may reach 30 ft (10 m) high with a rounded, umbrella-like crown consisting of clustered, stiff, lance-shaped, blue-green leaves about 24 in (60 cm) long and nearly 2 in (5 cm) wide. It bears insignificant flowers followed by berries in summer. Full-grown trees are usually only seen in botanic gardens. *Zones 10–11.*

DURANTA
Verbenaceae
Golden dewdrop, pigeon berry
A genus of evergreen trees and shrubs from the American tropics and subtropics, *Duranta* is represented in gardens by just one of its many species. The more vigorous growths are armed with spines, leaves are smallish and often toothed and the 5-petaled flowers, narrowed at the center into a short tube, appear in sprays from the upper leaf axils. They are followed by firm, fleshy fruits with hard stones, said to be poisonous. *Duranta* is a vigorous grower equally at home in the tropics and frost-free temperate regions.

Cultivation
Grow in a fertile, well-drained soil in full sun. Propagate from cuttings. They may be bothered by whiteflies.

Duranta erecta
Under good conditions this shrub can reach 15–20 ft (5–7 m) if trained to a single-trunked tree, with dense, slightly pendulous foliage. Flowers are a pale mauve-blue with darker streaks on the 2 lower petals and a cream 'eye', borne from late spring to autumn but continuing into winter in the tropics. The decorative fruits can appear in profusion, overlapping with the flowers in late summer and autumn and often persisting into winter. The cultivar 'Alba' has white flowers. *Zones 10–11.*

E

ELAEAGNUS
Elaeagnaceae

This genus consists of deciduous and evergreen shrubs, small trees and scrambling climbers mostly from Asia. All have simple, toothless leaves which, together with the twigs, flower-buds and fruits, glisten with tiny circular scales, either silvery or rusty brown. Flowers, clustered in the leaf axils, have 4 small, fleshy 'petals' (actually sepals) opening narrowly, with a bulge at the stalk end indicating the ovary.

Cultivation

Generally vigorous and trouble free, they thrive in most soils and positions. Propagate from seed for deciduous species and cuttings for evergreens.

Elaeagnus pungens

This vigorous, spreading, evergreen shrub of Japanese origin grows to 12 ft (4 m) tall and even wider, with long, horizontal branches. It is often used for screening and shelter. The leaves are green and shiny above and dull white beneath with scattered brown glandular spots. It has insignificant but fragrant bell-shaped white flowers in autumn. 'Aurea' has variegated foliage, with leaves having a wide irregular margin of golden yellow. *Zones 7–10.*

ENKIANTHUS
Ericaceae

About 10 species of deciduous shrubs make up this genus, which have small, bell-shaped flowers, densely clustered, and fine autumn foliage colors. Growth is rather open and the smallish leaves are clustered at the end of each season's growth, producing a layered effect. The stalked, pendulous flowers are produced in numerous short sprays from just below the leaves.

Cultivation

They like moist woodland conditions, with humus-rich, acid soil. Propagate from seed or from cuttings.

Enkianthus campanulatus

From Japan and southern China, this is the most popular species, making a shrub 9–12 ft (3–4 m) high of narrow, open habit and slow growth. The flowers, cream but heavily striped and tipped dull crimson, are produced in abundance in spring. In autumn the leaves turn to shades of gold, scarlet and dull purple. *E.* var. *palibinii* has more strongly reddish flowers. *Zones 6–9.*

Enkianthus perulatus

This is rather distinctive among *Enkianthus* species in its lower, bushier

Enkianthus campanulatus

Elaeagnus pungens

Erica carnea

Enkianthus perulatus

Erica × darleyensis

habit and more sparsely scattered waxy flowers that are pure white or greenish white, without markings and contracted at the mouth. They are borne on nodding stalks in early spring. It likes a cool, sheltered position. This species has by far the best autumn foliage color. *Zones 6–9.*

ERICA
Ericaceae
Heath

This genus is made up of small-leafed, free-flowering, evergreen shrubs. In Europe several *Erica* species plus the closely related *Calluna* (heather) dominate moorland vegetation. Not frost-hardy, they were popular in the early 19th century as greenhouse plants and some hybrids were developed then. The European species bear smaller flowers in a more limited white-to-deep-pink color range but are much more hardy, especially the many cultivars derived from *E. cinerea, E. × darleyensis* and *E. herbacea.*

Cultivation
They like full sun and perfect drainage, and are best grown in poor soil. Dead-heading is usually necessary.

Erica carnea
syn. *E. herbacea*
This evergreen, spreading shrub makes good ground cover. From early winter to late spring, it bears bell-shaped to tubular flowers in shades of red and pink (sometimes white). Its leaves are arranged in whorls. It grows to about 12 in (30 cm) high. *Zones 5–9.*

Erica × darleyensis
This hybrid forms a spreading mass of stems up to 24 in (60 cm) high with dark green foliage, covered from late autumn through spring in crowded short spikes of cylindrical pale rose flowers with protruding darker stamens. 'Darley Dale', has mauve flowers. 'Jack H. Brummage' has golden to red-tinted winter foliage. *Zones 6–9.*

ERIOBOTRYA
Rosaceae

This genus belonging to the rose family includes 10 species of evergreen shrubs or trees. It includes trees growing to 30 ft (10 m), all with leathery, deeply veined leaves with silvery or felty undersides. Insignificant, creamy white, scented flowers are held in loose sprays at the tips of the branches during autumn and are followed by edible fruit.

Cultivation
Easily grown, they are frost-hardy and tolerate dry as well as coastal conditions.

Eriobotrya japonica
Loquat

The loquat can grow to 20 ft (7 m), forming a dense, conical, shapely tree, but is kept compact by pruning, after harvesting the golden yellow fruit. The large, leathery, deep green leaves are pale and felty beneath. It blooms in late autumn and fruit ripens in spring. It is susceptible to fruit-fly, and birds can also damage the crop. It needs fertile, well-drained soil and ample moisture as fruit matures. *Zones 8–10.*

Eriobotrya japonica

Erythrina caffra

ERYTHRINA
Fabaceae
Coral tree

The 108 species of deciduous and semi-evergreen trees and shrubs in this genus originate in tropical and warm-temperate areas of Africa, Asia, Central America, the Caribbean and Hawaii. Ranging in height from 6–65 ft (2–20 m), trunk and branches are protected with short, sharp spines. Sweet-pea-like flowers in hues of scarlet, crimson or orange are borne in racemes toward the ends of branches at varying times, followed by narrow seed pods that dry and brown as they ripen.

Cultivation
Most species are not frost-hardy. They enjoy full sun and well-drained soil. Propagate from seed in spring or cuttings in summer, and from suckers.

Erythrina caffra
South African coral tree

This semi-evergreen tree with a broad, open crown quickly reaches about

35–60 ft (12–18 m) and is a popular shade tree in South Africa. The compound leaves have 3 sharp oval leaflets on long stalks. Clusters of brilliant orange-red flowers on almost bare branches (sometimes quite thorny) are borne from late spring to early summer. *Zones 9–11.*

Erythrina crista-galli
Cockspur coral tree

This species from Brazil is the best known coral tree in temperate climates, where it is treated almost as a herbaceous plant, being cut severely after the flowers are over, transferred to a large pot and overwintered under glass, or else grown permanently in the greenhouse. It grows about 6 ft (2 m) tall under these conditions. In subtropical climates, it grows into a gnarled tree 15–30 ft (5–10 m) tall and bears its scarlet or coral-red flowers in spring and summer. *Zones 8–11.*

ESCALLONIA
Escalloniaceae

These evergreen shrubs and small trees have smallish toothed leaves which are usually shiny and succulent. The flowers, crowded into dense panicles, have separate white or pink petals that in many species are pressed together to form a tube but with the tips recurving. The fruit is a small globular capsule, shedding fine seed. They are capable of sprouting profusely from the base after being cut back by frost. Their growth habit is untidy, but as hedges the shrubby kinds will thicken with trimming.

Cultivation

Propagate from softwood cuttings.

Escallonia 'Appleblossom'

Wind resistant and ideal for hedging in coastal gardens, this attractive, bushy, dense evergreen bears apple-blossom

Erythrina crista-galli

pink flowers in early to mid-summer. It has dark green, glossy leaves. Moderately frost hardy, it grows to about 6 ft (1.8 m) high and wide. *Zones 7–10.*

EUCALYPTUS
Myrtaceae

This diverse genus contains over 600 species of evergreen trees and large shrubs prized for their beauty, oils, timber and honey. Almost all originate in Australia, with a few species from New Guinea and nearby islands. The flowers have no separate sepals or petals as these have been fused together to form a cap which is pushed off by the densely packed emerging stamens which can be in shades of white, yellow, pink or red. Foliage varies from linear to heart shaped. Trees vary in hardiness, with wide variation in shape, size and habitat; some are able to withstand prolonged droughts, others are salt resistant and survive in swamps; others prefer cool mountain areas.

Cultivation

Propagate from seed in spring or fall.

Eucalyptus citriodora
Lemon-scented gum

This adaptable tree is tall and straight trunked, growing to 100 ft (30 m). It has

Eucalyptus citriodora

Eucalyptus ficifolia
Scarlet-flowering gum, red-flowering gum

A spectacular flowering eucalypt, *E. ficifolia* bears enormous terminal clusters of scarlet to orange flowers in late spring to summer, followed by large, urn-shaped fruits. It grows to about 30 ft (10 m) with rough bark and a spreading crown of lance-shaped foliage. *Zones 9–10.*

Eucalyptus pauciflora
Snow gum

This 30–65 ft (10–20 m) tree tends to have a rather twisted trunk that is often distorted by the exposed conditions in which it grows. The reddish brown or gray bark peels in irregular strips, revealing white and beige under bark. Small cream flowers in spring and summer are followed by small seed capsules. Its flowering is erratic — pauciflora means few flowers. Subspecies *niphophila*, which occurs at relatively cold high altitudes, is smaller and more low-branching. Both are grown successfully in England and Ireland. *Zones 7–9.*

Eucalyptus ficifolia

Eucalyptus pauciflora

smooth, sometimes dimpled bark in subtle shades of white, gray or pale pink which is shed during the summer. The foliage is held aloft on an open crown and, when crushed, the leaves have a lemony scent. Winter flowers are creamy white. Young plants may be damaged by frost, but once established it is fast growing and hardy. *Zones 9–11.*

Euonymus europaeus

Euonymus japonicus 'Ovatus Aureus'

EUONYMUS
Celastraceae
Spindle-tree

This genus consists of both deciduous and evergreen trees, shrubs and creepers with simple leaves in opposite pairs, usually with toothed margins. Flowers are inconspicuous, greenish or yellowish, in small groups along the lower parts of the current year's growth. The capsular fruits split open in autumn to reveal bright yellow, orange or red seeds against a contrasting capsule. Birds, attracted by the nutritious oily outer layer, distribute the seeds.

Cultivation

They like a sheltered position with ample sun and fertile, well-drained soil. The deciduous species are usually propagated from seed, the evergreen ones from cuttings.

Euonymus europaeus
European spindle-tree

'Tree' is a slight exaggeration, though this species is usually single stemmed at the base and occasionally reaches 20 ft (7 m). It grows in woodlands and often in limestone or chalk soils. It is a nondescript shrub until laden with pink or red fruit in late summer, which split open to reveal the large orange seeds. *Zones 6–9.*

Euonymus japonicus

Generally represented by its variegated cultivars, this spreading evergreen shrub

Euphorbia pulcherrima

has dark green shiny leaves, reaching heights of 10–13 ft (3–4 m). Pale greenish flowers appear in early summer, and autumn foliage may be enlivened by scattered pinkish capsules opening to reveal orange seeds. 'Ovatus Aureus' has broad, irregular margins of bright yellow. *Zones 8–10.*

EUPHORBIA
Euphorbiaceae

The genus includes annuals, herbaceous perennials, shrubs and some succulent species that resemble cacti. The flowers of all species are almost indistinguishable from each other. They are much reduced, consisting of only a stigma and a stamen, always green, and usually carried in small clusters. They are in fact a unique type of flower, called a cyathium.

Cultivation

Propagate from seed, from basal cuttings, or by division.

Euphorbia pulcherrima
Poinsettia, Christmas plant

Potted poinsettias are a familiar Christmas decoration in the northern hemisphere. In the garden it makes a gangly shrub up to 12 ft (4 m) tall, usually dropping its leaves as flowering starts. The bracts give each flower-cluster the appearance of a single huge flower. *Zones 10–11.*

EURYOPS
Asteraceae

Part of the large daisy family, this genus contains around 100 species of evergreen shrubs most of which come from southern Africa and have large yellow flower heads, held above the fern-like foliage.

Cultivation

They like well-drained soil and a position in full sun, otherwise the shrubs grow leggy and flowers are not as plentiful. Lightly prune after flowering.

Euryops pectinatus
Grey-leaved euryops

This widely cultivated shrubby evergreen from southwestern Cape, South Africa, grows well in most temperate conditions. Excellent for rock gardens and borders, it likes sun, partial shade in hot areas and moist, well-drained, gravelly soil. From winter to spring it bears bright yellow daisy flowers, for which the finely cut gray-green leaves are an attractive foil. It is a single, short-stemmed, bushy shrub growing to around 3 ft (1 m). *Zones 9–11.*

EXOCHORDA
Rosaceae
Pearl bush

These deciduous shrubs from central Asia and northern China have weak, pithy branches and thin-textured, paddle-shaped, untidy leaves, but in spring the branch ends are clustered with 5-petaled, delicate white flowers. The fruits are capsules with wing-like segments, splitting apart when ripe to release flattened seeds. Dry summers produce the best display of flowers.

Cultivation

A sheltered position in full sun and well-drained soil are desirable. Propagate from cuttings.

Exochorda × macrantha

This hybrid is a cross between *E. racemosa* and the central Asian *E. korolkowii.* Sometimes reaching 10 ft (3 m) tall, in mid- to late spring it produces elongated clusters of pure white flowers from every branch tip. *Zones 6–9.*

Euryops pectinatus

Exochorda × macrantha

F, G

FAGUS
Fagaceae
Beech

Beeches are large, long-lived, deciduous trees with distinctive pointed winter buds with brown scales. Flowers appear briefly in spring with the new leaves. The fruits are small shaggy capsules which in early autumn split open to release several strongly angled seeds, or 'beech nuts'. Their timber is used for flooring, furniture and small items. The oil-rich nuts are a major food source for wildlife.

Cultivation

Beeches have a shallow, dense root system that robs moisture and nutrients from plants beneath their canopy. They require an open, well-drained soil of reasonable fertility and need shelter from strong winds. Propagate from seed, which should be sown as soon as it falls.

Fagus sylvatica

Fagus sylvatica
Common beech, European beech

This is a large tree to 130 ft (40 m) high, with a long, smooth bole when close planted; in the open it is low branching, the crown spreading with age. In spring drooping balls of yellowish male flowers and less conspicuous greenish clusters of female flowers appear at the branch tips, while the nuts are shed in abundance in early autumn. Many cultivars have darker bronze or purple foliage, including 'Purpurea' and 'Cuprea'. 'Aspleniifolia' and 'Rohanii' have deeply cut leaves. 'Pendula' has branches drooping from a mushroom-shaped crown. *Zones 5–9.*

FATSIA
Araliaceae

The single evergreen species in this genus is closely related to ivy *(Hedera)*, a relationship evident in the flowers, fruit and leaf texture. However *Fatsia* is a shrub, with thick, erect, little-branched stems, and the deeply lobed leaves are larger than those of ivies. The creamy white flowers are in spherical heads grouped in a large panicle that terminates the shoot, and are followed by small black berries.

Cultivation

It has shade and cold tolerance and also adapts well to warmer-temperate and

Fatsia japonica

even subtropical climates, given shade and moisture. Propagate from seed or cuttings.

Fatsia japonica

Sometimes known by its earlier name *Aralia japonica*, this shrub reaches an average height of 8–9 ft (2.5–3 m). The leaves are 12 in (30 cm) or more across. In moist forest undergrowth in its native Japan it can reach small tree size and in New Zealand 12 ft (4 m) tall specimens are not uncommon. Flowers appear in late autumn, with fruits ripening in late winter. It should be protected from fierce summer sun or the leaves may be scorched. *Zones 8–11.*

FICUS

Moraceae

Fig

Figs range from climbers and shrubs to large trees, much planted in frost-free climates where there is room for their branches and invasive roots. The flowers are completely enclosed in what matures to fruit, and they need certain species of wasps to penetrate their protection and fertilize them. Once the fruit ripens, it is eaten by birds and bats which spread the seeds, often into the branches of other trees where the young fig trees germinate, to send down roots to the ground. These soon become woody trunks, and the host tree is eventually strangled;

strangler figs are one of the more dramatic features of the tropical rainforests.

Cultivation

Propagate from seed, semi-ripe cuttings or aerial layers.

Ficus elastica

India-rubber tree

This tree can grow to 100 ft (30 m), and forms massive aerial roots and high buttresses with age. The species and its variegated forms can be pruned to restrict size, but their aggressive root systems can damage foundations and drains. Its attractive rosy sheath of new leaves contrasts with the deep green, shiny mature leaves. A popular cultivar is 'Decora' with bronze colored new leaves. *Zones 10–11.*

Ficus macrophylla

Moreton Bay fig

This large, spreading evergreen tree occurs naturally in coastal rainforests of eastern Australia. It grows to about 130 ft (40 m) and has a buttressed trunk. The large, leathery, dark green leaves have rust-toned undersides. The fruit is reddish brown when ripe. It needs a subtropical or warm-temperate climate and its size restricts it to large gardens or public plantings. Well-drained sandy soils and moderate to high rainfall areas suit it best. *Zones 10–11.*

Ficus elastica 'Decora'

Ficus macrophylla

Forsythia × intermedia 'Spectabilis'

Forsythia suspensa

FORSYTHIA
Oleaceae

Forsythias bear brilliant yellow or gold blossoms in mid-spring. Deciduous shrubs of medium stature, they have soft-wooded stems branching from near the ground. The rather narrow, bluntly toothed leaves appear after the 4-petaled yellow flowers, which are paired or clustered at the twig nodes.

Cultivation

A sunny position aids flowering, but they virtually refuse to flower in warm climates, requiring winter temperatures below the freezing point. Propagate from hardwood cuttings in early summer.

Forsythia × intermedia

This hybrid was first recorded in Germany around 1885 and some fine cultivars were named in the following 50 years, including 'Lynwood' and 'Spectabilis'. In 1939 Karl Sax at the Arnold Arboretum in Massachusetts created the first artificial tetraploid 'Arnold Giant', and subsequent breeding work resulted in 'Beatrix Farrand' and 'Karl Sax'. They all carry profuse, large, gold flowers on vigorous plants up to about 10 ft (3 m) tall. *Zones 5–9.*

Forsythia suspensa

Indigenous to China, this species makes a shrub of 8–10 ft (2.5–3 m), or taller if supported, with dense, slender, arching branches. From mid-spring the branches are lined with profuse golden yellow blooms with narrow petals. *Zones 4–9.*

FRAXINUS
Oleaceae
Ash

This genus consists of mainly deciduous trees, with pinnate leaves consisting of a number of leaflets, and small flowers that in most species lack petals. The dry winged fruits or 'keys' are a characteristic feature. Several larger species have tough, pale timber.

Cultivation

Ashes make fast growth and survive in exposed or arid conditions, though most

Fraxinus angustifolia subsp. oxycarpa

Fraxinus americana 'Autumn Purple'

respond to shelter and fertile, moist soils with more luxuriant growth. Propagate from seed or, for cultivars, by grafting on to stock of the same species.

Fraxinus americana
White ash
This species occurs naturally through eastern USA and in southeastern Canada. In the wild it reaches about 80 ft (24 m) with a long straight bole and furrowed gray-brown bark and a somewhat domed canopy. The pinnate leaves have 7 to 9 large, dark green leaflets with silvery undersides. The inconspicuous flowers appear before the leaves. Autumn color is most commonly fine yellow to deep purple to maroon. A number of forms are available including *F. americana* var. *juglandifolia*, which has a slender, columnar habit, and 'Autumn Purple' with leaves that turn reddish purple in fall. *Zones 4–10.*

Fraxinus angustifolia
This name includes a range of forms from the Mediterranean and western Asia. The leaves are arranged in whorls of 3 to 4 on the main shoots. It is suitable for semi-arid climates with hot dry summers. The best known subspecies is *oxycarpa* (the desert ash), which is upright with smooth bark. *Zones 6–10.*

Fraxinus ornus

Fraxinus ornus
Flowering ash, manna ash
From southern Europe and Asia Minor, the flowering ash makes a round-topped tree of 30–50 ft (10–15 m) with a short, fluted trunk and smooth gray bark. Its sugary sap or 'manna' used to be used medicinally. The leaves consist of 5 to 9 oval leaflets, with downy undersides. In late spring foamy panicles of white blossoms are produced from branch tips followed by small, narrow fruits. *Zones 6–10.*

FREMONTODENDRON
Sterculiaceae
Fremontia

This genus is made up of evergreen shrubs or small trees from southwestern USA and adjacent areas of Mexico, usually of ungainly habit but bearing profuse, cup-shaped, bright golden flowers. The stems have a coating of felty or scurfy hairs, as do the strongly lobed leaves. The inner bark contains strong fibers and has a slippery layer of mucilage beneath it. The flowers lack petals but the large golden sepals are petal-like.

Cultivation

They like a sheltered, sunny position with well-drained soil, but they can be rather short lived. They do not perform well in climates with hot, wet summers.

Fremontodendron californicum

This is the best known and most cold-hardy species, and may eventually become a small tree of 30 ft (10 m), but is usually seen as a shrub of sparse, crooked form 10–13 ft (3–4 m) tall, with dark brown bark. From mid- to late spring it produces a succession of 2 in (5 cm) wide flowers that clothe the branches with gold. *Zones 8–10.*

Fremontodendron californicum

FUCHSIA
Onagraceae

The numerous hybrids of this genus with showy pendulous flowers in shades of red, white, pink and purple are technically shrubs but when raised for sale in pots or hanging baskets they are often treated as herbaceous plants. The genus is confined to South and Central America except for 4 species in New Zealand and one in Tahiti. Many larger-flowered American species inhabit areas of high rainfall, sometimes growing as epiphytes or on rocks in forests. The larger fuchsias have pale, spongy bark which peels off in thin flakes or strips.

Cultivation

Hardier fuchsias need adequate shelter and humidity, freedom from extremes of heat and cold, and a moist but well-drained, acid soil of open texture.

Fuchsia magellanica
Hardy fuchsia, ladies' eardrops

This hardy species is usually seen as a large evergreen shrub, with pendulous red-sepaled, purple-petaled flowers. The flowers can be white, red, pink, blue, purple or lavender — or any combination of these — many being double. They range from almost prostrate sprawlers to upright shrubs nearly 6 ft (2 m) tall. They like rich soil and dappled shade, and benefit from fairly hard pruning in early spring to keep them compact. *Zones 7–10.*

Fuchsia magellanica

Genista lydia

GARDENIA
Rubiaceae

Gardenias are delightfully fragrant flowers and are popular in warm-climate gardens worldwide. Evergreen shrubs or small trees with glossy leaves and white or cream flowers, they require a fertile, well-drained, slightly acid soil and are suited to lightly shaded gardens. Generous water in warmer months and a regular dressing of compost and fertilizer ensures good flowering and deep glossy green foliage. Frost-tender and lovers of humidity, they are grown in heated greenhouses in cooler climates.

Cultivation
Propagate from semi-ripe cuttings.

Gardenia augusta
Gardenia, Cape jasmine

Formerly known as G. *jasminoides*, this is the best known gardenia. It is from southern China, though long supposed native to the Cape of Good Hope, hence the common name. It is usually seen in one of its double-flowered cultivars, all with white, strongly perfumed flowers which change to pale yellow as they age. 'Magnifica' is larger though less generous with its flowers. Flowers appear over a long season from late spring. *Zones 10–11.*

Gardenia augusta

Genista × spachiana

GENISTA
Fabaceae
Broom

These shrubs bear small, fragrant, pea-like flowers. Many species have very reduced leaves, sometimes bearing their flowers on leafless green branches. In ancient times their flowers were used to make dyes.

Cultivation
Full sun and well-drained soil suit them best. Propagate from seed or semi-ripe cuttings.

Genista lydia

This deciduous shrub grows up to 24 in (60 cm), often spreading wider, in a domed shape with arching branches and bluish green leaves. It bears bright yellow flowers in spring and early summer. *Zones 7–9.*

Gleditsia triacanthos 'Sunburst'

Ginkgo biloba

Genista × spachiana
This dense evergreen may grow to 18 ft
(6 m) tall. Leaves are dark green and
shiny above, pale and silky beneath. A
profusion of yellow flowers are borne in
winter and spring. *Zones 9–11.*

GINKGO
Ginkgoaceae
Ginkgo, maidenhair tree
This single species, *Ginkgo biloba*, first
appeared about 300 million years ago. A
temperate climate tree, it is resistant to
pollution and pests, but needs shelter
from strong winds. It prefers deep,
fertile soil. Although female trees drop
smelly fruit, in China the seeds of the
female tree are prized for their nutri-
tional value. They do not appear before
the tree is some 35 years old.

Cultivation
Propagate from seed or autumn cuttings.

Ginkgo biloba
The ginkgo reaches a height of 80 ft
(25 m) or more, upright when young
and spreading to about 30 ft (10 m) with
age. Deciduous, long, matte green, fan-
shaped leaves turn bright golden yellow
in autumn. A fleshy, plum-like, orange-
brown fruit with an edible kernel
appears in late summer and autumn if
male and female trees are grown together. *Zones 3–10.*

GLEDITSIA
Caesalpiniaceae
Honey locust
Indigenous to North America and Asia,
these deciduous, broadly spreading,
usually thorny trees have attractive
foliage, and are popular shade trees.
They have inconspicuous flowers and
large, often twisted, hanging seed pods
filled with a sweetish, edible pulp.

Cultivation
Gleditsias grow best in full sun in good
alluvial soils but will tolerate higher land
if watered well in summer. They are fully
hardy although young plants need
protection from frost. Propagate selected
forms by budding in spring or summer
and species from seed in autumn.

Gleditsia triacanthos
Honey locust
Growing to 100 ft (30 m) high and 50 ft
(15 m) wide, this species has an open,
vase-shaped canopy and a thorny trunk.
Fern-like, shiny, dark green leaves turn
deep yellow in autumn. The variety
inermis is thornless. There are several
cultivars including 'Ruby Lace', with
reddish young growth turning dull
bronze in autumn, and 'Sunburst', with
bright yellow young leaves that turn to
pale green in summer and deep yellow in
autumn. *Zones 3–10.*

GREVILLEA
Proteaceae

This Australian genus is the largest protea, with around 350 species, ranging from prostrate shrubs to forest trees but all evergreen. Handsome foliage and a long blooming season means that the shrubby species are important indigenous garden shrubs in Australia; they are also popular in similar mild-winter, dry-summer climates. The tree species are long lived, but the shrubby ones often die after 10 years or so. Flowers are pollinated by nectar-eating birds.

Cultivation

Grevilleas need full sunshine and perfect drainage and should never be given fertilizers rich in phosphorus. Propagate from cuttings in summer; the species hybridize freely in cultivation.

Grevillea lanigera
Woolly grevillea

A bushy shrub, this species takes its name from the grayish, furry leaves with which the red and cream flower-clusters make a very pleasing contrast in late winter and spring. It varies in size, some forms being quite prostrate, others growing to about 3 ft (1 m) tall and wide. It is quite a cold-tolerant species, though it is inclined to be rather short lived in cultivation. *Zones 7–9.*

Grevillea lanigera 'Mt. Tamboritha'

Grevillea 'Robyn Gordon'

This is widely regarded as the best of the many hybrid grevilleas developed in recent years. It makes a dome-shaped bush a little more than 3 ft (1 m) tall and rather wider. The olive-green leaves are much divided and fern-like in effect though rather stiff and prickly. Red flowers appear in showy clusters almost all year, with peak displays in spring and autumn. *Zones 9–11.*

Grevillea rosmarinifolia
Rosemary grevillea, spider flower

This red or deep pink flowered species is usually taller than head high and spreads nearly as wide. The red spider-like flower clusters are borne in abundance in spring, but tend to be hidden among the leaves. It makes a good formal hedge as it can be clipped to shape and its prickly leaves make it quite impenetrable. *Zones 8–10.*

Grevillea rosmarinifolia

Grevillea 'Robyn Gordon'

GREWIA
Tiliaceae

Although there are over 150 species of this genus of trees, shrubs and climbers from tropical regions of Africa, Southeast Asia and Australia, there is really only one species, *Grewia occidentalis*, from southern Africa, which is commonly found in gardens. The genus is named after Nehemiah Grew, who was famous for his botanical drawings.

Cultivation

Propagate from seed or cuttings.

Grewia occidentalis
Four corners, cross-berry

This evergreen with deep green, oval, toothed, leathery leaves, is an upright shrub that can grow to 10 ft (3 m) high. The star-shaped, mauve-pink flowers, held in small clusters, are dotted over it during spring and summer. Brownish, 4-valved berries ripen in autumn. In a sheltered, sunny position with well-drained, humus-rich soil it will form a neat, rounded bush that needs occasional pruning to keep its shape. *Zones 9–11.*

GRISELINIA
Cornaceae

This genus is made up of 6 species of evergreen shrubs and trees from New Zealand and Chile. They have a bushy

habit, and tiny, inconspicuous, pale greenish flowers. The flowers are followed by black berries, though only on female plants. *G. littoralis*, especially, is a first-rate seaside shrub withstanding salty winds very well. It is well liked in England and popular in California.

Cultivation

A temperate climate, well-drained soil and sunshine are called for. With a little trimming, the shrubs make good hedges. Propagate from summer cuttings or seed.

Griselinia littoralis
Kapuka

Growing to a height and spread of 18–37 ft (6–12 m), this tree or shrub has densely packed, bright green foliage and insignificant yellow-green flowers followed by black berries. It prefers full sun to partial shade and fertile soil, is resistant to salt-laden winds and will withstand drought. It appreciates the protection of a wall if grown in colder areas. If used as a hedge, trim in summer. A popular cultivar is 'Variegata', with blotched white variegations. *Zones 8–10.*

Griselinia littoralis

Grewia occidentalis

H

HAKEA
Proteaceae

This genus consists of 130 species of evergreen shrubs and small trees from Australia. They are popular in Australia, New Zealand and California, but disliked in South Africa where several species have become weeds. Fast growing but not always long lived, they prefer mild-winter climates, sunshine and well-drained soil and dislike phosphorus-rich fertilizers. Many are drought resistant and do poorly in summer-rainfall climates. The bushier species make informal hedges, those with prickly leaves being impenetrable. Flowers are borne in small clusters, often half-hidden among the leaves.

Cultivation
Propagate from seed.

Hakea laurina
Pincushion bush
This shrub or small tree grows to 18 ft (6 m) tall, spreading to 10 ft (3 m). The long, narrow leaves are gray-green and leathery. Through winter and spring its fragrant, ball-shaped, crimson flower heads appear, with long creamy styles protruding like pins from a pincushion. Useful for hedges and screens, it needs perfect drainage and may become top heavy and liable to being toppled by strong winds. *Zones 9–11.*

Hakea laurina

HAMAMELIS
Hamamelidaceae
Witch hazel
These deciduous shrubs from East Asia and North America have fragrant flowers, borne on bare stems through winter. They are good shrubs for cool-climate gardens, preferring an open, sunny position (although they will tolerate semi-shade) in fertile, moist but well-drained loamy, acid soils. Old branches should be thinned out in spring to make way for new shoots.

Cultivation
Propagate selected forms by grafting in winter, from heeled cuttings in summer or by budding in late summer. Species can be raised from seed, but germination may take a full year.

Hamamelis × intermedia
Witch hazel
The name covers a group of cultivars derived from *H. japonica* and *H. mollis,* deciduous shrubs with oval leaves 3–5 in (7–12 cm) long that color well in autumn. Fragrant flowers appear on bare twigs in winter. Their color varies from light yellow to deep orange depending on the cultivar: 'Jelena' is bright orange. All cultivars have a preference for moist, well-drained, humus-rich soils in dappled shade. *Zones 4–9.*

Hamamelis × intermedia 'Jelena'

Hamamelis mollis
Chinese witch hazel

From central and western China this upright, open shrub has fragrant, golden yellow flowers, borne on bare branches from mid-winter to spring. It grows to a height and spread of 12 ft (4 m) and the large, thick leaves are mid-green above, downy beneath; they turn deep golden-yellow in autumn. 'Coombe Wood' has larger flowers. *Zones 4–9.*

HEBE
Scrophulariaceae
Veronica

These evergreen shrubs are native to New Zealand and Chile. They have luxuriant, dense spikes of tiny, 4-petaled, purple, white or cerise flowers, and are best suited to warm-temperate climates; only a few can be rated hardy in cooler places, none in cold climates. There are 2 main groups: the broad-leafed hebes, fast-growing shrubs with abundant spikes of small flowers in shades from white through pink to violet and blue; and the whipcord hebes, with small leaves and white or pale mauve flowers.

Cultivation

Hebes like moist but well-drained soil and the broad-leafed types benefit from a post-flowering trim. Propagate from summer cuttings.

Hamamelis mollis

Hebe speciosa

This evergreen, compact shrub grows to about 3 ft (1 m) high, spreading to 4½ ft (1.5 m) wide in a broad bun shape. It has oval, glossy foliage and bears a profusion of reddish purple flowers in terminal clusters from early summer to late autumn. Many attractive cultivars exist including 'Variegata', with creamy white leaf margins, and 'Alicia Amherst', with purple flowers. *Zones 8–9.*

Hebe 'Wiri' hybrids

'Wiri Joy' is a showy, large-flowered hybrid which grows into a rounded shrub with glossy oblong leaves. Purple-pink flowers appear in summer. 'Wiri Mist' is a low shrub to 18 in (45 cm) and can spread to 3 ft (1 m). Its thick leaves are margined with yellow. It is covered with white flowers towards the end of spring. *Zones 8–10.*

Hebe 'Wiri Mist'

Hebe speciosa

Hibiscus rosa-sinensis

Hibiscus syriacus

HIBISCUS
Malvaceae
While the genus name evokes the innumerable cultivars of *Hibiscus rosa-sinensis*, widely grown in tropical and subtropical gardens, the genus is large and diverse, including hot-climate evergreen shrubs and small trees, a few deciduous, temperate-zone shrubs and some annuals and perennials.

Cultivation
The shrubby species thrive in sun and slightly acid, well-drained soil. Propagate from late-summer cuttings.

Hibiscus rosa-sinensis
China rose, shoe flower
This is a glossy-leafed evergreen shrub, sometimes as much as 15 ft (5 m) high and wide, with blood-red flowers borne nearly all year. Its numerous cultivars vary in height from 3 ft (1 m) or so to 3 times that, and the flowers can be 5-petaled singles, semi-double or fully double, the colors ranging from white through pinks to red; the Hawaiian hybrids offer yellow, coral and orange, often with 2 or 3 shades in each flower. Flowers range upwards in size from about 5 in (13 cm). *Zones 10–11.*

Hibiscus syriacus
Rose of Sharon, blue hibiscus
This hardy hibiscus is of erect habit and while usually seen as a head-high shrub it can be trained into a small tree about 12 ft (4 m) tall. It flowers in abundance from late summer. Flowers can be single or double and white, pink, mauve or lilac-blue, according to the cultivar; they almost always have red or maroon blotches at the base of the petals. *Zones 5–10.*

HOVENIA
Rhamnaceae
This genus consists of 2 species of trees from Asia, only one of which is widely grown. Graceful, deciduous trees for temperate-climate gardens, they like full sun and well-drained, fertile soil.

Cultivation
Propagate from fresh seed in autumn or cuttings in summer.

Hovenia dulcis
Japanese raisin tree
This deciduous tree grows to 50 ft (15 m). Its large, heart-shaped leaves produce brilliant autumn hues. The summer flowers are inconspicuous and lightly fragrant and are borne in clusters on thick stalks. As the small capsular fruit ripen, the stalks become fleshy and are also edible. The fruit tastes like raisins. *Zones 8–10.*

HOWEA
Arecaceae

Two similar palms make up this small genus endemic to Lord Howe Island, halfway between Australia and New Zealand. They have a smooth, ringed, single trunk and arching, feathered leaves on long, smooth stalks. Flowers are light brown (male) or green (female), borne on the same plant; held on long stalks at the base of the leaves, they are followed by small fruit. The plants are frost-tender and need moist, humid conditions. Both are popular indoor plants; they tolerate less light and heat than many other palms.

Cultivation

Propagate from seed in spring.

Howea forsteriana
Kentia palm, thatch palm

Growing singly but in natural groves, these palms are best known as indoor plants. Outdoors in warm climates they are slow growing to about 30 ft (10 m) with a slender trunk. They like well-drained, humus-rich soil; regular mulching; fertilizer and adequate water during dry periods. *Zones 10–11.*

HYDRANGEA
Hydrangeaceae

The flower-clusters of these deciduous shrubs contain tiny fertile flowers and showy sterile ones with 4 petal-like sepals. Many cultivated forms have heads com-

Hovenia dulcis

posed almost entirely of sterile flowers called mobcaps, mopheads or hortensias. Intermediate forms with sterile flowers surrounding a central cluster of fertile flowers are called lacecaps. Flower color may vary with the soil's acidity or alkalinity—blue in acid, pink or red in alkaline; white cultivars do not change.

Cultivation

Grow these plants in shade. Soil should be constantly moist, rich in humus and well drained. Propagate from cuttings or seed.

Hydrangea macrophylla
Hortensia

The name usually covers a large race of hybrids. These are the best known

Hydrangea macrophylla

Howea forsteriana

Hymenosporum flavum

Hydrangea quercifolia

hydrangeas, few temperate-climate shrubs matching them for their summer display of flowers. Mobcaps are the most familiar, though there are some handsome lacecap cultivars such as 'Blue Sky'. The many named cultivars range in growth from less than 3 ft (1 m) tall and wide to twice that. **Zones 6–10**.

Hydrangea quercifolia
Oak-leafed hydrangea

This deciduous shrub grows to a height of 6 ft (2 m). The deeply lobed, dark green leaves change to orange-scarlet in autumn. Flowers are a mixture of small, fertile and sterile flowers. The white, sterile flowers eventually fade to pink and violet. It prefers dappled shade. *Zones 5–9*.

HYMENOSPORUM
Pittosporaceae
Australian frangipani

This genus consists of a single species of evergreen tree. It prefers moist, humus-rich soils and flowers best in full sun. It will tolerate some shade.

Cultivation

Propagate from seed or from cuttings.

Hymenosporum flavum

Growing to 30 ft (10 m), taller in its natural rainforest environment, this tree develops a straight, smooth trunk and open, columnar shape, with widely spaced horizontal branches and glossy leaves clustered towards the ends. In spring it bears profuse clusters of fragrant, trumpet-shaped cream flowers that age over several days to deep golden yellow. *Zones 9–11*.

HYPERICUM
Clusiaceae
St. John's wort

This is a large and varied genus of herbaceous plants, shrubs and a few small trees, some evergreen but mostly deciduous, with showy flowers in shades of yellow with a central mass of prominent golden stamens. *Wort* is the Anglo-Saxon word for 'medicinal plant'.

Cultivation

Mostly cool-climate plants, they do best in fertile, well-drained soil, with plentiful water in late spring and summer. Remove seed capsules after flowering and prune in winter. Cultivars are propagated from cuttings and species from seed or from cuttings.

Hypericum calycinum

One of the best ground covers for temperate climates, this species is a low-growing evergreen shrub only about 15 in (35 cm) tall but spreading rapidly by creeping, runner-like stems to cover quite a large area. The flowers appear in mid-summer, and are about the size of a rose. Any sort of soil suits and, though the plant will grow happily in dry shade, it flowers more profusely in sunshine. *Zones 6–10*.

I, J, K

Ilex aquifolium 'Ferox Argentea'

Ilex crenata 'Golden Gem'

Ilex × altaclarensis

ILEX
Aquifoliaceae
Holly

The evergreen and deciduous trees and shrubs which make up this genus come predominantly from cool northern hemisphere climates. Male and female plants must be grown together to obtain the small glossy berries. Berries are either red, yellow or black, and clusters of small, insignificant, greenish white blossoms precede them.

Cultivation

Hollies like deep, friable, well-drained soils with high organic content and an open, sunny position. Propagate from seed in spring or semi-ripe cuttings. Watch for holly aphid and holly leaf miner.

Ilex × altaclarensis
Highclere holly

This group of evergreen hybrid hollies, reaching a height of about 50 ft (15 m), differs from the English holly in having larger, less prickly leaves and larger flowers and berries. There are many cultivars, including 'Camelliifolia', a female with purple-tinged shoots, leaf stems and petal bases, larger berries and long leaves with only a few spines. *Zones 6–10.*

Ilex aquifolium
English holly

This evergreen ornamental is a popular Christmas decoration with its glossy, spiny-edged dark green leaves and bright red winter berries. It can reach a height of 50 ft (15 m) and spread of about 15 ft (5 m) with an erect, many-branching habit. Popular cultivars include 'Ferox', the hedgehog holly, with more compact growth to 18 ft (6 m) and 15 ft (5 m) spread, and leaves with spines over the entire surface; and 'Ferox Argentea', with cream-edged leaves. *Zones 6–10.*

Ilex crenata
Japanese holly

This compact, evergreen shrub has stiff branches, small scalloped leaves, dull white flowers and glossy black berries. It is often used for hedges and topiary. It can grow to a height of 15 ft (5 m) with a spread of 10 ft (3 m) but is usually smaller. A popular cultivar is 'Golden

Ilex verticillata

Ilex opaca

Gem', compact but rarely flowering, with soft yellow foliage. Variegated or pale-leafed forms do best in full sun, green-leafed forms do well in semi-shade. *Zones 6–10.*

Ilex opaca
American holly
The best known American species, this evergreen tree grows to a height and spread of about 40–50 ft (12–15 m); it has an erect habit and produces red berries in winter. The leaves are dull green above and yellowish underneath, with spiny or smooth edges. It prefers a sunny position and acid soil, and does not do well near the sea. *Zones 5–10.*

Ilex verticillata
Winterberry, black alder, coral berry
From eastern USA, this deciduous shrub grows 6–10 ft (2–3 m) high and has a spread of 4–10 ft (1.2–3 m). The toothed leaves are purple-tinged in spring and turn yellow in autumn. The bright red berries stay on the bare branches for a long period, persisting until spring. This shrub tolerates wet conditions. Cultivars include 'Cacapon', a female which produces abundant berries when grown with a male; 'Nana' (syn. 'Red Sprite'), a dwarf female which reaches 4 ft (1.2 m) tall and has a spread of 5 ft (1.5 m); and 'Winter Red', an extra vigorous female

with a height and spread of 10 ft (3 m) and good crops of bright red berries when grown with a male plant. *Zones 3–9.*

Ilex vomitoria
Carolina tea, Yaupon holly
An evergreen tree from southeastern USA and Mexico, this holly grows to a height of 20 ft (6 m) and has red berries and shallowly round-toothed glossy dark green leaves. A quick-growing species, it makes a good hedge or screen. Its leaves contain an emetic substance and were infused by Native Americans to prepare a purgative drink. The cultivar 'Fructoluteo' is a yellow-fruited clone. *Zones 7–10.*

INDIGOFERA
Fabaceae
This genus has over 700 species, and they come in just about every form imaginable: annuals, perennials, shrubs and small trees. One species, *I. tinctoria*, is the source of the blue dye indigo. The cultivated species are generally sub-shrubs or small, deciduous, woody plants with bright green pinnate leaves and panicles of sweet-pea-like flowers, usually in summer.

Cultivation
They prefer light yet moist, well-drained soil in sun or partial shade. Propagate from seed, cuttings or basal suckers.

Indigofera decora

This deciduous shrub grows to 24 in
(60 cm) high and wider in mild climates.
The stems may die back to ground level,
but the plant usually shoots again from the
rootstock. The light green pinnate leaves,
up to 10 in (25 cm) long, are composed
of 5 to 13 leaflets. Panicles of mauve-pink
pea-shaped flowers appear throughout
the warmer months. *Zones 7–11.*

IOCHROMA
Solanaceae

Members of the nightshade family, these
brittle-wooded shrubs from tropical and
subtropical areas of Central and South
America are best suited to warm, humid
climates. Usually erect, with soft-wooded,
arching branches, the evergreen shrubs
carry clusters of long tubular flowers in
shades of blue, purple, red or white.

Cultivation

Propagate from semi-ripe cuttings or
seed.

Iochroma cyaneum
syns *Iochroma tubulosum, I. lanceolatum*
Violet tubeflower

This fast-growing, semi-erect shrub
grows to 10 ft (3 m) high with a spread
of 5 ft (1.5 m). It brings a deep purple
accent to the warm-climate garden; it
can be grown in a greenhouse in cooler
areas. It has gray-green felty leaves;
deep purple-blue flowers are borne in
large pendent clusters through summer
and autumn. *Zones 9–11.*

Iochroma grandiflorum

This evergreen shrub or small tree
grows 10–18 ft (3–6 m) high and 6–12 ft
(2–4 m) wide. It has soft, pointed oval
leaves up to 8 in (20 cm) long that are
slightly downy when young. The
clustered flowers open in late summer
and autumn, and are long, pendent,
bright purple tubes with widely flared
mouths. They are followed by pulpy,
purplish green fruit. *Zones 9–11.*

Indigofera decora

Iochroma grandiflorum

Iochroma cyaneum

Jacaranda mimosifolia

Itea virginica

ITEA

Of the 10 species of evergreen and
deciduous shrubs and trees in this genus,
most are from tropical and temperate
Asia but one species is native to North
America. They bear showy, fragrant
autumn flowers and are frost hardy,
although in some colder areas they need
the protection of a wall. These are useful
plants for specimens or for growing in a
shrubbery. The name *Itea* comes from
the Greek, meaning 'willow', to which
some species bear a slight resemblance.

Cultivtion

They will thrive in anything but very dry
soil and prefer a part-shaded position, but
tolerate full sun. Propagate from cuttings
in summer and plant out in fall or spring.

Itea virginica
Sweetspire, Virginia willow

The best known member of the genus,
this deciduous North American shrub
of upright, slender form grows 3–5 ft
(1–1.5 m) tall and in summer bears
fragrant, creamy white flowers in semi-
erect panicles. Its finely toothed,
deciduous, bright green leaves do not
fall until early winter, when they
sometimes turn red. It is suitable for
mass planting. *Zones 5–9.*

JACARANDA
Bignoniaceae

This is a genus of about 50 species of
medium-sized to large trees from Brazil
and other parts of South America, all
with fern-like, bipinnate leaves and bell-
shaped flowers, which may be white,
purple or mauve-blue. The timber
known as Brazil rosewood is usually that
of *J. filicifolia*, a larger but less decorative
tree than *J. mimosifolia*, with white
flowers.

Cultivation

Propagate from seed in spring.

Jacaranda mimosifolia
Jacaranda

A broadly spreading tree to about 50 ft
(15 m) tall, the jacaranda has fern-like
leaves that are shed in early spring
(rather than in autumn as with most
deciduous plants). A few months later
the tree is covered in a mass of mauve-
blue flowers that last for just a few weeks.
The new foliage then appears, together
with round, flat seed pods. Pruning is
not desirable—if branches are removed
they are replaced by vertical shoots
which spoil the tree's shape. *Zones 9–11.*

JUBAEA
Chilean wine palm, coquito palm

Consisting of one species of palm, this
genus is named after King Juba of the
old African realm of Numidia, although
the plant comes from coastal Chile. It is
now rare in its natural habitat as it has
been consistently cut for its sugary sap,
which is distilled as palm wine or boiled
down to make palm honey.

Cultivation

Slow growing when young, this palm's growth is much quicker once a trunk has formed. More frost tolerant than most palms, and widely grown in temperate climates, it needs full sun and deep, fertile, well-drained soil. As both male and female flowers are held on the same plant, fertile seed is easily obtained in autumn; it must be sown while fresh, but can take 6 to 15 months to germinate.

Jubaea chilensis

syn. *Jubaea spectabilis*

With maturity, this handsome palm reaches 80 ft (24 m), with a distinctive thick, cylindrical gray trunk topped with a dense mass of long, straight, feathery, deep green fronds. The yellowish flowers are borne in spring and are followed in autumn by woody, yellow fruit that look like small coconuts. *Zones 9–11.*

Jubaea chilensis

JUNIPERUS
Cupressaceae
Juniper

This conifer genus has about 50 species of slow growing, long lived, evergreen shrubs and trees. Juvenile foliage is needle-like, but many adult species develop shorter scale-like leaves, closely pressed to the stem, with a pungent smell when crushed. Male and female organs usually occur on separate plants. The bluish black or reddish cones have fleshy, fused scales, or berries, used to flavor gin. The fragrant, cedar-like timber is soft but durable.

Cultivation

Junipers like a sunny position and any well-drained soil. Propagate from hard-wood cuttings in winter or from seed; cultivars can be propagated by grafting.

Juniperus chinensis
Chinese juniper

Native to the Himalayas, China, Mongolia and Japan, this frost-hardy species usually matures to a conical tree up to 50 ft (15 m) in height with a spread of 6–10 ft (1.8–3 m). Sometimes, however, it forms

Juniperus chinensis

a low-spreading shrub. Both adult and juvenile foliage may be found on adult trees. The berries are fleshy and glaucous white. 'Aurea' grows to at least 35 ft (11 m) tall, with a conical habit and soft, golden foliage; 'Blaauw' is somewhat spreading when young, but becomes an upright 5 ft (1.5 m) shrub; 'Kaizuka' is a small tree to 20 ft (6 m), with twisted spear-like branches. *Zones 3–9.*

Juniperus communis
Common juniper

This is either a slim, upright tree growing to 18 ft (6 m) or a sprawling shrub with a height and spread of 10–15 ft (3–5 m). Greenish berries, used for flavoring gin, take 2–3 years to ripen to black. Garden varieties include 'Depressa Aurea', a dwarf form with bronze-gold foliage, which grows to 20 in (50 cm) high with a spread of 6 ft (2 m); and 'Hibernica', reaching a height of 10–15 ft (3–5 m). *Zones 2–9.*

Juniperus communis 'Depressa Aurea'

Juniperus horizontalis 'Blue Chip'

Juniperus conferta
Japanese shore juniper

This prostrate, spreading shrub from Japan grows 12–18 in (30–45 cm) high with a spread of 6–8 ft (1.8–2.4 m). The soft foliage is a mixture of fresh, clear green and pale blue, aromatic, needle-like leaves. The berries are pale green. It makes a first-rate ground cover. *Zones 5–10.*

Juniperus horizontalis

This tough, prostrate shrub is fast spreading and its branches form a mat up to 20 in (50 cm) thick of blue-green or gray leaves. 'Wiltonii' is a blue cultivar with trailing branches; 'Blue Chip' is a blue-green cultivar. *Zones 4–10.*

Juniperus × media

These cultivars have mainly scale-like, dull green leaves with an unpleasant smell when crushed. Berries are white or blue-black. 'Pfitzeriana' is broadly pyramidal with wide-spreading branches with weeping tips and gray-green leaves, to 10 ft (3 m) tall with a spread of 10–15 ft (3–5 m). *Zones 4–10.*

Juniperus conferta

Juniperus virginiana
Eastern red cedar, pencil cedar
From North America, this is the tallest
of the junipers commonly grown in
gardens, reaching 50–60 ft (15–18 m)
high. It has a conical or broadly columnar
habit and both scale- and needle-like,
gray-green leaves. The berries are fleshy,
small, glaucous and brownish violet. The
wood is used in making lead pencils,
hence the common name. *Zones 2–9.*

JUSTICIA
Acanthaceae
These shrubs and woody perennials
have simple leaves in opposite pairs. The
tubular flowers come in shades of cream,
yellow, pink, orange or red.

Cultivation
Propagate from cuttings of non-flower-
ing shoots taken in spring.

Justicia brandegeana

Juniperus × media 'Pfitzeriana'

Justicia brandegeana
syns *Beloperone guttata, Drejerella guttata*
Shrimp plant
The curved spikes of salmon to rose-
pink or pale yellow bracts surrounding
the white flowers of this evergreen shrub
resemble shrimps, hence its common
name. It reaches a height of 3 ft (1 m)
and a spread of 24 in (60 cm) or more,
and can survive temperatures as low as
25°F (-4°C) by behaving like a perennial
when the tops are frozen back. *Zones 9–11.*

KALMIA
Ericaceae
The kalmias are evergreen North
American shrubs. They bloom in spring
and produce heads of pink flowers.

Cultivation
These hardy plants prefer a cool, moist
climate. Propagate from seed, cuttings,
or by layering.

Kalmia latifolia
Mountain laurel, calico bush
This shrub has leathery leaves and red-
brown bark. The clusters of distinctive,
bright pink buds open to heads of small,
pale pink flowers with stamens arranged
like umbrella ribs. It can grow to 12 ft
(4 m) but is more commonly 5 ft (1.5 m)
high and wide. *Zones 3–9.*

KALOPANAX
Tree aralia
This genus now contains only a single
species, the deciduous tree aralia,
indigenous to the cool deciduous forests
of China, Korea, Japan and eastern
Siberia. It has attractive foliage and fruit.

Cultivation
When grown in moist but well-drained,
fertile soil, it develops into a good shade
tree. It enjoys full sun, but will also grow
well in part-shade. Propagate from fresh
seed or from cuttings.

Kalmia latifolia

Kalopanax septemlobus
syn. *Kalopanax pictus*

This tree develops a single stout trunk and a low-branching habit with a dense, rounded crown, and may grow 40–50 ft (12–15 m) high in gardens. When mature it will generally retain prickles on its trunk, branches and new growth. The maple-like leaves are usually large, dark green and coarsely lobed, and may be as much as 15 in (38 cm) across on young saplings. The white summer flowers are held in large sprays radiating from the ends of branches. The small blue-black fruit, borne in autumn, are slightly split at the apex. *Zones 4–9.*

Kalopanax septemlobus

KERRIA
Rosaceae

This genus contains only one species, a deciduous shrub with many upright 6 ft (2 m), deep green stems emerging directly from the ground. The true species has simple, bright golden yellow flowers up to 2 in (5 cm) across.

Cultivation

This adaptable plant does well in any moist, well-drained soil. Propagate by basal suckers or from cuttings.

Kerria japonica
Japanese rose

The bright golden blossoms of this shrub make delightful cut flowers. The small leaves that follow, bright green and

Kerria japonica 'Pleniflora'

double toothed, only sparsely clothe the arching branches. Although the species is single flowered, the double form 'Pleniflora' is more common in gardens. *Zones 5–10.*

KOELREUTERIA
Sapindaceae

Grown for their foliage, flowers and decorative fruit, this small genus of deciduous trees is from East Asia. They prefer cool climates.

Cultivation

They thrive in full sun in fertile, well-aerated soil with free drainage. Seaside conditions do not suit them. Propagate from root cuttings or from seed.

Koelreuteria bipinnata
Pride of China, Chinese flame tree

From central and western China, this shapely tree grows 30–50 ft (9–15 m) tall with a single trunk and broadly conical crown. The bipinnate leaves are a clear yellow-green, turning deep golden in autumn. Bright yellow flowers, blotched scarlet at the base, are borne during summer. The fruit are like miniature Chinese lanterns, green at first then turning bright pink in fall and paper-brown in winter. *Zones 8–11.*

Koelreuteria paniculata
Golden rain tree, varnish tree

From China and Korea, this wide-spreading, medium-sized tree reaches a height of 30–50 ft (10–15 m), though it is usually smaller in gardens. Slow growing, it has a broad, convex crown and a single or divided main trunk. The mid-green leaves turn deep golden yellow in autumn and large, showy clusters of clear yellow flowers are borne in summer. *Zones 4–10.*

KOLKWITZIA
Caprifoliaceae
Beauty bush

This genus consists of a single species of deciduous shrub from China, much admired in temperate and cool-climate gardens for its lavish spring display, though its foliage is undistinguished for the rest of the summer. Place it where other plants can attract the eye.

Cultivation

It likes any well-drained soil, and does well in sun or light shade. Prune every 3 years or so after flowering. Propagate from root cuttings.

Kolkwitzia amabilis

This shrub develops into a mass of upright, whippy stems to 10 ft (3 m) high, with small side branches. The oval leaves are in opposite pairs, a feature common to the honeysuckle family. The pale pink, trumpet-shaped flowers, which open in spring as the new leaves are developing, form profuse clusters at the ends of the side branches. *Zones 4–9.*

Koelreuteria bipinnata

Koelreuteria paniculata

Kolkwitzia amabilis

L

Lagerstroemia indica

Laburnum × watereri 'Vossii'

LABURNUM
Fabaceae
Golden chain tree

These deciduous, fast-growing shrubs and small trees have attractive foliage and profuse clusters of bright yellow, pea-shaped flowers followed by brown, legume-like pods. The leaves and seeds are poisonous.

Cultivation

They prefer full sun and some humidity and tolerate any moderately fertile soil with free drainage. Prune in the early years to establish a tree-like form. Watch for leaf miner and snails. Species are propagated from seed in autumn and hybrids by budding in summer.

Laburnum × watereri 'Vossii'
Voss laburnum

This spreading tree reaches a height and spread of 30 ft (10 m). It has thick foliage and produces longer sprays of rich buttercup-yellow flowers up to 20 in (50 cm) in length. The fruit is sparsely produced, with only a few in each cluster. It is the cultivar most commonly seen in nurseries. *Zones 3–9.*

LAGERSTROEMIA
Lythraceae

These evergreen and deciduous shrubs and small trees are grown in warm and hot climates for their showy flowers. The timber of some species is highly prized for shipbuilding.

Cultivation

They thrive in freely drained, fertile soil, preferably with high organic content. They need shelter from strong summer winds. Propagate from semi-ripe cuttings in summer or from seed in spring. Watch for powdery mildew.

Lagerstroemia indica
Crape myrtle, pride of India

This deciduous small tree or large shrub grows up to 20 ft (7 m) tall with an open, spreading, rounded head. In mid- to late summer it bears large clusters of frilly flowers in tones of white, pink, lilac or dark purplish red. The flower heads appear at the tips of the current season's growth. Pruning promotes large, elongated flower heads, but is unnecessary. Older plants are prone to attack by powdery mildew in areas of high humidity, but newer cultivars seem to have overcome this problem. *Zones 6–11.*

LAGUNARIA
Malvaceae
Norfolk Island hibiscus, white oak

This genus consists of a single species, indigenous to the warm east coast of Australia as well as Norfolk and Lord

Lagunaria patersonia

Lantana camara 'Chelsea Gem'

Howe Islands off the coast. It is well suited to seaside situations as its leathery, gray-green foliage seems to be immune to salt spray. The seed pods of this plant contain spicules, or tiny needles, which can cause extreme skin irritation—hence another common name, cow-itch tree.

Cultivation
Propagate from seed.

Lagunaria patersonia
Usually seen as a neat, pyramid-shaped tree reaching up to 40 ft (13 m) high, this evergreen has oval, leathery leaves with a whitish bloom on the undersides. The pale to bright pink flowers that appear in the leaf axils during summer look like small hibiscus, with 5 reflexed petals surrounding a central column of stamens. It needs full sun, well-drained soil and adequate water; it tolerates occasional light frosts once established. *Zones 10–11.*

LANTANA
This genus of the verbena family consists of around 150 species of evergreen shrubs and cany stemmed perennials, native to warmer parts of the Americas except for a few in southern Africa. Several species are notorious weeds of tropical and subtropical regions. The plants have rough, slightly prickly stems with oval leaves in opposite pairs, their surfaces harsh and closely veined. Very small, trumpet-shaped flowers in compact button-like heads open progressively from the center of each head, their color changing in the older flowers towards the perimeter. Tiny fruits like blackberry drupelets may follow.

Cultivation
They prefer fertile, well-drained soil and full sun. Top-dress potted plants annually in spring; water well when in full growth, less at other times. Propagate from cuttings in summer or from seed in spring.

Lantana camara
Common lantana, shrub verbena
This plant is reviled in warmer, wetter parts of the world for its rampant invasion of forests and pastures and poisoning of cattle, but valued as an ornamental in cooler or drier regions. The weedy forms produce long scrambling canes and can mound up to 20 ft (6 m) even without trees to climb over, but garden forms are mostly rounded or spreading shrubs 2–6 ft (0.6–1.8 m) high. The tiny flowers typically open cream, yellow or yellow-red and age to pink, red, orange or white, the heads

appearing in a long succession from spring to autumn. Cultivars range in color from the golden orange and red of 'Radiation' to the white blooms of 'Snowflake'. 'Chelsea Gem' has profuse orange and red flowerheads. *Zones 9–11.*

Lantana montevidensis
syn. *Lantana sellowiana*
Trailing lantana
The slender, weak stems of this trailing species mound up into a dense mass making it a wonderful plant for a ground cover or low hedge. It grows 18–36 in (45–90 cm) tall and 6 ft (2 m) wide or more, with small, neat, closely veined dark green leaves. Throughout the year, but particularly in summer, it bears bright mauve-pink flowerheads, each with a yellow eye. There is also a white-flowered cultivar. *Zones 9–11.*

LARIX
Pinaceae
Larch
From cool mountainous regions of the northern hemisphere, these deciduous, fast-growing conifers are known for their strong, durable timber. Mainly conical in shape, they lose their leaves in autumn, bursting into leaf in early spring. At this time too they bear bright red or purple-red female 'flowers'. The cones are erect and persist on the tree after shedding their seeds. The bark has been used for tanning and dyeing.

Cultivation
They do best in well-drained, light or gravelly soils; most resent waterlogged soils. Propagate from seed. Larches are prone to several diseases, including larch canker or blister and infestation by larch chermes (a type of aphid).

Larix decidua
European larch
This tree reaches a height of 100 ft (30 m). Branches are widely spaced and have a graceful, weeping habit. The soft, bright green, needle-like leaves turn yellow before falling. In spring, the tree bears both drooping, yellow male flowers and upright, red female flowers. The cones are egg shaped, brown and upright. The gray bark becomes red-brown, fissured and scaly with age. It is a source of turpentine. *Zones 3–8.*

Larix kaempferi
syn. *Larix leptolepis*
Japanese larch
This fast-growing Japanese species is widely used for ornamental landscaping and is grown in forestry plantations in the UK. Broadly conical, it grows to a height of 100 ft (30 m) and a spread of

Larix decidua

Lantana montevidensis

20 ft (6 m). Its soft needle-like leaves are gray- to blue-green and the mature cones are brown and almost globular, their broad scales spreading at the tips to give a rosebud appearance. The scaly bark is reddish brown, or orange-red on older branches. *Zones 4–7.*

LAURUS
Lauraceae

Two evergreen trees from the Mediterranean region and Atlantic islands make up this genus, grown for their aromatic leaves which are used in cooking. They make dense, evergreen screen plants and patio tub specimens.

Cultivation

Moderately frost-hardy, they do best in sheltered positions in sun or semi-shade in fertile, well-drained soil. Propagate from seed or from semi-ripe cuttings.

Laurus nobilis
Sweet bay, bay tree, bay laurel, laurel

An evergreen, broadly conical tree, this species grows up to 37 ft (12 m) high and 30 ft (10 m) wide, but is generally smaller in cultivation. Its glossy, dark

Larix kaempferi

green leaves are smooth, leathery and highly aromatic when crushed. It produces small, star-shaped, fragrant yellow flowers in spring, followed by small, round green berries that ripen to dark purplish black in autumn. 'Aurea' is a yellow-leafed form. *Zones 7–10.*

LAVANDULA
Lamiaceae

These fragrant, evergreen, aromatic shrubs have silvery, lacy, fragrant foliage, and grow to 2–3 ft (60–90 cm) high and about as wide. The small mauve-purple flowers, held in silvery bracts, are borne in erect spikes above the foliage, mostly in spring. *Lavandula angustifolia* and *L. stoechas* have oil glands at the base of the flowers that produce the pleasantly pungent oil of lavender used in the perfume industry.

Cultivation

They prefer full sun and fertile, well-drained, alkaline soil. Propagate from cuttings.

Lavandula angustifolia
English lavender

This dense, bushy, evergreen shrub from the Mediterranean region grows to about 24 in (60 cm) tall with narrow, furry, gray leaves. It has long-stemmed heads of purple, scented flowers that

Laurus nobilis

appear in spring and through the warm months; these are dried for lavender sachets, potpourri and the like. It makes an attractive low hedge. 'Munstead' is an outstanding cultivar. *Zones 5–9.*

Lavandula dentata
French lavender

The densely packed, soft spikes of tubular, mauve-blue flowers remain on this shrub from autumn through late spring. It grows to a height and spread of about 3 ft (1 m). It is drought resistant and is often used as an edging plant. *Zones 8–10.*

Lavandula × intermedia
English lavender, lavendin

These naturally occurring and cultivated hybrids between *Lavandula angustifolia* and *L. latifolia* show considerable variation in plant size and flower form. Few exceed

3 ft (1 m) tall but they are otherwise something of a catch-all group. 'Provence' has green foliage and small-bracted spikes of mauve-pink flowers. *Zones 6–10.*

Lavandula stoechas
Spanish lavender, bush lavender, Italian lavender

This species has pine-scented, narrow, silvery green leaves with edges that curl inwards. A small, neat shrub 2 ft (60 cm) high and spreading to 3 ft (1 m) wide, it is covered with spikes of deep purple flowers in late spring and summer. Several bracts at the apex of each spike are elongated into pinkish purple petal shapes. It needs regular water and protection from frost. *Zones 7–10.*

LAVATERA

Closely related to the mallows and hollyhocks, this genus of 25 species of

Lavandula × intermedia 'Provence'

Lavandula dentata

Lavandula angustifolia 'Munstead'

Lavandula stoechas

annuals, biennials, perennials and softwooded shrubs has a scattered, patchy distribution around temperate regions of the world, mostly in Mediterranean or similar climates; some favor seashores. A few species are cultivated for their colorful mallow flowers, generally produced over a long season. These plants are upright in habit with simple to palmately lobed leaves, often downy to the touch. The shrubs and perennials are not very long-lived.

Cultivation

Moderately to very frost-hardy, they prefer a sunny site and well-drained soil Prune after flowering to encourage branching and more blooms. Propagate annuals, biennials and perennials in spring or early autumn from seed sown *in situ* (cuttings do not strike well), and shrubs from cuttings in early spring or summer.

Lavatera thuringiaca

This European perennial produces a glorious display of rose-pink, hollyhock-like flowers all summer on sturdy bushes up to 5 ft (1.5 m) in height. The mid-green leaves are an attractive foil for the flowers. Use at the back of a border or as a colorful hedge. Several cultivars with distinct flower colors are available. *Zones 6–10.*

LEPTOSPERMUM
Myrtaceae
Tea-tree

This genus of about 30 species of evergreen shrubs, sometimes small trees, from Australia and New Zealand, is not related to *Camellia sinensis* whose leaves are brewed into the familar drink; the name tea-tree arose because early sailors and settlers used the aromatic leaves as a substitute. They are rapid, upright growers with small, sometimes prickly leaves and 5-petaled flowers, mostly white or pale pink. Some attractive cultivars with double flowers in shades from white to red have been developed, mostly from the red-flowered New Zealand form of *Leptospermum scoparium.*

Cultivation

They like a mild-winter climate and sunshine, and most are drought resistant. Propagate from summer cuttings.

Leptospermum laevigatum
Coast tea-tree

This tall, bushy shrub or small tree bears attractive small white flowers in spring

Lavatera thuringiaca

Leptospermum laevigatum

Leptospermum scoparium 'Ruby Glow'

Lespedeza thunbergii

and early summer. The evergreen leaves are small, oval and gray-green. Preferring moist, well-drained soil, it grows to about 20 ft (7 m) tall, with a spread of about the same and a trunk that becomes gnarled with age, especially when buffeted by salt-laden winds. It is an excellent plant for seaside areas. *Zones 9–11.*

Leptospermum scoparium
Manuka, tea-tree
This species occurs throughout New Zealand and in the far southeast of Australia (mainly Tasmania). Many popular hybrids have been developed. It is an adaptable plant to 10 ft (3 m) tall with mainly erect growth, broadly needle-like foliage and sweetly scented, white or pale pink flowers. Among the many cultivars are 'Red Damask', with double crimson blooms; and 'Ruby Glow', with dark foliage and double, dark red blooms. Smaller hybrids include 'Kiwi' with red flowers and 'Pink Pixie' with pink blooms. *Zones 8–10.*

LESPEDEZA
This legume genus includes about 40 species of annuals, perennials and deciduous shrubs and subshrubs from across the northern hemisphere, extending to Southeast Asia and Australia. The leaves are made up of 3 leaflets, while the small pea-flowers are held in long sprays. The pods are small and one-seeded, falling without opening. Some species are grown for fodder or green manure.

Cultivation
These plants do best in a sunny position in well-drained soil, and prefer warmer climates where cold winters will not cut them back. Mulch well, especially at the limit of frost hardiness, and prune to rejuvenate in spring. Propagate from seed or cuttings, or by division.

Lespedeza thunbergii
Bush clover
This erect, open subshrub grows 3–6 ft (1–2 m) tall and has bright green leaves. The pendulous sprays of rose-purple flowers appear in late summer and are followed by flattish seed pods. 'Alba' bears white flowers. *Zones 5–8.*

LEUCOPHYLLUM
There are 11 species of slow-growing, low, spreading, evergreen shrubs in this genus from the Chihuahuan Desert of western Texas and northern Mexico. They have soft gray foliage and complement hedges or clumps of green shrubs.

Cultivation
They prefer a warm, sunny position, sheltered and frost free, in sandy, well-drained soil. Propagate from seed or cuttings.

Leucophyllum frutescens

Leucothoë fontanesiana

Leucophyllum frutescens
Texas ranger, Texas sage, silverleaf, cenizo
This species is the most frost hardy and
the most commonly seen in gardens. Its
dense, upright form—usually 6–8 ft
(2–2.5 m) tall and almost the same in
width—is covered with reddish lavender
flowers following a good rain. Very
tough and tolerant of heat and dry
conditions, nurseries are now offering
selections with flowers of pink, white or
purple on plants that may be low and
compact or tall and slender. *Zones 8–11.*

LEUCOTHOE
This genus, containing about 50 species
of deciduous and evergreen shrubs allied
to *Pieris*, is widely distributed in cool- to
warm-climate regions from southern
USA to the mountains of South
America, with a few in East Asia. They
have simple, alternate leaves and
produce white or pink flowers in short
axillary or terminal spikes. The fruits are
small capsules containing many seeds.

Cultivation
These shrubs prefer moist, acidic, well-
drained soil and a sheltered position in
sun or part-shade. Propagation is from
seed, cuttings or from the suckering root
sections of the plant, or by division.

Leucothoë fontanesiana
syn. *Leucothoë catesbaei*
Pearl flower, drooping leucothoë
Indigenous to the southeastern states of
the USA, this evergreen shrub grows
3–5 ft (1–1.5 m) tall. The arching stems
bear leathery, long-pointed dark green
leaves and pendulous spikes of small
bell-shaped white or pinkish flowers
through spring. 'Rainbow' (or 'Golden
Rainbow'), is a very popular cultivar,
with cream and pink-mottled green
leaves. *Zones 4–8.*

LEYCESTERIA
This genus of 6 deciduous or semi-
evergreen shrubs from the western
Himalayas and western China form
clumps of arching, suckering, cane-like
stems and grow from 4–8 ft (1.2–2.5 m)
tall, depending on species. The leaves,
usually borne in pairs, are from 2–8 in
(5–20 cm) long, oval with pointed tips
and finely serrated edges. The small,
tubular or trumpet-shaped flowers,

carried in whorls on pendulous or arching racemes, may be partly obscured by colored bracts and are followed by clusters of soft berries. The flowers open over a long period and the berries ripen quickly, so racemes may bear flowers and fruit at the same time.

Cultivation

Grow in any well-drained soil in sun or part-shade. In cool but mild, wet climates some species can become weeds of disturbed forests. Most are frost hardy. Propagate from seed or by removing rooted suckers.

Leycesteria formosa
Himalayan honeysuckle

This deciduous shrub from the Himalayas measures 8 ft (2.5 m) tall and 6 ft (2 m) wide. It has a woody stem, leafy chains of purple and white flowers and interesting fruit of purple-black berries in purple leafy sheaths. *Zones 7–10.*

LIGUSTRUM
Oleaceae
Privet

This temperate-climate genus of some 50 or so species grows in almost any soil or position. They range from shrubs to small trees, some evergreen, others deciduous; all grow rapidly and bear

Leycesteria formosa

Ligustrum japonicum 'Rotundifolium'

abundant sprays of small white flowers in spring. They follow up with black berries. Birds love these and can easily overpopulate the whole area with privet seedlings.

Cultivation

Privets grow easily from seed but selected varieties need to be propagated from cuttings.

Ligustrum japonicum
Japanese privet

This bushy, evergreen shrub with a dense habit reaches 10 ft (3 m) tall with a spread of 8 ft (2.5 m). From Asia, it has oval, glossy, dark green leaves and bears large conical panicles of flowers from mid-summer to early autumn, followed by blue-black berries. It can be used as a hedge plant. 'Rotundifolium' is dense and slow growing, with thick, rounded leaves. *Zones 7–11.*

Ligustrum lucidum
Common privet

An evergreen, upright shrub or tree, popular for hedging, this species can reach 30 ft (10 m) in height with a spread of 25 ft (8 m). Large panicles of small white flowers are borne among the leaves in late summer and early autumn. It can become invasive, its seed spread by birds which eat the small black fruit. Prune after flowering to avoid this problem. The leaves of 'Tricolor' are variegated with yellow, pink when young. *Zones 7–11*.

LINDERA

This genus of the laurel family consists of 80 species of evergreen and deciduous trees and shrubs, indigenous to eastern Asia and North America. Only a handful of cool-climate, deciduous species are grown in gardens. The leaves are variable, often lobed; when crushed, the foliage releases a pungent, spicy odor. Male and female flowers, both yellow, are borne on the bare branches of separate plants in early spring. The fruits are globular and berry-like.

Cultivation

They grow naturally in part-shade in acidic, humus-rich soil. Though tolerant of extreme cold, they do best if protected from late spring frosts. Propagate from

Ligustrum lucidum 'Tricolor'

seed, which should be cleaned of pulp and sown fresh, or from cuttings taken in late summer.

Lindera obtusiloba

Native to Korea, China and Japan, this shrub or small tree may grow as high as 20 ft (6 m). The leaves, usually 3-lobed, turn pale gold in autumn. The small, yellow-green flowers appear in spring, followed by shiny, black, globular fruit. *Zones 6–10*.

LIQUIDAMBAR
Hamamelidaceae

This is a genus of deciduous trees belonging to the witch hazel family, grown for their shapely form, handsome foliage and superb autumn colors. The leaves are deeply lobed, resembling a maple leaf. Some species produce a resinous gum known as liquid storax that is used to scent soap, as an expectorant in cough remedies and as a fumigant in the treatment of some skin diseases. They are best allowed to develop their lower branches to ground level.

Cultivation

They require sun or semi-shade and fertile, deep loamy soil with adequate water during spring and summer. They will not thrive in shallow, sandy soil. Propagate by budding in spring or from seed in autumn.

Lindera obtusiloba

Liquidambar styraciflua
Liquidambar, sweet gum

This deciduous tree reaches a height of 130 ft (40 m) and spread of 70 ft (22 m). Young branches and twigs are often ridged with a distinctive, corky bark and the wood, known as satin walnut, is used for furniture-making. It bears palmately lobed, glossy dark green leaves that turn orange to red and purple in autumn.

Liquidambar styraciflua

Liriodendron tulipifera 'Aureomarginatum'

Small, yellow-green flowers appear with the new growth, followed by spiky, ball-like fruit clusters. The deeply furrowed bark yields liquid storax. 'Variegata' has leaves with paler green and yellowish blotches and streaks; 'Worplesdon' has leaves that turn orange in autumn. *Zones 5–11.*

LIRIODENDRON
Magnoliaceae
Tulip tree

Some botanists dispute there being two species in this genus, and prefer to recognize only one, *Liriodendron tulipifera*, regarding *L. chinense* as merely a variety. The majority, however, accept the two. Their leaves distinguish them from other trees: they have 4 lobes and look like their ends have been cut off. The distinctive flowers are pale green with orange at the base of the petals and numerous stamens. They don't look very much like tulips. They are recommended only for large gardens.

Cultivation

They prefer a temperate climate and deep, fertile soil. Propagate from seed or by grafting.

Liriodendron tulipifera
Tulip tree

This tree reaches 95 ft (30 m) or more with a spread of about 50 ft (15 m). A vigorous grower with a broadly conical habit, it bears deep green, lobed leaves that turn rich golden yellow in autumn. Orange-based, pale green flowers are borne singly at the ends of new shoots in mid-summer, followed by conical brown fruit. An important timber tree in the USA, 'yellow poplar' is light and strong and used in furniture-making. The bark is said to have medicinal properties. 'Aureomarginatum' has green leaves heavily edged with yellow. *Zones 4–10.*

Livistona chinensis

Lonicera fragrantissima

LIVISTONA
Arecaceae
This genus of medium to tall fan palms found in the wetter parts of Southeast Asia and Australia feature large, round, pleated fronds up to 5 ft (1.5 m) across and a dense crown. The leaf stalks are usually long and are edged with sharp teeth. They are popular for outdoor landscaping; their clusters of blue, purple-black or, rarely, reddish, fruit and tapering leaves are shown to great effect. They make excellent potted plants.

Cultivation
Most survive warm-temperate and subtropical climates, but prefer mild, frost-free areas. They prefer deep, sandy soil and, while they tolerate full sun, they produce better deep green foliage in dappled shade. Propagate from seed.

Livistona chinensis
Chinese fan palm
This palm will reach a height of 20–40 ft (7–13 m); it is quite fast growing in the tropics, slow in temperate climates. Its single trunk is heavily textured and the large circular fronds held on relatively short stalks droop attractively from the crown to give good foliage cover. A useful container specimen, it is one of the most frost-hardy palms and has been grown outdoors in sheltered gardens in England. *Zones 8–11*.

LONICERA
Caprifoliaceae
Honeysuckle
The best known species of this genus of 180 species, found all over the northern hemisphere, are climbers, but there are some attractive shrubs among them. The chief attraction is the often delicious scent of the flowers, though there are also scentless ones. The species here are plants of temperate climates, easily grown in sun or light shade and not fussy about soil.

Cultivation
Prune occasionally. Propagate from cuttings.

Lonicera fragrantissima
Winter honeysuckle
This bushy, deciduous (sometimes evergreen) shrub reaches a height of 10 ft (3 m) with a spread of 12 ft (4 m). The most fragrant of the shrubby species, it bears tubular, paired, creamy white flowers, in some forms stained with rose-carmine, in winter and early spring. The dark green oval leaves appear shortly after the flowers. Except in the coldest climates, many will hang on the plant through winter. *Zones 4–9*.

Lonicera × heckrottii
Everblooming honeysuckle, goldflame honeysuckle
This deciduous, woody vine bears magnificent flower colors over an

exceptionally long period: late spring through summer with an occasional recurrent bloom in autumn. In bud the flowers are brilliant carmine, revealing a lustrous yellow throat as the corolla opens. Once opened the outside changes to a true pink. The foliage emerges reddish purple and matures to a lustrous blue-green. It reaches 10–20 ft (3–6 m) in height. *Zones 4–9.*

Lonicera nitida
Box honeysuckle

This evergreen shrub forms a dense bush composed of masses of fine twigs covered with tightly packed, leathery, bronze-green leaves. Gold and variegated foliage forms are available. The small, creamy white, spring-borne flowers are not showy and the purple

Lonicera × heckrottii

Lonicera nitida

fruit is rarely seen in cultivation, so it is best regarded as a foliage plant. It is often used for hedging. *Zones 7–9.*

LUMA

This genus consists of 4 species of evergreen shrubs and trees from Argentina and Chile, closely related to *Myrtus* in which genus they were formerly included. They have small, leathery, pointed, oval, deep green leaves and a dense, bushy growth habit. The small, creamy white, starry flowers appear from mid-summer. The attractive bark of most species is a reddish brown and flakes off to reveal white to pink new bark.

Cultivation

They prefer moist, well-drained soil in sun or light shade. Propagate from seed or cuttings in late summer.

Luma apiculata
syns *Myrtus luma, Eugenia apiculata*

This upright species grows to around 50 ft (15 m) tall in the wild but can be kept to 10 ft (3 m) high with regular trimming and may be used for hedging. The small leaves are aromatic and the flaking bark is cinnamon brown with white wood underneath. The flowers have conspicuous stamens and smother the bush from mid-summer to mid-fall. *Zones 9–11.*

Luma apiculata

M

MACLURA
syn. *Cudrania*

This genus of 15 species of deciduous and evergreen thorny trees, shrubs and scrambling climbers is scattered widely throughout warmer parts of the world. The usually green flowers appear in racemes or clusters. Both male and female trees bear flowers and both are needed for fruits to grow.

Cultivation

Fully frost hardy, they do best in full sun and in areas with hot summers. They grow well in a wide range of soils. They have spreading roots and are resistant to very dry conditions. Propagate from seed in autumn, or from cuttings in summer or late winter.

Maclura pomifera
Osage orange

This deciduous tree from southern USA can reach 50 ft (15 m) in height with a spread of 40 ft (12 m). It has dark brown, fissured bark, and its thorny branches form an open, irregular crown with oval, dark green leaves. Tiny yellow flowers, borne in summer, are followed by large, wrinkled, pale green fruit. The hard, flexible timber is used for archery bows. *Zones 4–9.*

MAGNOLIA
Magnoliaceae

This large and varied genus of deciduous and evergreen trees and shrubs occurs in the wild in East Asia and the Americas. Leaves are mainly oval and usually smooth edged; flowers are generally large and solitary. Flower colors are shades of white, yellow, pink or purple, but the flower shapes have great variety.

Cultivation

Magnolias require deep, fertile, well-drained, mildly acid soil, well aerated by fibrous matter. They thrive in either sun or part-shade but need protection from strong or salty winds. Propagate from semi-ripe cuttings in summer, seed in autumn, graft cultivars in winter.

Magnolia campbellii

This broadly conical deciduous tree can grow to a height of 80 ft (25 m) and spread of 40 ft (13 m) with a forked trunk and a broad, irregular crown. Very large, slightly fragrant, pale to deep pink to purplish pink or white flowers are carried on leafless branches from late winter to mid-spring. On plants raised from seed, flowers are only produced after 20 or more years growth. 'Lanarth' has larger flowers. *Zones 7–10.*

Magnolia denudata

Maclura pomifera

Magnolia denudata
Yulan magnolia

Sometimes known as *M. heptapeta*, this small, deciduous tree grows to a height and spread of 30 ft (10 m). It has spreading branches and produces masses of scented, pure white flowers from mid-winter to early spring, before the oval, mid-green leaves with downy undersides appear. The flowers are followed by rectangular cones containing orange seeds. In ancient Chinese paintings it is a symbol of purity and candor. *Zones 5–8.*

Magnolia grandiflora
Southern magnolia, bull bay

One of the few cultivated evergreen magnolias, this species forms a dense broad dome up to 60 ft (20 m), if the climate is sufficiently warm. It has thick, deep green, leathery leaves with rusty tones on the undersides. The cup-shaped white or cream blooms appear during late summer, and are followed by reddish brown cones. The typical species prefers warm, moist conditions, but there are many cultivars which are hardier in more temperate conditions. *Zones 6–11.*

Magnolia campbellii

Magnolia liliiflora

A deciduous, bushy shrub, this Chinese species also known as *M. quinquepeta*, reaches a height of 10 ft (3 m) with a spread of 12 ft (4 m). The oval, dark green leaves are downy on the undersides and taper to a point. Fragrant, narrow, purplish pink flowers, whitish inside, are borne among the leaves from mid-spring until mid-summer. 'Nigra' has large, dark wine-purple flowers that are pale purple inside. *Zones 5–8.*

Magnolia liliiflora

Magnolia grandiflora

Magnolia stellata

Mahonia aquifolium

Magnolia × soulangiana

Magnolia × soulangiana

This cross between *M. denudata* and *M. liliiflora* grows up to 24 ft (8 m) tall and 15 ft (5 m) wide. The leaves are tapered at the base and rounded at the tip, with a short point. Goblet- to cup- or saucer-shaped, white to pink or deep purple-pink flowers are borne from late winter to mid-spring. 'Brozzoni' has white flowers, shaded purple at the base; 'Lennei' bears beetroot-purple flowers that are white to pale purple inside. *Zones 5–10.*

Magnolia stellata
Star magnolia

A smaller growing magnolia, this deciduous shrub reaches a height and spread of about 15 ft (4.5 m). Its bark is aromatic when young. Fragrant, star-like, pure white flowers open from silky buds in late winter and early spring. A bush of spreading, though compact growth, it flowers when quite young. Protect from wind and frosts. It has several cultivars in pink shades. 'Waterlily', the most prolific flowerer, has more petals and slightly larger flowers. *Zones 4–9.*

MAHONIA
Berberidaceae

This genus of evergreen, low-growing to tall flowering shrubs has beautiful foliage, often fragrant yellow flowers, blue-black fruits which usually have a bloom of whitish or blue-gray wax, and interesting bark on some taller species and cultivars. The berries resemble miniature grapes and make an excellent jelly. They make good specimens, hedges, windbreaks and ground covers.

Cultivation

They require a sunny aspect and a well-drained, fertile soil with adequate water. In warmer climates they do better in part-shade. Propagate species from semi-ripe cuttings, basal suckers or seed.

Mahonia aquifolium
Holly grape, Oregon grape

An evergreen shrub with a dense, bushy habit, this species grows to 6 ft (2 m) high and wide with 8 in (20 cm) long pinnate leaves made up of 5 to 9 holly-like, glossy, deep green leaflets. In the cooler months the foliage develops purple tones. Clustered heads of small, bright yellow flowers appear in spring, followed by the fruits. *Zones 5–8.*

Mahonia lomariifolia

One of the tallest and most elegant mahonias, this shrub grows 10–15 ft (3–5 m) tall with a spread of about 6–10 ft (2–3 m). It has many erect bamboo-like shoots. The long, dark green leaves are mainly confined to the ends of the shoots and have narrow, holly-like spiny leaflets. Dense, upright racemes of fragrant, bright yellow flowers are borne during late autumn and winter, followed by purplish fruits. *Zones 7–10.*

MALUS
Rosaceae

The fruit of most varieties of this genus of deciduous flowering and fruiting trees is edible and is used in sauces, jams and preserves. It also contains many varieties of apple. Leaves are simple and toothed or sometimes lobed and the flowers are borne in clusters, varying from white to deep rose-pink or deep reddish purple.

Cultivation

They grow best in a cold, moist climate, preferring full sun but tolerating part-shade. Plant in a fertile, well-drained loamy soil with protection from strong winds. Cut out dead wood in winter and prune to maintain shape. Propagate by budding in summer or grafting in winter.

Malus × domestica
Common apple

This large hybrid group includes upright and spreading trees, usually with dark gray-brown scaly bark. They can grow 30 ft (9 m) tall and 15 ft (5 m) wide.

Malus × domestica 'Delicious'

Mahonia lomariifolia

The white flowers are usually suffused with pink. The juicy, sweet fruit are green or yellow to red. These common orchard trees are distinguished from the wild crab (*Malus sylvestris*) by their downy shoots, blunter leaves and juicy fruit that sweeten on ripening. Apples are not completely self-fertile and for fruit production, a different cultivar growing nearby is needed. Advice on compatible pollinating cultivars should be obtained before buying apple plants. There are hundreds of cultivars; among the best known are 'Discovery', 'Delicious', 'Golden Delicious', 'Golden Harvest' and 'Granny Smith'. *Zones 3–9.*

Malus floribunda
Japanese crab

Regarded as one of the most beautiful crab apples, this tree grows to a height of 24 ft (8 m) with a spreading, broad-domed crown of about 30 ft (10 m). Pale pink flowers, red in bud, almost cover the entire tree in early spring, followed by tiny, pea-shaped crab apples in autumn. *Zones 4–9.*

Malus ioensis
Iowa crab

Growing to about 25 ft (8 m) tall with a spread of 24 ft (8 m), this leafy tree bears clusters of large, fragrant, pale pink flowers in late spring—it is one of the last of the crabs to flower. It has a very heavy crop of flowers, good color and sweet perfume. 'Plena' (the Bechtel crab) has double flowers and is more widely grown than the species. *Zones 2–9.*

Malus sargentii
Sargent's crab apple

A spreading shrub, this crab apple reaches a height and spread of about 8 ft

Malus floribunda

(2.5 m). It has oval, dark green leaves with serrated margins and bears masses of white flowers in spring, followed by tiny, deep red fruits that last well into winter. Some branches may have thorns. *Zones 4–9.*

Malus sylvestris
Crab apple, wild crab

This parent of orchard apples can grow to a height of 30 ft (10 m) with a spread of 10 ft (3 m). It has a rounded crown and dark bark. In spring it bears white

Malus ioensis

Malus sargentii

flowers, flushed with pink, followed by yellow, flushed orange-red fruit that, although rather sour and bitter, make delicious conserves. The leaves have a partly red stalk and some branches may bear thorns. *Zones 3–9.*

MALVAVISCUS
Malvaceae
This genus of soft-wooded, frost-tender, evergreen shrubs and small trees from South America is named from the Latin *malva* (mallow) and *viscidus* (sticky). They prefer a warm, humid climate but are successful in subtropical areas where there is no danger of frost.

Cultivation
They like a well-drained soil of a loamy nature, and must have ample summer moisture. Cuttings taken towards the end of summer will strike easily.

Malvaviscus arboreus
Cardinal's hat, sleeping hibiscus
This Mexican shrub grows to 10 ft (3 m) tall and almost as wide. It has large, mid-green leaves and bright red flowers. It

Malvaviscus arboreus

Malus sylvestris cultivar

prefers well-drained moist soil either in sun or part-shade. In early spring, prune back by half the last season's growth. The form with long, pendulous, mostly scarlet flowers is now treated as a distinct species, *M. penduliflorus. Zones 9–11.*

MELALEUCA
Myrtaceae
The evergreen trees and shrubs of this genus are indigenous to Australia, except for a few species from New Guinea, Indonesia and Southeast Asia. They have brush-like flowers with showy stamens. The profuse blooms produce nectar, making them an excellent food source for many native birds and animals. They tolerate pollution, salt winds and saline soils.

Cultivation
Melaleuca species tolerate wet and even boggy conditions (but they prefer well-drained soil) and, although they are warm-climate plants, most species also withstand cold if they are given full sun. They can be grown from seed or cuttings which should be taken just as the current season's growth begins to form. They are remarkably free from pests and disease.

Melaleuca fulgens
Honey-myrtle

A shrub growing up to 5 ft (1.5 m), the honey-myrtle has an erect, open habit and yellow-tipped, bright scarlet flower-spikes that open during spring and summer. The seed capsules remain on the bush for some time. It does best in full sun and a well-drained position. Tip prune regularly. *Zones 9–11.*

Melaleuca linariifolia
Flax-leafed paperbark, snow-in-summer

A fast-growing 30 ft (9 m) tree with a spreading crown and white, papery bark, this species derives one of its common names from its flax-like leaves. Short white flower spikes bloom at the branch tips from late spring into summer. It grows naturally around swamps, but adapts to most garden soil types. An essential oil is extracted from its leaves. 'Snowstorm' is a dwarf form that grows to around 6 ft (1.8 m) tall. *Zones 9–11.*

Melaleuca linariifolia

Melaleuca nesophila
Western tea myrtle, pink melaleuca

This bushy shrub, native to Western Australia, bears summer flowers that are brushes of mauve, gold-tipped stamens, fading to white, giving it a multicolored effect. It grows 10 ft (3 m) tall and 6 ft (1.8 m) wide. *Zones 9–11.*

Melaleuca thymifolia

An upright or spreading shrub, this species grows to a height and spread of about 3 ft (1 m). This vase-shaped shrub has small, erect blue-green leaves that give off a spicy aroma when crushed. Pale purple flowers with incurving stamens are borne from late spring to autumn. *Zones 9–11.*

Melaleuca nesophila

Melaleuca thymifolia

Melaleuca viridiflora
Broad-leafed paperbark

This attractive species grows to about
30 ft (10 m), the trunk and branches
clothed with thick cream papery bark.
The leaves are among the largest in
melaleucas, up to 4 in (10 cm) long and
2 in (5 cm) wide, very thick and stiff.
The bottlebrush-type flower-spikes are
most commonly greenish cream, but
pink and bright red forms also occur. It
tolerates poorly drained soil. *Zones 10–11.*

MELIA
Meliaceae

Recent botanical studies have shown
that this genus consists of only one very
variable species of deciduous tree,
ranging across Asia from Iraq to Japan,
and south to Australia. This is *Melia
azedarach*, a favorite small to medium-
sized tree in warm but not tropical
climates. The name *Melia* is Greek for
the ash *(Fraxinus)*, though the only
connection is that the pinnate or doubly
pinnate leaves are vaguely similar.

Cultivation
Propagate from seed.

Melia azedarach
Chinaberry, white cedar, Persian lilac

A fast-growing, spreading tree to about
30 ft (10 m), the Chinaberry is popular
in arid climates, though not always very
long lived. Large sprays of small,
delicately scented lilac flowers appear in
late spring or early summer, followed by
bunches of pale orange berries, each
containing a single woody seed. These
are poisonous to humans, but are eaten
by birds. The form *australasica* occurs in
northern and eastern Australia, and is
one of the few deciduous trees native to
Australia, though most trees there have
been propagated from seed originating
in Iraq. *Zones 8–11.*

Melia azedarach

METASEQUOIA
Taxodiaceae
Dawn redwood

Until shortly after World War II,
Metasequoia glyptostroboides was known
only as a fossil. Then a stand of living
trees was discovered in western China
and from these it has been propagated,
to be widely planted in temperate-
climate gardens. It is one of the few
deciduous conifers. It grows very
rapidly and, as the timber is durable and
of fine quality, it is a very promising tree
for cool-climate forestry.

Cultivation
It prefers a deep, fertile soil, good
summer rainfall, and shelter from strong
winds. Propagate from seed or cuttings
taken from side shoots in autumn.

Metasequoia glyptostroboides
Its gracefully conical outline and delicate
foliage, light green in spring and summer
and russet and gold in autumn, have
given the dawn redwood wide accep-

tance in parks and large gardens. It is rapid in growth if the climate is moist and the soil fertile, and it is thought that old trees will achieve 200 ft (60 m). As trees mature, the rough textured bark turns from reddish to dark brown to gray. *Zones 5–8.*

METROSIDEROS
Myrtaceae

The 20 or so species in this South Pacific genus are not all trees; some are shrubs or even vines. They are especially important in New Zealand where several species yield rata, the hard dark-red timber prized by the Maori for sculpture. They typically have hard,

Metrosideros excelsus

Metrosideros kermadecensis 'Variegata'

leathery, evergreen leaves, often with an attractive gray tinge, and red (sometimes bright yellow) summer flowers whose chief beauty comes from their long colored stamens. The shrubby species do very well as container plants.

Cultivation

They do best in subtropical or warm-temperate climates, and are adaptable to most soils.

Metrosideros excelsus
Pohutukawa

Growing to around 37 ft (12 m), these trees begin as shrubs with masses of low-growing branches forming a dense outline. As they mature a stout main trunk forms and an umbrella-shaped canopy develops. The oblong leaves are a dull deep green above with a gray felty texture underneath. Crimson stamens stand out from the flowers making a showy display in warmer climates. *Zones 10–11.*

Metrosideros kermadecensis
Kermadec pohutukawa

Growing to much the same height as *M. excelsa*, it is more often seen in its

Metasequoia glyptostroboides

variegated-leaf forms. 'Variegata' forms a neat shrub for many years before eventually becoming tree-like to around 18 ft (6 m). The gray-green leaves are edged with an irregular creamy yellow margin. The species and cultivars make good hedges and screens. *Zones 10–11.*

MICHELIA
Magnoliaceae

Closely related to the magnolias, the 50 or so species of *Michelia* are to be found in tropical and subtropical Asia, with a few species in the cooler foothills of the Himalayas. They range from shrubs to quite substantial trees, mainly evergreen, the chief attraction being the often intense fragrance of their flowers. Some species are widely cultivated in India for the extraction of fragrant oil from these blooms, for use in the perfume and cosmetic industry.

Cultivation

They like frost-free climates and fertile soil. They do not like being transplanted. Propagate from seed or summer cuttings.

Michelia doltsopa

Growing to around 30 ft (10 m), this tree has a slender habit while young which tends to a broader crown with age. The large, scented, white flowers appear in the leaf axils in late winter and early spring. *Zones 9–11.*

Michelia figo
Port-wine magnolia, banana shrub

A slow-growing, compact, evergreen shrub from western China, the port-wine magnolia is usually seen as a dense shrub of about 10 ft (3 m) but eventually grows to twice that. The small, shiny, deep green leaves virtually obscure the tiny spring-blooming cream flowers which are streaked with purple and heavily scented. *Zones 9–11.*

MICROBIOTA

There is just one species in this genus, a dwarf evergreen conifer that is excellent as a ground cover, as a specimen on its own, or grouped with other low-growing conifers or heathers. It also makes a good foil for other more colorful plants.

Michelia figo

Michelia doltsopa

Cultivation

Very frost hardy, it does best in free-draining soil with an open aspect. Prune only if absolutely necessary and then only into the new wood. Propagate from seed or from tip cuttings.

Microbiota decussata
Russian arbor-vitae

This conifer from Siberia grows to only 18 in (45 cm) high with a spread of up to 10 ft (3 m). Its branches nod at the tips and bear flat sprays of scale-like, yellowish green leaves (bronze in winter). Its small, round cones are pale brown and contain one fertile seed each. *Zones 3–9.*

MORUS
Moraceae
Mulberry

The 12 or so species of deciduous trees in this genus originate mostly in eastern Asia. They have broad, heart-shaped leaves with closely toothed margins and inconspicuous greenish flowers on short catkins, the male and female flowers on separate catkins. Female catkins bear tiny fruits so closely packed together that they appear as a single fruit, the mulberry. Some species have been cultivated for centuries, both for edible fruit and for silk production, the silkworm larvae feeding on the leaves.

Microbiota decussata

Cultivation

They do best in fertile, well-drained soils and a sunny, sheltered position. Propagate from cuttings.

Morus alba
syn. *Morus bombycis*
White mulberry, fruitless mulberry, silkworm mulberry

This vigorous, low-branching tree has sustained the silk industry of China and Japan. It grows up to 30 ft (9 m) tall, and has a broadly spreading crown and rather pendulous smaller branches. The leaves are a fresh green to yellow color, strongly veined, with sharp marginal teeth. The rather rubbery fruit are cylindrical, sometimes lanceolate, and color varies from white through pink or red to purple-black. *Zones 5–9.*

Morus nigra
Black mulberry

Grown mainly for its fruit, this mulberry has a thick trunk, a compact crown and dark green foliage. The leaves have a velvety down on the undersides and blunt marginal teeth. Fruits are dark red and slightly acid, though quite sweet when fully ripe. *Zones 6–10.*

Morus alba

Murraya paniculata

Morus nigra

MURRAYA

Allied to *Citrus*, this small genus of evergreen trees and shrubs comes from India and Southeast Asia. They have aromatic foliage and creamy white flowers, which resemble those of the orange and are often strongly scented. The fruits are small, oval berries.

Cultivation

They flourish in warm, frost-free climates in full sun or part-shade and humus-rich, moist but well-drained soil. When grown in borderline temperate situations, they need shelter. Gardeners in cooler areas should substitute the similar (though not so tall growing) *Choisya ternata*, from Mexico. Propagate from seed or cuttings.

Murraya paniculata
syn. *Murraya exotica*
Orange jessamine, mock orange
Widely distributed in tropical Asia, this compact, rounded bush up to 10 ft (3 m) tall is densely covered with shiny, dark green leaflets. The small, creamy white, perfumed flowers are held in dense clusters at the branch tips in spring and at intervals thereafter. Red berries may appear after each flowering. *Zones 10–11.*

MYRICA

Myrica is a genus of about 50 species of evergreen or deciduous shrubs and trees of worldwide distribution ranging in

Myrica californica

height from 5 ft (1.5 m) to 100 ft (30 m). Their fruits are clusters of bluish black berries enclosed in a white waxy crust. Tiny flowers appear in late spring; both sexes are borne on the one plant.

Cultivation

Moderately frost hardy to frost tender, they thrive in part-shade, but will not grow in alkaline or chalky conditions. Do not allow to dry out. Propagate from seed or cuttings, or by layering.

Myrica californica
Pacific wax myrtle
An evergreen shrub or small tree, this native of the west coast of the USA has dark green leaves and a decidedly upright habit, except where sheared by coastal winds. It grows 25 ft (8 m) or more in height, less in spread. *Zones 7–10.*

Myrsine africana

Myrtus communis 'Microphylla'

MYRSINE

This is a small genus of 5 species, all evergreen shrubs or small trees with inconspicuous flowers—male on one plant, female on another. If both sexes are present attractive berries will form, but it is for the pleasant foliage that these plants are usually grown. The leaves alternate up the stems and can be linear or lance-shaped or even rounded. The genus has a disjunct distribution in Africa, the Azores, the Himalayas and China. Sometimes the genus Rapamea is merged with Myrsine, resulting in a genus of over 150 species.

Cultivation

Species vary from fully frost hardy to frost tender. They grow in sun or part-shade, and are not fussy about soil types, although do not thrive in shallow, dry soil. They can be raised from seed, but plants of known sex are probably better struck from summer cuttings.

Myrsine africana
Cape myrtle, African boxwood

Although its botanical and common name suggests an African origin, this species is also native to the Himalayas and China. It is a slow-growing, upright, leafy shrub to 4–8 ft (1.2–2.4 m) tall by 30 in (75 cm) wide. The aromatic foliage is ¾ in (18 mm) long and glossy dark green, and the berries are pale blue in color. *Zones 9–11.*

MYRTUS
Myrtaceae
True myrtle

The name 'myrtle' is used here in the narrow sense following most present-day botanists who separate the southern hemisphere myrtles off into other genera including *Lophomyrtus, Luma* and *Ugni,* leaving *Myrtus* with the single species *M. communis.* Myrtles are usually densely foliaged evergreen shrubs with starry white flowers in spring. Flowers may be followed by blackish purple berries.

Cultivation

They prefer moist, well-drained soil and will grow in sun or light shade. Propagate from semi-ripe cuttings or from seed.

Myrtus communis

This is an erect shrub to around 10 ft (3 m) with dense, small, deep green leaves, fragrant when crushed. The fragrant white flowers appear in spring, followed by edible berries ripening to blue-black with a delicate whitish waxy bloom. This myrtle was prized by the ancient Greeks. A number of cultivars exist, including 'Flore Pleno' with double white flowers, 'Microphylla' with tiny leaves and flowers, and 'Variegata' with leaves edged white. *Zones 8–11.*

NANDINA
Berberidaceae
Sacred bamboo, heavenly bamboo

Nandina is a genus of a single species from China and Japan, related not to the bamboos—though it is rather bamboo-like in its habit and the elegance of its compoundly pinnate leaves—but to the barberries. It grows as a clump of thin, upright stems, and bears sprays of white flowers in summer and red berries in autumn and winter. The plants come in male and female and both are needed to enjoy the fruit, though hermaphrodite cultivars are available.

Cultivation
They like shade and fertile soil and a warm-temperate or subtropical climate.

Nandina domestica
This shrub has strongly upright, cane-like stems growing to 6 ft (2 m) high. The evergreen foliage is composed of many elliptical leaflets, which are red when young, become green and then develop intense yellow, orange and red tones in cold weather. Small white flowers appear in terminal panicles in summer. Although separate clones are usually needed to see the red berries that follow, self-fertile cultivars such as 'Nana' and 'Richmond' are available. *Zones 6–9.*

Nandina domestica

NERIUM
Apocynaceae
Rose-laurel, oleander

This small genus consists of evergreen shrubs native to northern Africa and southwest Asia. The most important is *N. oleander*, cultivated (and often naturalized) through the drier subtropics and popular in warm-temperate climates for its lavish display of perfumed flowers. The wild form is pink, but cultivars offer shades from white to red. It is a straggling bush with dull green pointed leaves and flourishes in any sort of soil, as long as it gets plenty of sunshine. *Nerium* species are poisonous.

Cultivation
Propagate from summer cuttings.

Nerium oleander
Oleander
Depending on the cultivar, the plants can grow 6–12 ft (2–4 m) tall. Cultivars have long, deep green leaves and the flowers, ranging from white to salmon to deep pink, appear in late summer onwards and are held in clusters. Blooms can be single or double, while some have variegated foliage. Popular cultivars include 'Album', with single white flowers with a cream center; and 'Punctatum', with single, pale pink blooms. *Zones 8–11.*

Nerium oleander 'Album'

NOTHOFAGUS
Fagaceae
Southern beech

Nothofagus is a genus of over 25 species of fast-growing evergreen and deciduous trees. The foliage of several of the deciduous species displays rich bronze hues before dropping. The small fruits each contain 3 triangular seeds known as beechnuts. Thought to have originated in Antarctica before spreading to Australia, New Zealand and South America, they grow in a variety of climates but need protection from winds.

Cultivation
They prefer deep acid soil. Position in full sun. Propagate from cuttings in summer or seed in autumn.

Nothofagus cunninghamii
Tasmanian beech

This tree grows to 160 ft (50 m) in the cool, mountainous regions in the south of its native Australia. An evergreen, it is one of the faster growing species in the genus, and is valued for its reddish timber. Its small, dark green, triangular-toothed leaves are held in fan-shaped sprays and the young foliage is a deep bronze shade in spring. Small catkin flowers are borne in early summer. *Zones 8–9.*

Nothofagus fusca
New Zealand red beech, tawhairaunui

This erect evergreen has a dome-shaped crown and averages 18–37 ft (6–12 m) in height when cultivated. The egg-shaped foliage is roughly serrated, the immature leaves turning reddish bronze in cooler weather. Small green flowers are followed by seed cups, each containing 3 angular seeds. *Zones 7–10.*

Nothofagus cunninghamii

Nothofagus fusca

Nyssa sylvatica

Olea europaea

NYSSA
Nyssaceae

Occurring naturally in southern Asia and North America, the trees in this genus need adequate year-round water to survive. Fast growing and wind tolerant, they must be left undisturbed after planting and may reach a maximum height of 110 ft (35 m). Small clusters of greenish white flowers appear in summer, followed by vivid, dark purple berries. Autumn foliage is red, crimson, yellow and orange.

Cultivation

They need acid soil and a cool climate. Prune only to remove dead or crowded branches. Propagate from seed in spring.

Nyssa sylvatica
Black tupelo, sour gum

This elegant, deciduous tree loves swampy conditions. The leaves are a glossy dark or yellowish green turning red, often with shades of orange and yellow, and are slightly wider towards the tip than the base. Growing to 65 ft (20 m) with a broad columnar conical habit, its trunk is covered with brownish gray bark which breaks up into large pieces on mature specimens. *Zones 4–9.*

OLEA
Oleaceae

There are about 20 species in this genus, all long-lived evergreen trees or shrubs, the most important of which is the common olive *(Olea europaea)* — the source of olive oil. They have leathery, gray-green leaves and tiny off-white flowers, followed by the fruit, known botanically as a drupe.

Cultivation

They require a frost-free climate, but winters need to be sufficiently cool to induce flowering while summers must be long and hot to ensure growth of the fruit. Propagate from seed in autumn, from heel cuttings in winter, or from suckers.

Olea europaea
Olive

The olive has many cultivars. Selection depends on whether black fully ripe olives, green almost-ripe ones, or olive oil are wanted. This is the best cooking oil — it has a fine flavor and is free of saturated fats — and has long been used in cosmetics and lamps. The fruit must be treated with lye before being pickled in brine or preserved in its own oil. It grows slowly to about 30 ft (10 m) and is very long lived. It does not come into full bearing for about 10 years. *Zones 8–11.*

OLEARIA
Asteraceae
Daisy bush

Indigenous to Australia and New Zealand, this large genus of evergreen shrubs and small trees are characterized by daisy-like flower heads which can be white, cream, blue, lavender, purple or pink and which appear from spring to autumn. They make excellent hedges.

Cultivation

Olearia can grow in alkaline soils and most are tolerant of salt, wind and atmospheric pollution. Propagate from seed or semi-ripe cuttings in summer.

Olearia macrodonta

This New Zealand shrub has 2–4-in (5–10-cm) long, holly-like leaves. They are deep green above with grayish white hairs below. The flower heads are white and yellow in the middle and the bush blooms heavily from early summer. It grows to about 6 ft (2 m) in cultivation and prefers moist, well-drained soil in sun or light shade. *Zone 8–10.*

Olearia phlogopappa
Dusty daisy bush

This 6 ft (2 m) rounded bush bears numerous white, blue or purple flowers. The oblong leaves, held on a single, many-branched stem, are grayish green, under 2 in (4 cm) long with serrated margins. Its height makes *O. phlogopappa* an effective screen or windbreak for seaside gardens or parks. Prune hard to encourage flowering or it can become very straggly. *Zones 8–10.*

OSMANTHUS
Oleaceae

Originally from the Himalayas, China and Japan, these evergreen flowering shrubs are prized for their fragrance. The white or cream flowers are almost inconspicuous. The Chinese use the flowers to enhance the scent of tea. The plants are slow growing, with some species eventually reaching 45 ft (14 m). The dense foliage comprises thick, rigid leaves which may be edged with stout, often hooked, spiny teeth.

Cultivation

Plant in rich, well-drained soil. Propagate from semi-ripe cuttings.

Osmanthus × burkwoodii
syn. *Osmarea burkwoodii*

This is a hybrid between *Osmanthus delavayi* from China and the rare *O. decorus* from the Caucasus. Profuse small, very fragrant flowers appear in the latter half of spring. It reaches a height of 6 ft (1.8 m) and has a dense, rounded habit with glossy, dark green foliage. *Zones 8–10.*

Osmanthus delavayi
syn. *Siphonosmanthus delavayi*
Delavay osmanthus

This species grows to a height and spread of around 6 ft (1.8 m). It has serrated, oval,

Olearia macrodonta

Olearia phlogopappa

Osmanthus fragrans

Oxydendrum arboreum

dark green leaves held on arching branches. Tubular white flowers are borne profusely in the leaf axils and at ends of branches in summer. *Zones 7–9.*

Osmanthus fragrans
Sweet osmanthus, sweet olive
Usually seen as a shrub with a height of around 10–20 ft (3–6 m), this species can be trained as a small tree and can also be grown in containers. Its broad, deep green leaves act as a foil to the clusters of very small creamy white or yellow flowers, which are held towards the ends of the branches. It flowers intermittently from spring to autumn. *Osmanthus fragrans* f. *aurantiacus* has dull orange flowers. *Zones 7–11.*

OXYDENDRUM
Sorrel tree, sourwood
The single deciduous tree species in this genus is a native of eastern USA and is grown for its autumn foliage and flowers. The leaves are alternate and finely toothed; the fragrant, small urn-shaped flowers are held in drooping terminal panicles. The genus, which is related to *Pieris*, takes its name from Greek words meaning 'sour tree', a reference to the sour-tasting foliage.

Osmanthus delavayi

Cultivation
For the best fall colors, it should be planted in an open position in sun or part-shade in moist, acid soil. An occasional dressing of iron and/or ammonia after flowering may be required. Propagate from cuttings in summer or seed in fall.

Oxydendrum arboreum
Making a 20–40 ft (6–12 m) tree, this species tolerates frost better than dry conditions. The trunk is slender and the crown pyramid-shaped. Streamers of small white lily-of-the-valley-like flowers appear in late summer sometimes prior to, sometimes coinciding with, the display of deep scarlet foliage. *Zones 4–9.*

P

PACHYSTEGIA
Asteraceae

These evergreen shrubs are closely related to other New Zealand bush daisies such as *Olearia* and *Brachyglottis*. The large, thick, leathery leaves have glossy, wax-coated upper surfaces and felted undersides—superb protection against salt spray and coastal storms. They plants produce showy white daisy-like flowers in summer followed by attractive seed heads.

Cultivation

The rock daisy is generally undemanding. It grows in any well-drained soil in sun or light shade. Propagate from seed or cuttings.

Pachystegia insignis
Marlborough rock daisy

The height of this attractive seaside plant is variable—1–5 ft (30 cm–1.5 m)—while it can spread to 3 ft (1 m). In early summer the white daisy-like flower heads open; they have golden yellow central florets. Fluffy brown seed heads follow. The leaves are heavy and leathery, 3–7 in (8–18 cm) long, deep glossy green above with heavy white felting below. *Zones 8–11.*

Pachystegia insignis

PAEONIA
Paeoniaceae

This genus is made up of about 30 herbaceous perennials and deciduous shrubs. The shrubby species are known as 'tree peonies', which usually reach the size of a large rose bush. Peonies have large, lightly scented flowers, which come in every shade from white through pink to red, as well as orange; and the form varies from poppy-like singles to extravagantly frilled doubles with 80 petals or more.

Cultivation

They prefer a cool climate and partial shade (in hot climates), and rich, moist but well-drained soil. Peonies are difficult to propagate.

Paeonia lutea
Yellow tree peony

This large shrub can reach a height and width of about 6 ft (2 m). In late spring to early summer it bears single, clear yellow flowers about 6 in (15 cm) across, which tend to hide among the leaves. The dark green leaves have saw-toothed margins. *P. lutea* is the parent of some beautiful hybrids with *P. suffruticosa. Zones 6–9.*

Paeonia lutea

Paeonia suffruticosa
Tree peony, mudan

This handsome shrub reaches a height and width of 3–6 ft (1–2 m), and produces very large, single or double, cup-shaped flowers in spring. Depending on the variety, these are white, pink or red or yellow, and are set among attractive, large, mid-green leaves. *Zones 4–9.*

PARROTIA
Hamamelidaceae
Persian witch hazel

From Iran and the Caucasus comes this genus of a single species cultivated for its rich autumnal hues and unusual flowers. The petal-less flowers consist of upright, wiry, dark red stamens enclosed in brown bracts and appear in early spring before the leaves. These are about 4 in (10 cm) long and have undulating edges. The branches on older trees dip down towards the ground. The genus was named after F. W. Parrot, a German botanist.

Parrotia persica

Cultivation

Propagate from softwood cuttings in summer or from seed in autumn.

Parrotia persica

A spreading, short-trunked, deciduous tree with flaking bark, this species can reach about 40 ft (13 m) in the wild, but is usually about 25 ft (8 m). The roughly diamond-shaped leaves with wavy margins turn yellow, orange and crimson in autumn. A lime-tolerant tree, it is said to achieve these splendid hues best on a slightly acid soil. The tree grows well in full sun and in fertile soils in temperate climates. *Zones 5–9.*

PAULOWNIA
Bignoniaceae

Originally from China and Japan, the genus is named for Anna Paulowna, a daughter of Paul I, Tsar of Russia. *Paulownia* species may grow to 8 ft (2.5 m) in their first year, reaching an eventual height of 50 ft (15 m). Big, heart-shaped leaves and dense clusters of elegant flowers make them distinctive shade trees. The flower-spikes, similar to foxgloves, appear in spring with the new leaves, and are followed by capsules containing winged seeds.

Paeonia suffruticosa

Paulownia tomentosa

Persea americana

Cultivation

They do best in well-drained, fertile soil, with ample moisture in summer and shelter from strong winds. Propagate from seed or root cuttings.

Paulownia tomentosa
syn. *P. imperialis*
Princess tree

This species has large, heart-shaped leaves and pale-violet, fragrant flowers. The paired leaves can be as long as 12 in (30 cm) as can the erect flower spikes. Drought-tender, the tree reaches a height and width of 40 ft (13 m). It can suffer damage to the flower buds if late frosts strike. If pruned almost to the ground each winter it will develop branches about 10 ft (3 m) long with enormous leaves, though it will then not flower. *Zones 5–9.*

PERSEA

This genus is made up of about 150 species of evergreen trees and shrubs mostly from tropical parts of Central and South America with a few from Asia and one, *P. indica*, from the Azores and Canary Islands. The best known member of the genus is the avocado. They are large trees with deep green, elliptical leaves and inconspicuous unisexual flowers followed by the familiar large, rough-surfaced, pear-shaped fruits.

Cultivation

Frost tender and fast growing, they can be untidy trees as they drop leaves constantly. Although self-fertile, at least 2 trees are required for good crops. *Persea* demand rich soil, perfect drainage, ample moisture when fruiting and full sun. Shelter from strong winds. Cutting-grown or grafted plants are superior to seedlings.

Persea americana
syn. *Persea gratissima*
Avocado

This species can reach a height of 60 ft (18 m). Its glossy, dark green leathery leaves are shed all year. The small greenish flowers, held in the axils, are followed by pear-shaped, nutritious, green or black fruit. The stem is usually erect. The avocado is tender to both frost and dry conditions, and can be nurtured in mild climates well south and north of the tropics. There are many named cultivars, each with different growth patterns and requirements. *Zones 10–11.*

PERSOONIA
Proteaceae

Persoonia species are evergreen shrubs native to Australia where about 60 different species occur. Some have a prostrate habit and are used as ground

Persoonia pinifolia

covers, but most are tall—up to 15 ft (5 m)—open-growing shrubs or small trees. The 4-petaled flowers are yellow, and are followed by fleshy berries that are edible but rather astringent.

Cultivation
They grow best in full sun and acid, sandy soil. They are hard to propagate. Try freshly harvested seeds that have first been soaked in warm water for 24 hours to soften the hard seed coat.

Persoonia pinifolia
Pineleaf geebung
This shrub has soft, delicate, bright green and pine-like foliage with long arching stems. It reaches a height of 12 ft (4 m) and is nearly as wide. The small golden yellow flowers are borne in large clusters at the branch tips throughout summer and autumn. An additional highlight is provided by bunches of small, succulent green berries. By winter these have attractive red to purple tonings and they persist for several months. They make excellent cut foliage for flower arrangers. *Zones 10–11.*

PHILADELPHUS
Hydrangeaceae
Mock orange, syringa
This genus of deciduous shrubs comes from the temperate regions of the northern hemisphere, mainly from East Asia and North America. They grow to about 10 ft (3 m) high and wide and have light green, roughly elliptical leaves to around 3 in (8 cm) long. They flower in late spring and early summer and bear 4-petaled flowers in loose clusters. The flowers are often strongly scented of orange blossom, hence the common name.

Cultivation
They prefer moist, well-drained soil and a position in sun or light shade. Propagate from seed or from cuttings.

Philadelphus coronarius
A native of southern Europe and Asia Minor, this species grows to around 6 ft (2 m) and has very fragrant 2 in (5 cm) wide white flowers. Its oval bright green leaves are slightly hairy on the undersides. 'Aureus' is a cultivar with bright yellow new growth and smaller flowers. *Zones 4–9.*

Philadelphus coronarius

Philadelphus 'Lemoinei'

This hybrid was introduced in the late 1880s by the famous French hybridist Lémoine, who also raised many hydrangeas and lilacs. It grows to around 8 ft (2.4 m). The flowers are white, very fragrant and usually carried in clusters of up to 7 blooms. *Zones 5–9*.

Philadelphus 'Virginal'

Fully hardy, this vigorous shrub grows to a height and spread of a little under 9 ft (3 m). From late spring to early summer, it bears large, fragrant, semi-double flowers set among dark green oval leaves. *Zones 5–9*.

PHILODENDRON

This genus of up to 500 species includes many well-known houseplants as well as some shrubs and small trees. Native to tropical America and the West Indies, they are mainly epiphytic, evergreen vines and creepers with aerial roots, some dainty but others quite robust. They have lush foliage, often with a dramatic outline or deep lobes, mostly green but sometimes attractively marked with white, pink or red. The petal-less flowers are inconspicuous. All parts of the plants are poisonous.

Philadelphus 'Virginal'

Cultivation

They need plenty of moisture and a tropical or subtropical climate to be grown outdoors. They like a sheltered, shady spot with well-drained, humus-rich soil. Water and fertilize houseplants regularly. Propagate from cuttings or from seed.

Philodendron bipinnatifidum
syn. *Philodendron selloum*
Tree philodendron

This upright, robust species from Brazil grows to 10 ft (3 m) tall. It has shiny, oval, deep green leaves, 15–24 in (38–60 cm) long and many-lobed; in some hybrids, the leaves can be up to 3 times as large. Leaf outline is variable; the common form with irregular lobing is sometimes known under the synonym. Other cultivars and hybrids include some of the most spectacular of all foliage plants. *Zones 10–11*.

Philadelphus 'Lemoinei'

Philodendron bipinnatifidum

PHLOMIS

This genus consists of around 100 species of often downy-leafed perennials, sub-shrubs and shrubs found from the Mediterranean region to China. Although variable, their leaves are mostly large and densely covered with hair-like felting. The tubular flowers, borne on upright verticils, curl downwards and have 2 lips at the tip, the upper lip hooded over the lower. They occur in clusters of 2 to 40 blooms, depending on species.

Cultivation

Hardiness varies, though most tolerate moderate frosts. Species with heavily felted foliage suffer in prolonged wet weather and are best grown in exposed positions where the foliage dries quickly after rain. Plant in moist, well-drained soil in full sun or part-shade. Propagate from seed, small cuttings, or by division.

Phlomis fruticosa
Jerusalem sage

This evergreen shrub, a native of southern Europe, bears strikingly beautiful yellow flowers in whorls from early to mid-summer, among oval, wrinkled, felty green leaves. It tolerates coastal areas and grows to a height and spread of 30 in (75 cm). To keep its habit neat, prune to about half its size in autumn. *Zones 7–10.*

Phlomis fruticosa

PHOENIX
Arecaceae

These evergreen feather palms are native to subtropical and tropical parts of Asia, Africa and the Canary Islands. Some are a source of food (dates and also palm sugar) while others are popular as house-plants or decorative trees. The long fronds have stiff, sharp spines at their bases and form a dense crown. Small yellow flowers grow in clusters, followed by the fruit. Male and female plants have to be planted to ensure pollination.

Cultivation

They prefer full sun though they will tolerate partial shade, hot winds and poor soil, given good drainage. Propagate from seed.

Phoenix canariensis
Canary Island palm

This massive palm is a popular land-scape feature in warm-temperate zones. It grows up to 50 ft (15 m) tall with a spread of 30 ft (10 m), the trunk being thick and sturdy—up to 3 ft (1 m) across. The deep green fronds are up to 12 ft (4 m) long. In summer small yellow flowers are arranged in large, drooping clusters. These are followed by orange-yellow, inedible acorn-like fruit. *Zones 9–11.*

Phoenix canariensis

Phoenix roebeleni

Photinia × fraseri 'Robusta'

Photinia serrulata

Phoenix roebeleni
Dwarf date palm

This versatile small palm from Laos is suitable for the hot-climate garden and also as a potted specimen indoors. It will grow to 10 ft (3 m) tall with a similar spread, given enough room. It has dark green arching fronds. The short, slender stem is rough because the bases of the old leaves persist. Fruit are small, black, egg-shaped drupes. Plant outdoors in a sunny or partly shaded location but shelter it from frosts. Keep soil or potting mix moist. *Zones 10–11.*

PHOTINIA
Rosaceae

These evergreen or deciduous shrubs and small trees of Asian origin have brilliant young foliage and, in the case of the deciduous species, wonderful autumn color. The majority are fast growing. The leaves are alternate and the flowers mostly white, followed by either red or dark blue berries. They make excellent hedges and should be pruned to promote bushiness.

Cultivation

Plant in sun or partial shade in fertile, well-drained soil. Propagate from seed or cuttings in summer, or by grafting on to hawthorn or quince stock.

Photinia × fraseri

The young growths on these evergreen shrubs are attractive shades of bright red, bronze-red and purple-red. The mature leaves are glossy and green. 'Robusta' bears eye-catching coppery-red young leaves. The height of the shrub varies with the cultivar, but most are in the 9–12 ft (3–4 m) range. *Zones 7–10.*

Photinia serrulata

Indigenous to China, this small evergreen tree or shrub can grow to a height of 21 ft (7 m) with a bushy crown, but can also be kept to lower heights and clipped to form hedging. The glossy oval leaves are large, serrated and bronze tinted in spring. The small white spring flowers are followed by small, red berries. The plant is also listed as *P. serratifolia*. Zones 7–10.

PHYSOCARPUS
Ninebark
The unusual inflated fruits of this genus of deciduous shrubs from Asia and North America are not edible—the 11 or so species are admired for their flowers and foliage. In the wild, they reach a height of 10 ft (3 m) The leaves are prominently veined, lobed and serrated, and change to a dull yellow in autumn. The small, 5-petaled, white or pink flowers, appearing in spring or early summer are borne in decorative clusters.

Cultivation
They require fertile, well-drained soil and a sunny position. They resent soil with a high lime content and dry roots. Thin out crowded plants by cutting back some of the arching canes after flowering. Propagate from seed or cuttings of semi-ripened wood in summer.

Physocarpus monogynus
Mountain ninebark
This species from central USA grows to around 3–4 ft (1–1.2 m) tall with arching, spreading stems. The new stems are bright brown, sticky, often with fine hairs; the young leaves are light green. The 2-in (5-cm) wide foliage is 3- to 5-lobed with serrated edges. Flat 2-in (5-cm) wide heads of small white flowers open from late spring. Zones 5–7.

PICEA
Pinaceae
Spruce
A large genus of evergreen conifers, *Picea* contains about 45 species. They are

Physocarpus monogynus

fast growing, sometimes reaching an impressive 220 ft (70 m). They develop a stiff, narrow, conical, sometimes columnar growth-habit, with short, upward-pointing branches. The leaves are arranged spirally on short pegs and appear in a range of shades from bright green to glaucous blue. *Picea* species bear large cones which hang downwards. They will not survive transplantation when large, nor grow well in heavily polluted environments. Some cultivars make ideal bonsai specimens; others make excellent groundcovers.

Cultivation
They can tolerate poor soil, some lime and heat, although they are prone to fungal infections in warm, humid climates. Propagate from seed or cuttings in autumn or by grafting.

Picea abies
Norway spruce, common spruce
The traditional European Christmas tree, the trunk of *P. abies* has orange-brown, maturing to reddish, bark which it sheds in scales. Leaves are dark green and rectangular and the reddish cones are cigar-shaped. Dwarf shrubby cultivars have been propagated from 'witches' brooms', tight clumps of congested foliage that sometimes appear on the plant. Shallow rooted, it can be

upended by strong winds. 'Maxwellii' is a low-growing, compact form ideal for rockeries and borders. 'Pumila Glauca' is a semi-erect dwarf form with lime green foliage. 'Pygmaea' is a slow-growing dwarf form. 'Reflexa' is a weeping cultivar distinguished by growing tips that point upwards when young. *Zones 3–8.*

Picea glauca
White spruce
Grown commercially for the paper industry, this tree reaches a height of 80 ft (25 m) when mature, but is relatively slow growing. Characterized by the bright green shoots that appear in spring, it prefers sharply drained soil. The drooping branchlets carry the 4-angled needles that are strongly aromatic. Cones are small and narrow. 'Conica', known as the dwarf Alberta spruce, is a compact, erect, cone-shaped shrub with grass-green foliage, and suits rockeries. *Zones 2–6.*

Picea pungens
Colorado blue spruce
This beautiful spruce grows to 110 ft (35 m) in the wild, although it is usually much smaller in gardens. It has a

Picea abies 'Maxwellii'

pyramid of bluish green foliage composed of stiff and sharply pointed needles; the bark is gray. 'Glauca', a commonly grown cultivar, is slightly smaller than its parent and is slower growing. Its strong steel-blue new foliage makes it a striking specimen tree in large gardens and parks. 'Hoopsii' is prized for its even bluer foliage; 'Koster' is another striking blue cultivar. *Zones 3–8.*

Picea pungens

Picea glauca 'Conica'

Pieris japonica 'Christmas Cheer'

Pieris formosa var. forrestii

PIERIS
Ericaceae
This genus consists of evergreen shrubs and, more rarely, small trees from North America and East Asia. The shrubby species have a neat compact habit, attractive foliage and flowers. The height of the shrubs rarely exceeds 12 ft (4 m) and is often less. The flower buds are held throughout the winter, and in spring open into clusters of small, waxy, usually white flowers.

Cultivation
They require a temperate climate, moist, peaty, acidic soil and a partially shaded site. Propagate from seed in spring or from cuttings in summer, or by layering.

Pieris formosa
This dense, bushy shrub from western China carries glossy, dark green leathery leaves and bears sprays of small, bell-shaped white flowers in mid-spring. Frost resistant, it grows well in both cool and mild climates but is drought-tender. It grows to 12 ft (4 m). *P. formosa* var. *forrestii* is usually smaller with scarlet-bronze young growth. *Zones 6–9.*

Pieris japonica
Lily-of-the-valley shrub
This Japanese shrub can grow to 12 ft (4 m) high, but usually only reaches around 6 ft (2 m). It has pointed, elliptical, deep green leaves that are reddish copper when young. Panicles of small, white, bell-shaped flowers appear from early spring. The many cultivars include 'Bert Chandler', with pink and cream new growth; 'Christmas Cheer', with early, pale pink flowers; and 'Variegata', with cream-edged foliage. *Zones 4–10.*

PINUS
Pinaceae
Pine
This genus of about 90 species of conifers, ranging from large shrubs to very large trees, includes some commercially important trees. Their timber is used extensively in construction, manufacturing and as wood pulp for paper. The resin of some species yields turpentine. Not suitable for small gardens, pines can be beautiful where they have room to develop and are good shelter trees. Some are tolerant of drought and dry, sandy soil and some

can withstand strong winds and coastal conditions. The pollen released from late winter can irritate hay-fever sufferers.

Cultivation

They need good drainage and plenty of sun. Pines can often be transplanted if a large rootball is preserved. Propagate from seed.

Pinus canariensis
Canary Islands pine

This moderately fast-growing tree from the Canary Islands, though adaptable and tolerant of dry conditions, prefers an open, sunny spot where the soil is rich and moist yet well drained. It matures to a spreading tree, up to 80 ft (24 m) high. The upright trunk has reddish brown, fissured bark. The densely packed, shiny, grass-green needles are 11 in (30 cm) long and are carried in groups of three. The oval, brown cones are 8 in (20 cm) long. *Zones 8–11.*

Pinus contorta
Shore pine, beach pine

This species from the west coast of North America grows quickly to 30 ft (9 m) tall then develops horizontal branches and grows slowly to 70 ft (21 m). It has pairs of dark green, 2 in (5 cm)

Pinus canariensis

needles and small yellow-brown cones. It does not thrive in hot, dry areas. *Pinus contorta* var. *latifolia*, the lodgepole pine, is a straight-trunked, tapering tree to 80 ft (24 m) in its native Rocky Mountains but is slow growing, low and bushy in cultivation. It has yellowish green, 2–3-in (5–8-cm) long needles in pairs and small, oval cones that release fine seeds that are carried by wind. *Zones 6–9.*

Pinus densiflora
Japanese red pine

This lovely tree is grown for its red bark and naturally twisted shape. Although reaching 100 ft (30 m), and widely used as a timber tree in its native Japan, in cultivation it is slow growing, often multi-trunked, and is also popular as a bonsai specimen. Ovoid, yellow-purplish cones stand out boldly from the bright green foliage. The dwarf cultivar 'Umbraculifera', the Tanyosho pine, has an umbrella-like canopy. The bark on the multiple trunks is an appealing orange-red and flaky. 'Oculus-draconis', the dragon's eye pine, has yellow-banded needles. *Zones 4–9.*

Pinus contorta var. latifolia

Pinus densiflora

Pinus halepensis

Pinus mugo 'Mops'

Pinus halepensis
Aleppo pine

From the eastern Mediterranean area, this pine is the most resistant to dry conditions, in fact tolerating most conditions except severe frost when young. Fast growing to 50 ft (15 m), it has a spreading crown and a distinctive rugged character. The young bark is ash gray, but ages to reddish brown. The soft, light green needles are usually carried in pairs; the 3–4 in (8–10 cm) cones are reddish brown. *Zones 7–10.*

Pinus mugo
Mountain pine, Swiss mountain pine

This small tree grows slowly to 25 ft (8 m). Its windswept appearance reflects its alpine habitat and makes it an interesting plant for bonsai work. Its pairs of bright green needles develop from very resinous buds. The oval, dark brown cones are 1–2 in (2–5 cm) long. This species is hardy but does not tolerate extreme heat or drought. 'Mops' matures to 16 in (40 cm) over 10 years; var. *pumilio,* the dwarf Swiss mountain pine, grows into a compact, rounded bun achieving 32 in (80 cm) in 10 years. *Zones 3–8.*

Pinus nigra
Austrian black pine, European black pine

This European pine grows to 110 ft (36 m) or more in the wild, though cultivated specimens rarely exceed 35 ft (10.5 m). It has an open, conical habit with a whitish brown trunk, whorled branches and a dense crown of dark green, 6 in (15 cm) long, paired needles; its cones are 3 in (8 cm) long. It grows in chalk and clay and tolerates coastal conditions. *Pinus nigra* var. *maritima,* the Corsican pine, forms a denser crown and is slower growing; its gray-green twisted needle pairs can exceed 6 in (15 cm) and it has cracking bark and a very straight trunk. *Zones 4–8.*

Pinus parviflora
Japanese white pine

This pine usually matures to a height of 40 ft (13 m) in cultivation. It produces some of the shortest needles in the genus, and forms a dense, bluish green foliage which, combined with its slow growth-habit, makes it a popular bonsai subject. 'Brevifolia' is upright and sparsely foliaged. 'Glauca' is a blue-foliaged cultivar that takes many years to reach 5 ft (1.5 m) high. *Zones 3–9.*

Pinus patula
Mexican yellow pine, spreading-leafed pine

This elegant pine, with long, slender, drooping needles and a spreading canopy eventually reaches a height of 50 ft (15 m) with a 15 ft (5 m) spread. The needles are soft pale green to grayish green, and grouped in threes. The clustered cones are 4 in (10 cm) long and oval in shape. *Zones 9–11.*

Pinus pinea
Roman pine, stone pine, umbrella pine

The seeds of this species are edible and known as pine nuts. The tree has a

Pinus nigra var. maritima

Pinus pinea

Pinus patula

Pinus parviflora 'Brevifolia'

flattened crown atop a straight, though often leaning trunk. It copes with extremes of drought and heat when established. It can reach a height of 80 ft (25 m). The trunk has furrowed, reddish gray bark; the rigid paired needles are 4–8 in (10–20 cm) long and bright green. Globe-shaped cones are shiny and brown. *Zones 8–10.*

Pinus strobus
Eastern white pine, Weymouth pine
Occurring naturally in eastern North America, where it is valued for its timber, this species grows to 200 ft (60 m) in the wild but to less than 50 ft (15 m) in cultivation. It has deeply fissured, grayish brown bark and whorled branches. Its fine, bluish green needles are carried in groups of five. The pointed cones, clustered at the branch ends, produce copious amounts of white resin. It develops rapidly if grown away from a polluted environment and, though cold hardy, it dislikes dry conditions and windburn. 'Prostrata' is a low-growing, spreading cultivar mounding to around 18 in (45 cm) high at the center. *Zones 3–8.*

Pinus sylvestris
Scots pine
This fast-growing species, found throughout northern Europe and

western Asia and the only pine indigenous to the UK, is the most commonly grown pine in Europe and is often used in forestry. It reaches 100 ft (30 m) with a rounded head of foliage and orange-red bark. Twisted, bluish green needles grow in pairs and are 3 in (8 cm) long. It grows well in poor sandy soil but does not tolerate dry conditions. 'Watereri' only grows 2–3 in (5–8 cm) a year and can be thought of as a dwarf, blue-foliaged form of the Scots pine. It is ideal for rock gardens or collections of dwarf conifers. *Zones 3–7.*

Pinus thunbergii
Japanese black pine
This tree is commonly grown in Japan as an ornamental where its irregular,

Pinus strobus 'Prostrata'

Pinus thunbergii

Pinus sylvestris

Pistacia chinensis

layered, horizontal branches have long
been an inspiration for artists and bonsai
masters. It does very well in containers.
Also known as *P. thunbergiana*, it has a
rugged trunk and intricate framework of
branches and will grow to 130 ft (40 m)
if left untrimmed. It has purplish black
bark, pairs of thick needles and conspicuous white buds. *Zones 5–8*.

PISTACIA
Pistachio

This small genus consists of 9 species of
deciduous and evergreen trees and
shrubs occurring naturally in the warm-
temperate regions of the northern
hemisphere. It includes the familiar
edible pistachio nuts as well as ornamental deciduous species that develop vivid
foliage tones in autumn, and species
grown for their resins and oils. The
tallest species grow to 80 ft (24 m). The
leaf arrangements are compound,
usually composed of an even number of
leaflets. The flowers are generally
inconspicuous, male and female flowers
occurring on separate plants. Female
plants display clusters of small berries or
fleshy fruits in fall and early winter.

Cultivation

A well-drained soil in full sun is preferred. Propagate from seed sown in fall
and winter, or by budding or grafting.

Pistacia chinensis
Chinese pistachio

Growing to 35 ft (10.5 m) in gardens,
this deciduous species has glossy green
leaves consisting of up to 10 pairs of
leaflets that in autumn turn yellow,
orange and scarlet. The inconspicuous
flowers, borne in panicles, are followed
in summer by small red spherical seed
pods that turn blue in fall and attract
birds. An excellent decorative tree, it
also makes a good canopy for shade-
loving shrubs. It often forms a double
trunk. *Zones 6–9*.

PITTOSPORUM
Pittosporaceae

These evergreens make good specimen
plants, screens and windbreaks or dense
hedges in mild-winter climates. There
are some 150 species, mostly from
tropical and subtropical regions of
Australasia. The leaves are arranged
alternately along the stems, or in whorls.
Several species have striking foliage.
Fragrant flowers are followed by fruit
consisting of a hard outer capsule
surrounding round seeds with a sticky
covering. Some of the species are frost
tolerant.

Cultivation

Grow them in full sun or partial shade,
choosing a sheltered position in colder
areas. The soil must be well drained and
kept moist over summer. Propagate from
seed in autumn or spring, or tip cuttings
in summer.

Pittosporum crassifolium
Karo

This New Zealand native forms a tall
shrub or small tree, rarely over 25 ft
(8 m) tall with a spread of 10 ft (3 m).
The single trunk bears low-growing
branches and has a dense, domed
canopy. Clusters of fragrant, star-

Pittosporum eugenioides

Pittosporum crassifolium

Pittosporum tenuifolium 'Tom Thumb'

shaped, reddish purple flowers appear in spring. Fleshy, greenish white, oval fruit follow. The karo is drought tolerant and copes well with exposed seaside locations. *Zones 8–10.*

Pittosporum eugenioides
Tarata, lemonwood

The tarata is a densely foliaged large shrub to small tree from New Zealand. Mature specimens reach up to 40 ft (13 m) tall. The shiny dark green oval leaves have a citrus-like aroma when crushed. Terminal clusters of small, star-shaped yellow flowers with a honey-like perfume appear in spring. Large clusters of green oval fruit follow. 'Variegatum' has mid-green leaves blotched along the edge with white. It grows to a height of 9–15 ft (3–5 m) and is suitable for clipped hedges. *Zones 9–11.*

Pittosporum tenuifolium
Kohuhu

The kohuhu is a New Zealand native that grows to 30 ft (10 m) tall. The pale green leaves have a wavy edge. Small, dark chocolate flowers appear in late spring, either singly or in small clusters. Their sweet perfume is most intense at night. In late summer, round fruit that turn from green to almost black when ripe are produced. It likes an open, sunny site with light to medium soils enriched with organic matter. There are a number of cultivars with variegated or purple-toned foliage suited to floral arrangements. *Zones 9–11.*

Pittosporum tobira
Japanese mock orange

From Japan and China, this shrubby species eventually reaches 12 ft (3.5 m). Its oval to oblong shiny green leaves, 4 in

Pittosporum tobira

Platanus × *acerifolia*

(10 cm) long, occur in whorls along the stems. Star-shaped, cream flowers with an orange blossom scent appear in late spring and summer. It thrives in mild climates in an open, sunny position. It is a good hedge plant in coastal regions. 'Wheeler's Dwarf', a mound-like shrub, grows to 24 in (60 cm); 'Variegatum' has an irregular silvery white edge to its leaves. *Zones 9–11.*

PLATANUS
Platanaceae

A genus of large, vigorous, wide-crowned, deciduous trees from Eurasia and North America, it contains some of the world's largest deciduous shade trees for dry summer climates. The most conspicuous feature is the mottled bark that is shed in winter. The 5-lobed leaves are large and maple-like, and the brown seed balls hang in clusters in winter. The flowers are of little visual significance. The majority tolerate severe pruning, air pollution and hard man-made substances, such as paving, partially covering the root run.

Cultivation
They thrive in deep, rich, well-drained soil in a sunny site. Propagate from seed, cuttings or by layering.

Platanus × *acerifolia*
London plane
A popular decorative tree, the plane is resistant to leaf blight and can withstand poor atmospheric conditions, deep shade, hot sunlight, severe pollarding and a concrete cover over its roots. However, the roots can lift paving and the large, bright green, leathery leaves can block small drains. It can reach heights of 120 ft (38 m). The trunk, blotched in gray, brown and white, is straight and erect. Decorative brown seed balls hang through the winter months. *Zones 4–9.*

PLATYCLADUS
Cupressaceae

Platycladus is an evergreen conifer with flat, fan-like sprays of aromatic foliage. It is a tall, conical tree but there is a wide choice of small to dwarf varieties. All the branches are retained right down to the ground, so they make excellent informal hedges and screens, rock garden features or tub specimens. Leaves are tiny, scale-like needles that clasp the twigs. Female trees have small, erect, fleshy brown cones with overlapping scales hidden among the foliage.

Cultivation
It prefers a warm climate, shelter from strong winds, a partly shaded position

Platycladus orientalis

Plumbago auriculata

and moist, well-drained soil. Propagate from seed, or from cuttings taken in the cooler months.

Platycladus orientalis
Oriental arbor-vitae

This conifer grows into a densely branched large shrub or small tree, up to 40 ft (13 m) tall, and features sprays of bright green foliage held vertically when young, but almost horizontal on older branches. Better known are the smaller-growing varieties. Some have very dense, crisp foliage and a symmetrical shape while others are softer looking with a more irregular form. They are good accent plants in a rock garden or can be grown in tubs. *Zones 6–11.*

PLUMBAGO
Plumbaginaceae

The leadworts are a small genus of perennials, evergreen shrubs and scrambling climbers and semi-climbers with clusters of blue, white or red flowers. The flowers have 5 petals narrowing to a long slender tube and are massed together on short stems near the tips of the arching branches. The leaves are arranged alternately.

Cultivation

Plumbagos grow best in warm climates. They require well-drained soil, perhaps enriched with a little organic matter.

Pruning in late winter ensures a good flower display, as flowers are produced on the new growth. Propagate from tip cuttings taken in the warmer months.

Plumbago auriculata
Blue plumbago

Originating in South Africa, *P. auriculata* (formerly known as *P. capensis*) has beautiful sky-blue flowers. It flowers prolifically through the warmer months, and will quickly increase its size and sprawling habit unless pruned once or twice a year. It makes a striking hedge. Often grown in a large pot or hanging basket, it is a popular conservatory or cool greenhouse plant. 'Royal Cape' has flowers of a more intense blue that hold their color and is considered slightly more tolerant of frost and drought. *Zones 9–11.*

PLUMERIA
Apocynaceae
Frangipani, temple tree

The genus contains 8 species of mainly deciduous shrubs and trees, originally from Central America. They can reach a height of 30 ft (10 m), though they are generally much smaller. Their fleshy branches contain a poisonous, milky sap. In the tropics the fragrant terminally held flowers (generally white) appear before the leaves and continue to flower for most of the year. In subtropical climates, flowers appear in spring after the leaves and continue growing until the next winter. In colder climates, it can be grown in a greenhouse.

Cultivation
Propagate from cuttings in early spring.

Plumeria rubra
This deciduous large shrub or small tree can grow to a height of 24 ft (8 m). It is distinguished by its pale pink to crimson flowers which are used extensively for decoration. *P. rubra* var. *acutifolia* is usually seen more commonly than the species. It features creamy white flowers, sometimes flushed pink, with a yellow center. *Zones 10–11.*

PODOCARPUS
Podocarpaceae
Plum pine
These evergreens vary in size from ground covers of 3 ft (1 m) to large trees of 145 ft (45 m). The flat, generally narrow leaves are spirally arranged. Male plants have catkin-like yellow cones. Female plants have naked seeds held on short stalks that later develop into the fleshy, berry-like 'fruit' that give them their common name. The fruit ranges from plum purple to blue-black to red.

Plumeria rubra

Cultivation
Podocarpus is moderately fast growing and reliable in a range of soils, either in full sun or part-shade, though warm-temperate climates suit them best. Leave unpruned unless grown as a hedge. Propagate from seed or cuttings.

Podocarpus elatus
Plum pine, brown pine
Its dense canopy makes this a good shade tree. It has flaky dark brown bark and shiny, dark, oblong green leaves that end in a sharp point. They are up to 4½ in (11 cm) long. The edible fruit are rounded and purplish to black. It can tolerate mild frosts, but must be watered in dry periods. *P. elatus* copes with heavy pruning, best done during the growing season which extends throughout the warmer months. It makes a good clipped hedge. *Zones 9–11.*

Podocarpus macrophyllus
Kusamaki
This large-leafed species prefers moist, humus-rich soil and is relatively tolerant

Podocarpus elatus

Podocarpus macrophyllus

of cold. Its informal pyramidal crown with a height of 65 ft (20 m) and spread of 12 ft (4 m) in the wild is composed of thick, dark green leaves that are crowded onto the branchlets. Also known as the Buddhist pine because it is often grown near Japanese temples, it bears little black berries. 'Maki' has a distinctly erect habit with almost vertical branches. *Zones 8–11.*

POPULUS
Salicaceae
This genus of 35 to 50 species of majestic, deciduous trees are fast growing, and are popular in parks, large gardens and as street trees as windbreaks and screens. They are also valued for their soft white timber. Male and female flowers, borne on separate trees, are hanging catkins and appear in late winter and early spring before the leaves. The fruit is a capsule containing seeds covered with fine hairs.

Cultivation
Plant in deep, moist, well-drained and fertile soil in full sun. They dislike arid conditions. Many have vigorous root systems, so are not suitable for small gardens. Propagate from cuttings.

Populus nigra
Black poplar
This tree is often included in small gardens where its stature of 100 ft (30 m) is out of place and its suckering habit a nuisance. The diamond-shaped leaves are bronze when young, becoming bright green and then yellow in autumn. These large leaves are held on thin stalks and give an impression of constant movement. The male trees produce black catkins in the mid winter. There are many cultivars, including 'Aurea', the golden poplar, and 'Italica', the Lombardy poplar. *Zones 3–9.*

Populus tremula
Aspen
A vigorous, spreading tree from Europe for cool climates, this species grows to about 50 ft (15 m). The rounded, toothed leaves are bronze-red when young, gray-green in maturity and turn a clear yellow in autumn. They are held on

Populus nigra

Populus tremula

Potentilla fruticosa 'Tangerine'

slim, flat stems. In late winter the tree carries long gray catkins. *Zones 1–7.*

POTENTILLA
Cinquefoil

This genus of 500 or so perennials, some annuals and biennials, and deciduous shrubs is indigenous mainly to the northern hemisphere, from temperate to arctic regions. Many have 5-parted leaves (hence the common name cinquefoil), and range from only 1 in (25 mm) or so tall to about 18 in (45 cm). They bear clusters of rounded, bright flowers in profusion through spring and summer.

Some are used medicinally—the root bark of one species is said to stop nose bleeds and even internal bleeding.

Cultivation

Plant in well-drained, fertile soil. Although they thrive in full sun in temperate climates, the colors of pink, red and orange cultivars will be brighter if protected from very strong sun. Perennials are generally frost hardy. Propagate shrubs from seed in fall or from cuttings in summer.

Potentilla fruticosa
Bush cinquefoil

This dense, deciduous shrub, found in many parts of the temperate northern hemisphere, grows up to 4 ft (1.2 m) tall with a spread of 4 ft (1.2 m) or more. From early summer to autumn, garden varieties bear 1 in (25 mm) wide flowers in shades from white to yellow and orange, the orange ones often fading to salmon pink in the sunshine. The flat, mid-green leaves comprise 5 or 7 narrow elliptical leaflets arranged palmately. 'Tangerine' has golden orange flowers; 'Primrose Beauty', up to 3 ft (1 m) tall, has primrose-yellow flowers very reminiscent of a small wild rose. *Zones 2–7.*

PROSOPIS
Mesquite

Although typically thought of as trees of the American southwest, this legume genus includes some 44 species of deciduous and evergreen subshrubs, shrubs and trees found not only in the warmer parts of the Americas but also in southwest Asia and Africa. They are often thorny stemmed and have lush, ferny foliage. The flowers are pea-like, usually creamy green to yellow and are borne on spike-like racemes that form in the leaf axils. Bean-like seed pods follow the flowers.

Prunus × *blireiana*

Prosopis glandulosa

Cultivation

Most tolerate only very light frosts and prefer a warm, dry climate. The soil should be light and well-drained with moisture at depth. They tolerate dry conditions and alkaline soil. Plant in full sun. Propagate from seed or cuttings.

Prosopis glandulosa
Honey mesquite, Texas mesquite

This is an important tree in arid regions, where its low, spreading canopy provides needed shade for patios and garden beds. Seldom more than 30 ft (9 m) tall with a similar width, its deciduous leaves are compound with many tiny leaflets giving a fine texture to the foliage mass. Spiny stems discourage close contact. In spring the trees are covered with fluffy spikes of yellow flowers, popular with bees. It has become a problem in some regions where it develops impenetrable thickets. *Zones 8–11.*

PRUNUS
Rosaceae

Prunus is a large genus that includes the edible stone fruit—cherries, plums, apricots, nectarines and almonds—as well as ornamental species and cultivars. While the genus includes several shrubby species, most are trees growing on average to 15 ft (5 m). All but a few are deciduous and bloom in late winter to spring with scented, 5-petaled, rose-like, pink or white flowers. All produce a fleshy fruit containing a hard stone. *Prunus* species vary in hardiness, some being warm-temperate in origin, others from cold climates.

Cultivation

Plant in moist, well-drained soil in sun with protection from strong wind. Ornamental plants are usually grafted or budded on to species seedlings.

Prunus × blireiana
Double-rose cherry-plum

This popular deciduous hybrid grows up to 12 ft (4 m). It has a squat appearance with slender arching branches and red-purple elliptical leaves that change to golden-brown in autumn. Its red-pink, semi-double flowers, blooming in early spring, are fragrant. *Zones 5–10.*

Prunus campanulata
Taiwan cherry, carmine cherry

This slow-growing, narrow, deciduous tree can grow to 30 ft (10 m) but like most cherries, it resists pruning. One of the earliest flowering *Prunus* species, it looks spectacular in late winter when its bare branches are festooned with clusters of single, bell-shaped, carmine or pale pink flowers. The fruit that follow are a

Prunus cerasifera

Prunus campanulata

Prunus laurocerasus

Prunus mume 'Geisha'

deep red. Its bright green foliage turns bronze-red in fall. *Zones 7–11.*

Prunus cerasifera
Purple-leafed plum, cherry plum, myrabolan

A deciduous, decorative tree, this species can grow to about 30 ft (10 m). A profusion of small white flowers appears before the leaves, in spring in cool climates and in late winter in milder ones. These are followed by edible, yellow-red cherry plums. Some cultivars have pink flowers. 'Nigra' has blackish purple leaves and single, pink or white blossoms. 'Elvins' grows to 12 ft (4 m), with rose-tinged white flowers. *Zones 4–8.*

Prunus laurocerasus
Laurel cherry, cherry-laurel

This handsome evergreen bears large, shiny, bright green, pointed leaves that are up to 7 in (17 cm) long. A vigorous grower, it is sometimes used as a hedge, but if unclipped it can grow to 50 ft (15 m). It tolerates alkaline soils and withstand low temperatures and shade. It bears upright sprays of small, sweetly scented, single, white flowers in mid to late spring; these are followed by red berries that ripen to black. *Zones 6–8.*

Prunus mume

This flowering species is a 15 ft (5 m) high, round-headed tree with sharply pointed leaves. Flowers are white to deep pink and carried in small clusters along the stems. They are lightly scented and are followed by yellowish apricot-like fruit. It features prominently in Chinese and Japanese paintings; and is popular for bonsai work. 'Geisha' has semi-double deep rose flowers. *Zones 6–9.*

Prunus persica
Peach

The peach bears profuse pinkish red blooms. Its delicious fruit is also pinkish red and covered with a velvety down. Growing to 12 ft (4 m), peach trees look best when mass planted, but can also make attractive formal standards. 'Versicolor' bears semi-double white and red-striped flowers on the same tree. *Zones 5–9.*

Prunus sargentii
Sargent cherry

This cherry is covered with single pink flowers with deeper pink stamens in spring. Its sharply pointed foliage, which opens at the same time as the blossoms, gives a brilliant display of young reddish bronze leaves. These are among the first leaves to turn in autumn, giving a splendid display of orange and reddish hues. It can

Prunus persica 'Versicolor'

Prunus serrula

grow to 50 ft (15 m). It performs best away from polluted environments. *Zones 4–7.*

Prunus serrula
Tibetan cherry

A deciduous, neat, round-headed tree growing to about 50 ft (15 m), this species has spectacular gleaming mahogany-red bark. Clusters of small white flowers appear in spring. *Zones 5–9.*

Prunus serrulata
Japanese cherry, Oriental cherry

This cherry from China is believed to be the main ancestor of the Japanese

Prunus serrulata

Prunus sargentii

flowering cherries (*Prunus*, Sato-zakura Group). It has similar foliage though the teeth on the leaves are not so noticeably bristle-tipped. It makes a spreading tree of about 30 ft (9 m) high and bears pink-flushed white flowers before or with the leaves in mid- to late spring. *Zones 5–9.*

Prunus subhirtella
Higan cherry, rosebud cherry

This deciduous spreading tree produces a profusion of pale pink flowers early in spring. Leaves are dark green, pointed and fade to shades of yellow before dropping. It grows to a height of 30 ft (9 m). 'Pendula' carries pink flowers in spring on the weepiest of branches from late winter into spring. *Zones 5–8.*

Prunus × yedoensis

This hybrid grows rapidly to about 30 ft (10 m) high and wide. The massed display

Prunus subhirtella 'Pendula'

of fragrant, white or pale pink flowers usually opens before the new foliage develops. It is an excellent lawn specimen or decorative tree. It comes from Japan where it is extensively cultivated, and is the famous flowering cherry so prominently featured in Washington, DC. *Zones 5–8.*

PSEUDOPANAX
Araliaceae

Members of this genus of 15 species of evergreen trees and shrubs are endemic to New Zealand with 1 each in Tasmania, New Caledonia and Chile. The leaves are simple when young, becoming compound as they mature. The 5-petaled, greenish summer flowers are inconspicuous. They are followed by clusters of berries. They are good tub specimens and house plants.

Cultivation

Grow in well-drained soil enriched with organic matter, either in sun or part-shade. Propagate from seed or semi-hardwood cuttings.

Pseudopanax lessonii
Houpara

Rich green, leathery leaves are featured on this shrub or small tree that reaches a height of 20 ft (7 m). Each leaf consists of 3 to 5 oval to lance-shaped leaflets up to 4 in (10 cm) long and has smooth or toothed edges. In warm-temperate areas,

Pseudopanax lessonii

Prunus × yedoensis

the leaves may be tinged bronze to purple in winter. The houpara grows into a well-branched, slender plant that maintains its fresh, rich foliage even in exposed windy conditions. There are hundreds of different forms with variable leaf shapes and colorings. *Zones 9–10.*

PSIDIUM
Myrtaceae
Guava

Named after the Greek word for pomegranate, this genus of evergreen shrubs, growing to 30 ft (10 m) high, originated in Central and South America. The clusters of 5-petaled white flowers are usually large and are followed by the decorative fruit. Each fruit is a globular to pear-shaped berry with red or yellow skin. The fruit is mostly used to make jellies, jams and juice.

Cultivation

Guavas need a warm to hot climate, a protected position and rich, moist, free-draining soil. Propagate from seed or cuttings, or by layering or grafting.

Psidium cattleianum
Strawberry guava

The strawberry guava has an upright trunk with smooth, beautifully mottled

bark, growing to a height of 20 ft (7 m). Its shiny green leaves are leathery in texture and rounded, and form a canopy to 12 ft (4 m) across. Single white flowers have 5 petals. Var. *littorale* has yellow fruit; 'Lucidum' has sweet purplish fruit. *Zones 9–11.*

PTELEA

From the cooler parts of North America, this is a genus of 11 species of small, deciduous trees or large shrubs that grow slowly to an eventual height of 25 ft (8 m). The branching stems carry bushy foliage with leaves composed of 3 oblong leaflets. In common with the citrus family, to which they are related, the leaves have oily glands that release a scent when crushed. They turn a beautiful shade of gold in autumn. The small, fragrant, greenish white flowers appear from late spring to early summer.

Cultivation

Plant in a shady site in free-draining soil and keep well watered. Propagate from seed in fall or by layering and grafting in spring.

Ptelea trifoliata
Hop tree, water ash, stinking ash

This tree can grow to 25 ft (8 m), given the shade of taller trees and plenty of

Ptelea trifoliata

Psidium cattleianum

mulch in the warmer months to conserve soil moisture. The bark is a rich brown, and the oval, dark green leaflets are up to 4 in (10 cm) long. The fruit resembles bunches of keys. This tree makes an attractive ornamental. 'Aurea' has soft yellow leaves when young that mature to lime green. *Zones 3–9.*

PTEROCARYA
Wing nut
Ranging from the Caucasus to China, this genus consists of about 10 species of deciduous trees bearing handsome leaves and pendent flowers. Reaching a height of 100 ft (30 m) or more, they have spreading crowns with abundant, pinnate, bright green leaves, each leaflet 4 in (10 cm) or more long. The spring flowers appear as yellowish green catkins and grow to 18 in (45 cm) long. Winged nutlets, forming chains up to 18 in (45 cm) long, hang from the branches in ribbons and are an eye-catching feature.

Cultivation
These very frost-hardy trees prefer full sun and fertile, deep, moist but well-drained soil. Propagate from cuttings in summer or from suckers or seed in autumn.

Pterocarya stenoptera
This Chinese species grows to at least 50 ft (15 m) tall with leaves up to 15 in (38 cm) long made up of up to 23 leaflets. The new foliage and young shoots are covered with fine down. The catkins are as long as or slightly longer than the foliage. *Pterocarya stenoptera* var. *brevialata* has short-winged catkins. *Zones 6–8.*

Pterocarya stenoptera

Punica granatum var. 'Nana'

Pterostyrax hispida

PTEROSTYRAX
Styracaceae

This genus consists of 3 species of deciduous shrubs and trees reaching up to 50 ft (15 m) with a spread of 37 ft (12 m). Creamy white, fluffy flowers are produced in pendulous sprays up to 10 in (25 cm) long. Fruits appear as bristly seed capsules from which the plant can be propagated in the cooler months. They are useful shade trees.

Cultivation
Plant in deep, moist, well-drained soil in sun or partial shade. Propagate from seed, from cuttings or by layering.

Pterostyrax hispida
Epaulette tree

This lovely species attains a height of 50 ft (15 m). Rich green, oval leaves, with wedge-shaped bases and downy undersides, form a dense crown. During summer it displays fragrant white flowers in drooping sprays. Gray, furry, 10-ribbed fruits appear in early autumn and stay on the bare branches during winter. *Zones 4–8.*

PUNICA
Punicaceae

This deciduous shrub or small tree has blunt-tipped, glossy leaves and large, 8-petaled flowers. Pomegranates can be grown in a wide range of climates, but the red or orange fruit will only ripen where summers are hot and dry.

Cultivation
Plant in deep, well-drained soil, in a sunny spot. Propagate from seed or cuttings, or by removing suckers.

Punica granatum
Pomegranate

Long cultivated for its edible fruit, the pomegranate grows to 15 ft (5 m) tall and 10 ft (3 m) wide. From spring to summer there are red-orange flowers held at the branch tips. Each bloom is funnel shaped with crinkly petals. These are followed by the fruit. 'Nana' is a dwarf cultivar growing up to 3 ft (1 m) high. *Zones 8–11.*

PYRACANTHA
Rosaceae
Firethorn

These large shrubs grow up to 20 ft (7 m). Clusters of small, white flowers are borne on short spurs and crowd along the branches in spring. Firethorns can adapt to a wide range of soils from sandy to clay. They tend to naturalize and become invasive where conditions suit. Choose a sunny position for the brightest berry display, and ensure adequate moisture. It should be borne in mind when pruning that fruit are produced on second year wood.

Cultivation
Propagate from seed or cuttings. The diseases fireblight and scab can be a problem.

Pyracantha angustifolia
Orange firethorn
This species can reach a height and width of 10 ft (3 m) or more. A dense shrub with graceful, horizontal branches, this firethorn has narrow,

Pyracantha angustifolia

Pyracantha coccinea 'Lalandei'

oblong, dark green leaves, with gray downy undersides. The leaves are clustered in whorls on the flowering twigs but spirally on new shoots. It bears clusters of small, white flowers from late spring to early summer. The yellow-orange berries persist for most of the winter. *Zones 5–11.*

Pyracantha coccinea
The popular *P. coccinea* produces a spectacular display of fiery scarlet fruit that resemble tiny apples. It is originally from southern Europe, and both fruit and foliage will become darker if grown in cool climates. *P. coccinea* reaches a height of 15 ft (5 m) and its arching branches spread to about 6 ft (2 m). The cultivar 'Lalandei' is a vigorous plant with erect branches that display abundant fruit which ripen to bright red. *Zones 5–9.*

PYRUS
Rosaceae
Pear
The 20 or so species in this genus are slow-growing deciduous or semi-evergreen trees occasionally reaching 80 ft (25 m) but often smaller. They have

Pyrus calleryana

grainy-textured, sweet, yellowish green stone fruit, not all of which are pear shaped. Many species have attractive fall foliage and clusters of 5-petaled fragrant white flowers (sometimes tinged with pink) which appear at the same time as the new leaves in spring.

Cultivation

They have modest moisture requirements and are suitable for coastal conditions, thriving in heavy, sandy loams with good drainage in a sunny position. Cross-pollinate to produce fruit. Propagate from seed or by grafting.

Pyrus calleryana
Callery pear

This semi-evergreen tree has showy clusters of white flowers in early spring, followed by small, brown, inedible fruit.

The grayish green leaves stay on the tree until late fall when they turn shades of rich purplish claret, red, orange or yellow. Reaching about 60 ft (18 m) with a broad canopy, and tolerating heat, drought, wind and poor soil, it makes an ideal decorative tree. It is not very long lived. 'Bradford', the Bradford pear, is a common cultivar which flowers pro-fusely and grows well in poor conditions. Zones 5–9.

Pyrus communis
Common pear

The parent of many garden cultivars, the wild pear is grown for its beautiful single, pinkish white flowers with red stamens. Long lived, it reaches 50 ft (15 m) but its short branches can look unappealing when not covered in flowers. The bark is

Pyrus communis 'Beurre Bosc'

Pyrus kawakamii

Pyrus salicifolia 'Pendula'

famous English Williams pear; in North America it is known as the Bartlett pear and is grown for canning. *Zones 4–9*.

Pyrus kawakamii
Evergreen pear

From Japan, this graceful, evergreen tree with somewhat pendulous branches grows to 25 ft (8 m) tall and wide. White flowers are produced in late winter, attractive against the glossy green leaves. The fruit are tiny and hard. It is susceptible to fire blight. *Zones 4–10*.

Pyrus salicifolia
Willow-leafed pear, silver pear

This tree comes from the Caucasus and Iran. Its beautiful willow-like foliage is long, silver-gray and covered with silky down when young. It bears small creamy white flowers but these are somewhat hidden by the foliage. Small, brown fruit are pear shaped and ripen in autumn. Growing to about 25 ft (8 m), its slender branches arch. 'Pendula' is of willowy habit. Its foliage is smaller than that of its parent. *Zones 4–7*.

dark gray or brown and cracks into small plates. The dark green, leathery leaves have serrated margins and long stalks. The greenish fruits ripen to yellow and are usually gritty with a dull flavor—the fruit of the cultivars are sweeter and best when picked before fully ripe. 'Beurre Bosc' is widely cultivated for its heavy crops of large, soft, sweet, brown-skinned pears which are good for baking. 'Bon Chrétien', cultivated since medieval times, has medium-sized, succulent, musky-flavored fruit and is the parent of the

Q, R

QUERCUS
Fagaceae

This diverse genus contains 450 or so species of evergreen and deciduous trees and shrubs, mostly from the northern hemisphere. Oaks range from small shrubs to tall trees, and are very long lived. Most are suitable only for large gardens. Their leaves, mostly lobed and leathery but in some species thin and lustrous, provide a dense canopy for a multitude of animals, birds and insects and make wonderful compost for acid-loving plants.

Cultivation

Quercus species thrive in a range of soils providing they are deep, damp and well drained. They are susceptible to oak-leaf miner in humid climates, as well as oak root fungus and aphids. Propagate from seed in autumn.

Quercus alba
American white oak

This deciduous oak grows up to 100 ft (30 m) high with a similar spread. It has scaly, fissured, pale ash-gray bark and oblong, lobed leaves that are up to 8 in (20 cm) long and turn purplish red in autumn. Its acorns are small. Its timber is important commercially, particularly in eastern USA and Canada where it is an important part of mixed hardwood forests. It is one of the stateliest of the American oaks. *Zones 3–9.*

Quercus coccinea
Scarlet oak

This deciduous oak has deeply lobed, glossy, bright green leaves with bristle tips. The leaves turn brilliant scarlet in a cool, dry autumn, and stay on the tree for a long time. It reaches 80 ft (25 m) on a strong central leader and is distinguished by its drooping branches. The bark is gray, darkening as it matures. The small acorns are cone-shaped, ripening in their second year. This can be brilliant for autumn color but trees often disappoint by merely turning brown. *Zones 4–9.*

Quercus ilex
Holm oak, holly oak

This oak grows up to 60 ft (18 m) tall, with gray rough bark that breaks into distinctive small squares. It is one of the largest, broad-leafed evergreen trees for cool-temperate climates and grows well in exposed seaside locations and lime-

Quercus alba

Quercus coccinea

stone soils. On young trees and lower branches of mature trees, the leaves are prickly, which discourages grazing animals. Acorns are small, appearing in groups of 1 to 3, and maturing from green to chocolate. *Quercis ilex* can be clipped to formal shapes or grown as a tall hedge. *Zones 7–10.*

Quercus palustris
Pin oak

This species tolerates dry, sandy soil. Moderately fast growing, it matures to a height of 80 ft (25 m). Its smooth, gray trunk supports horizontal branches towards the top of the tree, while the lower branches droop gracefully, so it needs plenty of room. Its deeply lobed, lustrous green leaves become crimson-red in autumn. They persist on the tree well into winter. *Zones 4–8.*

Quercus ilex

Quercus palustris

Quercus robur

Quercus virginiana

Quercus robur
English oak, pedunculate oak

Arguably the most famous oak with a life span of 600–700 years, *Q. robur* likes heavy clay soils where its roots can penetrate deeply. Acorns are held, often in pairs, on long stalks, and are partially enclosed in small cups. It is slow-growing, eventually reaching 110 ft (35 m). The timber is used for building, and wine barrels. 'Fastigiata' has a narrow, upright habit. 'Concordia', the golden oak, grows to 30 ft (10 m). It produces bright yellow, juvenile foliage that becomes a light greenish yellow in summer. *Zones 4–8.*

Quercus virginiana
Live oak

This evergreen species grows up to 60 ft (18 m) tall, with a short trunk that supports horizontally spreading branches. The dark green leaves are white and downy underneath. Acorns are small, arranged singly or in twos or threes, ripening to very dark brown. *Zones 7–11.*

RADERMACHERA
Bignoniaceae

This genus is made up of evergreen trees from tropical Asia, though only one, *R.*

sinica, is seen in gardens. Native to the tropical regions of China, this small tree has large bipinnate leaves up to 3 ft (1 m) long. The panicles of white trumpet-shaped flowers are held either terminally or in the axils of the branches and are followed by slender capsular fruit.

Cultivation

Provide a sheltered spot and choose a light, sandy soil. Propagate from seed, cuttings or by layering.

Radermachera sinica
China doll, Asian bell-flower

This attractive tree is native to southern China where it grows to 35 ft (11 m) tall. It has an upright habit and features glossy, dark green bipinnate leaves with leaflets up to 2 in (4 cm) long. Mature trees have large clusters of trumpet-shaped white flowers at the branch tips during summer and autumn. The fruit is a capsule up to 16 in (40 cm) in length. *Zones 10–11.*

RHAMNUS
syn. *Frangula*
Buckthorn

This genus of 125 species of deciduous and evergreen shrubs and small trees occurs in a range of climates, mostly in the northern hemisphere. It tolerates dry conditions and salt-laden atmospheres. They are distinguished by smooth, dark bark and simple green leaves, often with serrated edges. The flowers, borne in clusters, are insignificant. The fruits are fleshy, pea-sized berries popular with birds. Some species are thorny, some produce dyes that are used commercially, and the bark of some species is the source of the purgative cascara sagrada.

Cultivation
These versatile plants require moderately fertile, well-drained soil and full sun or part-shade in hot areas. Propagate the deciduous species from seed and the evergreen species from cuttings in summer.

Rhamnus alaternus
Italian buckthorn, alaternus
This large, evergreen, multi-stemmed shrub from the Mediterranean is valued in its native lands for its tolerance of dry conditions and polluted environments. It grows quickly to 15 ft (4.5 m) and its thorny branches bear a mass of small, glossy dark green leaves. These hide the tiny greenish yellow flowers, which attract all kinds of insects. Its berries are purple-black. It can become invasive in certain areas. 'Argenteovariegatus', which is more decorative than its parent but is less frost hardy, has leaves that are marbled with gray and edged with creamy white. *Zones 8–10.*

RHAPHIOLEPIS
Rosaceae
Indian hawthorn
These are slow-growing but tough evergreen shrubs, suitable for warm-temperate climates only. Leaves are leathery and have pale undersides. New shoots are often coppery red. The attractive, 5-petaled flowers are white or pink and are arranged in loose clusters that are often held rigidly away from the foliage at the branch tips. The fruit is a berry, usually blue-black.

Cultivation
They do best in a sandy soil enriched with organic matter and thrive in seaside gardens. Grow in full sun or heavy shade. Propagate new plants from seed, from semi-hardwood cuttings or by layering.

Rhaphiolepis indica
Indian hawthorn
Contrary to its common name, the Indian hawthorn originates in southern China. It is a compact shrub up to 8 ft

Radermachera sinica

Rhamnus alaternus 'Argenteovariegatus'

Rhododendron arboreum

Rhaphiolepis umbellata

Rhaphiolepis indica

(2.5 m) high and wide. During late winter and spring it bears perfumed flower clusters. Each flower is white with a pink blush, made more appealing by the central, long, pink stamens. Flowers are followed by black berries with a bluish tinge. The shiny, dark green leaves are narrow and pointed with a serrated edge. New foliage is reddish and downy. *Zones 8–11.*

Rhaphiolepis umbellata
Yeddo hawthorn

A dense, rounded mound normally 6 ft (2 m) tall, this shrub has paddle-shaped, quite thick leaves with a smooth edge. Newly emerging leaves are covered with gray, downy hairs. Clusters of perfumed white flowers are a summer feature and in warm climates the flowers spot bloom for much of the year. The fruit ripen to bluish black berries arranged in clusters and persist into winter. It is adapted to seashore conditions. *Zones 8–11.*

RHODODENDRON
Ericaceae

Rhododendrons are a diverse genus of deciduous, semi-evergreen and ever-green trees and shrubs, numbering some 800 species with thousands of cultivars. There are 3 divisions: azaleas, Vireyas and 'true' rhododendrons, ranging from miniature shrubs to small trees. Flowers come in a range of colors. The bell- to funnel-shaped flowers have 5 or more petals and are usually held in clusters at the branch tips. In some cultivars either the calyx or stamens develop into petal-like structures—known as 'hose in hose'.

Cultivation

Most require semi-shade and prefer light, well-drained but moist soil with slightly acid pH, enriched with organic matter with a cool root run. They do not tolerate lime. Protect from afternoon sun and strong winds. They are prone to

Rhododendron augustinii

Rhododendron degronianum

infestation by thrips, two-spotted mite (red spider mite) and powdery mildew in humid areas. Propagate from cuttings, or by layering, or grafting.

Rhododendron arboreum

This attractive tree can grow to 40 ft (13 m) and forms a narrow, cylindrical crown. The evergreen leaves are rough and leathery and have whitish or rust-colored undersides with quite prominent veins. Depending on the cultivar, red, white or deep pink, bell-shaped flowers appear in dense globular heads in very early spring. It needs a mild but cool climate to flourish and is the parent of many cultivars. *Zones 7–11.*

Rhododendron augustinii

This species has unusually small ever-green leaves that are dark green and tapered, with a prominent midvein. A medium-sized shrub reaching a height and width of 5 ft (1.5 m), *R. augustinii* is covered in late spring by a profusion of tubular blue or violet flowers, ranging from pale to deep hues—the deeper the color, the more tender the plant. The flowers occur in clusters of 3 or 5. It performs best in dappled shade. It is the parent of many blue-flowered hybrids. *Zones 6–9.*

Rhododendron fastigiatum

Rhododendron degronianum

This neat small shrub grows 2–3 ft (0.6–1 m) high, and has a domed crown. It produces long, dark green leaves with light brown, fuzzy undersides. Its bell-shaped flowers are a delicate, soft pink and appear in late spring. *Zones 7–9.*

Rhododendron fastigiatum

In the wild, this alpine species from China grows at altitudes of up to 15,000 ft (4,500 m). It has blue-gray leaves and is a wiry-stemmed, 18–30 in (45–75 cm) tall shrub. It flowers in mid-spring when it is smothered in purple or lavender blooms, and is a superb plant for a rock garden or mountain home. *Zones 6–9.*

Rhododendron griffithianum

This evergreen, rather tender rhododendron reaching 18 ft (6 m) has reddish brown peeling bark and unusually large, oblong leaves up to 12 in (30 cm) long. It holds its enormous, bell-shaped, white flowers tinged with pink in loose trusses of 6 blossoms, each 6 in (15 cm) in diameter. Flowers are faintly speckled with green and sweetly perfumed, peaking in late spring. *Zones 8–9.*

Rhododendron kiusianum

The foliage of this shrub develops yellow, red and purple tones as it ages and then most of the oval, hairy leaves are dropped by the end of winter, despite its classification as an evergreen. A very dense, twiggy bush that forms a rounded hummock to around 3 ft (1 m)

Rhododendron kiusianum

high and 5 ft (1.5 m) wide, from early spring it is hidden beneath masses of tiny pinkish purple flowers. White and light pink-flowered forms are also available. This is one of the parents of the Kurume azalea hybrids. *Zones 6–10.*

Rhododendron nuttallii

This species can grow to 25 ft (8 m) but usually makes a shrub 6 ft (2 m) high in gardens. The flowers are among the largest of any rhododendron, up to 5 in (12 cm) wide. Fragrant and funnel shaped, they form loose trusses of 3 to 9 blooms. They are white, tinted with yellow and pink. Leaves are metallic purple when young, becoming dark green and wrinkled as they mature. *Zones 9–10.*

Rhododendron occidentale
Western azalea

This deciduous azalea has oval, glossy green leaves that color richly in autumn. Its fragrant, funnel-shaped flowers are creamy white to pale pink with yellow or orange throats and appear in early summer. It grows to 8 ft (2.5 m). 'Exquisita' has fragrant, frilled flowers that are flesh pink inside and deep pink outside. *Zones 6–9.*

Rhododendron 'Patty Bee'

This pretty little dwarf hybrid develops into a mound of bright green elliptical

Rhododendron nuttallii

Rhododendron griffithianum

leaves. From early mid-season it is smothered in 6-flowered clusters of soft yellow, funnel-shaped flowers up to 2 in (5 cm) wide. It is ideal for rock gardens or containers. *Zones 6–9*.

Rhododendron sinogrande

This evergreen rhododendron is distinctive for its huge, glossy green leaves that reach 32 in (80 cm) in length and 12 in (30 cm) in width and are silvery underneath. These are matched in spring by enormous trusses of bell-shaped creamy white to yellow flowers with crimson blotches. Growing to a height of 40 ft (13 m), it needs a sheltered spot and a cool but mild climate. *Zones 8–10*.

Rhododendron, Azaleas

Azaleas are spectacular cool-temperate flowering shrubs. Flowers are white, yellow through pink and orange to flame blaze undiluted with green. Most in gardens are hybrids, grouped as Mollis hybrids, Ghent hybrids, Knap Hill hybrids, Exbury hybrids, and others. They make wide-spreading shrubs up to 10 ft (3 m) tall. The evergreen azaleas prefer warm-temperate gardens. The most important are the Indica azaleas

Rhododendron occidentale

Rhododendron sinogrande

Rhododendron 'Patty Bee'

Rhododendron, Kurume Azalea, 'Addy Wery'

Rhus aromatica

which may be from 18 in (45 cm) to up to 10 ft (3 m) high and smothered in single or double flowers in shades of pink, rose, red or white. Some of the Belgian Indicas have flowers up to 5 in (12 cm) wide. Other groups include the Gumpo, Satsuki and Kurume azaleas. *Zones 7–11*.

RHUS
Anacardiaceae

Rhus is a large and diverse genus of both deciduous and evergreen species shrubs and trees. One group of species contains trees and shrubs notorious for their allergy-causing properties; they include the creeping American poison ivy shrubs. Most species are relatively innocuous, but the sap may cause irritation to the skin. Some of the deciduous species have attractive foliage, often turning brilliant shades of red, purple, orange, yellow and bronze in autumn; others have dense clusters of reddish or brownish velvety fruit. In many species, male and female flowers occur on different trees.

Cultivation

They like a sunny position with adequate moisture and protection from wind. Propagate from seed or cuttings, or by division of root suckers.

Rhus aromatica
Fragrant sumac

This sprawling, deciduous species from eastern USA reaches 5 ft (1.5 m) tall and 5 ft (1.5 m) wide. Tiny yellow flowers, borne in spikes on bare stems, are followed by downy, deep green, coarsely toothed and aromatic foliage maturing to spectacular shades of orange and purple in autumn. Small red berries appear in mid-summer on female plants only. 'Gro-Low' is a very low-growing form with fragrant flowers that are a deeper yellow than those of the species. *Zones 3–9*.

Rhus ovata
Sugar bush

A large evergreen shrub, this native of southern California produces sugar-coated fruit that makes a refreshing citrus-like drink. Reaching a height and spread of 10–12 ft (3–4 m), it makes a good screening plant. Its oval leaves are very tough and leathery. Clusters of tiny pink and white flowers appear in late winter. It needs little or no water once established. *Zones 9–11*.

Rhus typhina
Stag's-horn sumac

This deciduous shrub or small tree has a slender erect trunk or frequently suckers from the roots to produce a thicket of

Rhus ovata

stems. It is usually under 15 ft (5 m) high with a spreading crown up to about 12 ft (4 m) wide. The clusters of terminal flowers are yellowish green and insignificant; it has brown stems, bunches of red fruit and intense scarlet, red, yellow and orange autumn foliage. Tannin is produced from this species. *Zones 4–9*.

RIBES
Grossulariaceae
Currant, gooseberry

The fruit of this genus of evergreen and deciduous trees is a juicy berry varying in color from white, scarlet, purple, green to black. These hardy shrubs can grow to 10 ft (3 m) with long arching stems. The lobed, mid-green leaves are pungent when crushed. Masses of blossoms in shades of yellow, red or pink cover the bushes in late winter or early spring. Stems must be thinned by one quarter after flowering to encourage growth, but remember that flowers and fruit are produced on the previous year's

Rhus typhina

growth. Some species are unisexual and must be planted in groups to ensure good displays of flowers and fruit.

Cultivation
They need moist, rich soil and full sun to semi-shade. Propagate from seed or cuttings.

Ribes odoratum
Buffalo currant, golden currant

A spreading shrub with an attractive, downy young stem growth, this species can reach about 8 ft (2.5 m). The 3-lobed leaves are shiny and color well in fall. The clustered, down-turned flower heads are large and greenish yellow, turning a deeper shade as they age. They exude a spicy, clove-like fragrance. The berries are black. It does not bear prickles. *Zones 4–7.*

Ribes sanguineum
Flowering currant

This is an ornamental shrub, deciduous and prickle free. The aromatic, lobed

Ribes odoratum

Ribes sanguineum

leaves are held on arching stems that can reach 12 ft (4 m). The deep pink or red flowers, appearing in late spring, are borne on erect to drooping spikes. Bluish black berries follow in summer. Popular cultivars include 'King Edward VII' with carmine flowers; 'Brocklebankii' with golden leaves and pink flowers; 'Tydeman's White' with white flowers; and 'Pulborough Scarlet' which carries a mass of deep red flowers. *Zones 5–10.*

ROBINIA
Fabaceae
Black locust

These deciduous shrubs and trees can reach a height of 80 ft (25 m) but many are shrub-like, maturing to 6 ft (2 m). Leaves are divided pinnately into small, oval leaflets. There is commonly a pair of spines on the branch at the leaf base. Fragrant pea flowers are clustered in pendulous sprays of pink, purple or white blossoms in spring. The fruit is a flat pod less than 4 in (10 cm) long. Pruning is only necessary to contain growth, and can be difficult as some species are very spiny.

Cultivation

Preferring poor, moist soil in a sunny position, they do well anywhere except

Robinia pseudoacacia 'Umbraculifera'

where exposed to strong winds. Propagate from scarified seed or cuttings, or by suckers or division.

Robinia pseudoacacia
Black locust, false acacia

This tree is fast-growing up to 80 ft (25 m). Leaves are fern-like. White, scented pea flowers are borne in late spring or summer, followed by reddish brown seed pods that persist into winter once they have released their black, kidney-shaped seeds during autumn. It suckers strongly so site carefully. 'Frisia' carries an airy head of distinctive golden foliage. It is thornless. 'Tortuosa' has short, twisted branches. 'Umbraculifera', the mophead acacia, rarely flowers but carries a neat rounded dense dome of foliage and is thornless. These cultivars rarely exceed 30 ft (10 m). *Zones 4–10.*

ROSA
Rosaceae

Roses have been popular since ancient times. Most of the roses grown today are hybrids many generations removed from their wild parent species. They come in a variety of flower forms and colors. Fragrance is variable, some cultivars intensely fragrant, others not at all. Roses range from only a few inches (or centimeters) high to giant climbers.

Cultivation

Roses prefer cool to cool-temperate conditions and sunny positions, which reduces the incidence of fungal diseases. They prefer a fairly rich soil with regular spring watering and occasional mulching. They are prone to aphids, mites and thrips. Most may be propagated from stratified seed or cuttings.

Rosa banksiae

This rose has long, arching, thornless canes. Leaflets are slender, pointed, dark green, smooth and leathery; foliage is evergreen and disease free. The sweetly scented, small white flowers appear in spring, are double and grow in clusters of three to seven flowers. It rarely bears hips, which are small and dull red. It requires a warm, sunny situation. It can be severely cut back immediately after flowering. *Zones 7–10.*

Rosa chinensis

A near-evergreen shrub or scrambler, this rose grows to around 15 ft (5 m) high and wide. It bears widely spaced prickles; its leaves are divided into 3 or 5 leaflets. The 5-petaled flowers, usually borne in small groups, open pink and rapidly age to red, followed by orange hips. Its repeat-flowering habit was a vital ingredient in the development of modern garden roses. *Rosa chinensis* 'Viridiflora' is reported to have been in cultivation in England as early as 1743. *Zones 6–10.*

Rosa banksiae

Rosa foetida

Rosa chinensis

Rosa foetida
Austrian briar

This deciduous species develops into a dense, twiggy shrub up to 10 ft (3 m) high and wide with numerous prickles. The branches carry pinnate leaves with between 5 and 9 leaflets. Flowers are 5-petaled and bright yellow. 'Bicolor' has flowers that are yellow on the outside and coppery red inside. *Zones 4–9.*

Rosa gallica
French rose, red rose

A suckering species, this is a dense, low-growing, 3 ft (1 m) tall shrub that bears few prickles. The leaves are divided into 3 or 5 leathery leaflets, and the slightly scented flowers are pink. Because of its tendency to produce double flowers, it has been an important species in the development of modern roses. 'Officinalis' has semi-double, deep pink flowers. *Zones 5–9.*

Rosa moyesii

Native to western China, this densely suckering rose bears rich crimson flowers in a single summertime flush.

Rosa gallica 'Officinalis'

The branches carry straight prickles and the dark green leaves are divided into between 7 and 13 leaflets. This plant can reach 10 ft (3 m). The pendent, deep scarlet flask-shaped hips may persist into winter. A popular hybrid is 'Geranium' with paler leaves, carmine-red petals and an eye-catching display of scarlet hips. This grows to about 6 ft (2 m) high and wide. 'Highdownensis' has more compact, bushy growth and profuse flowers. *Zones 5–9.*

Rosa rugosa

This hardy, sprawling shrub has thick, glossy, deep green, heavily veined leaves that are divided into as many as 9 leaflets. Its habit is dense and bushy to about 5 ft (1.5 m) high and wide, with branches thickly covered with prickles and bristles. It blooms in repeated flushes over a long season. The 5-petaled, white to deep pink flowers are followed by showy, large, pinkish orange-red hips. This disease-resistant species has given rise to a group of hybrids known collectively as Rugosas. 'Alba' is a white-flowered cultivar. *Zones 2–10.*

Rosa sericea var. pteracantha
Broad-spined rose

This large, cool-climate rose bush reaches about 10 ft (3 m). It has huge, broad-based prickles, deep red on young shoots. As the shoot matures, the prickles turn pale gray and opaque. Its leaves are divided into a large number of leaflets, as many as 17. The single burst of charming, white, 4-petaled flowers appears in late spring and is followed by small, oval, orange-red hips and attractive autumn foliage. *Zones 6–10.*

Rosa moyesii

Rosa sericea var. pteracantha

Rosa gallica 'Anaïs Ségales'

Rosa, Hybrid Rugosa, 'Sarah van Fleet'

Rosa rugosa

Rosa, Cluster-flowered Climber, 'Iceberg'

Roses, old garden roses

These are the groups that were developed before the rather arbitrary date 1867, when 'La France', first of the Hybrid Teas (Large-flowered roses) was introduced. There are literally hundreds to choose from.

Old garden roses are classified as **Gallicas** (such as 'Anaïs Ségales', a small bush with deep pink, double flowers); **Albas** (such as 'Alba Maxima' up to 8 ft (2.4 m) tall with white, double flowers); **Damasks** (such as 'Omar Khayyam', a fragrant mid-pink double dating from 1893); **Centifolias** (like 'Petite de Hollande', a small bush with masses of strongly scented pink blooms); **Moss** (such as 'Chapeau de Napoleon' with fragrant mid-pink, double flowers); **China** (such as 'Mutabilis', with light, yellow-orange flowers that age to crimson); **Tea** (such as 'Lady Hillingdon' with loose double, golden-yellow flowers); **Bourbon** (such as 'Boule de Neige' with white double flowers opening from red buds); **Portland** (such as 'Comte de Chambord' with sweetly scented, pink, double flowers); **Hybrid Perpetual** (such as 'Champion of the World', a deep pink double that is always one of the first to bloom);

Noisette (such as 'Alister Stella Gray' with light golden-yellow, fragrant double blooms).

Roses, modern garden roses

Most roses grown today are modern roses. Again, there are many hundreds to choose from, so make sure you select the right one for your garden. Modern garden roses are classed as **Bush** roses (**Large-** or **Cluster-flowered**) which make compact, upright bushes about 3 ft (1 m) tall (often more in mild climates). 'Peace' is a Large-flowered rose with perfectly formed, soft yellow flowers edged rose pink; 'Iceberg', a Cluster-flowered rose, is covered in heads of pure white blooms over a long season.

Shrub roses are taller, less upright growers, mostly repeat flowering, and include 'Buff Beauty', a **Hybrid Musk**, with soft yellow, aging to cream flowers; 'Sarah van Fleet', a **Hybrid Rugosa**, a tall, prickly bush with scented, double, deep pink flowers; 'Charles Austin', an **English rose**, with large, fragrant blooms in a dusky buff to yellow shade; 'Fritz Nobis', growing to 6 ft (1.8 m) with clusters of pale pink to white, semi-double flowers.

Miniature roses make lovely shrubs. 'Anita Charles' has deep pink, double flowers with an amber reverse to the petals; and 'Si', the smallest of all roses, has tiny, perfectly formed pink rosebuds.

ROSMARINUS
Lamiaceae

Some botanists recognize a dozen species in this genus but most suggest

Rosa, Miniature, 'Anita Charles'

there is only one, *R. officinalis*. An evergreen shrub native to the Mediterranean region, it has long been used in medicine, the perfume industry and the kitchen. These small shrubs, rarely growing more than 4 ft (1.2 m), have narrow, needle-like leaves that are dark green and aromatic. The blue flowers are held in short clusters.

Cultivation

They prefer a sunny site and tolerate salt-laden air. Prune regularly in summer. Propagate from seed or cuttings to keep it compact and promote new growth.

Rosmarinus officinalis 'Prostratus'

Rubus 'Benenden'

Rosmarinus officinalis
Rosemary

Widely grown as a culinary herb, this aromatic shrub is also an attractive ornamental plant. The habit is upright with strong woody branches that are densely clothed with narrow, deep green leaves. Simple, lavender blue to deep blue flowers smother the bush in autumn, winter and spring. It can also be grown as a low hedge. 'Prostratus' is a ground cover form that is ideal for spilling over walls or covering banks. *Zones 6–11.*

RUBUS
Roseaceae
Bramble, blackberry, raspberry

These deciduous and evergreen shrubs and scrambling climbers can grow to a height and width of 8 ft (2.5 m). Canes bear flowers and fruit in their second year. Leaves are mostly compound with 3–7 leaflets arranged pinnately or palmately and are usually felted underneath. The white, pink or purple flowers appear in summer. The sweet, juicy fruits are a mass of tiny drupes and are usually either red or black.

Cultivation

They like moist, well-drained soil in a sunny position. They are moderately to fully frost hardy. Some forms have naturalized and have become a menace. After fruiting, cut the canes back to ground level. Propagate by division of roots in winter or from seeds, cuttings or suckers.

Rubus 'Benenden'

This deciduous, arching, thornless shrub has peeling bark and lobed, deep green leaves. Reaching 10 ft (3 m) in height and spread, it bears pretty, large, pure white flowers in late spring and early summer. *Zones 5–9.*

S

SABAL
Arecaceae
Palmetto palm

Some species of these palms have erect tall trunks while others feature short stems. Leaves are fan shaped and deeply cut into segments of irregular size. Clusters of creamy flowers appear among the leaves, their stalks enclosed by tubular bracts at the base. Leaves are traditionally used for thatching roofs while some buds are one source of hearts-of-palm, or millionaire's salad. They suit warm to hot climates and moist or dry conditions.

Cultivation
They prefer a sheltered sunny spot in well-drained soil rich in organic matter. Propagate from fresh seed.

Sabal palmetto
Palmetto, cabbage palm

This evergreen tree thrives in swampy coastal areas. It can reach a height of 80 ft (25 m), with a sturdy trunk, scarred where the leaf bases have been. Leaves are up to 6 ft (2 m) long. Each leaf is divided into regular segments cut two-thirds of the way to the main axis and split at the tips. Small, whitish flowers are held in long, branched clusters. The fruit is a small black berry. *Zones 8–11.*

Salix alba var. *sericea*

SALIX
Salicaceae
Willow

This genus of about 300 species of deciduous trees, shrubs and ground-covers are grown for their timber, their twigs which are used in basket-making, and their strong suckering habit which aids soil retention. Willow bark was the original source of aspirin.

Cultivation
Willows like clearly defined seasons and prefer cool, moist soil with sun or partial shade. Propagate from hardwood or semi-ripe cuttings, layers or seed.

Salix alba
White willow

This adaptable tree grows to about 60 ft (18 m) high. Leaves are narrow, bright green above with flattened silky hairs on the undersides. It makes a good wind-break tree, albeit with invasive roots. It is often pollarded to gain long, flexible shoots for basket-making. *Salix alba* var. *caerulea,* has attractive blue-green leaves; and var. *sericea* has very silvery foliage. *Zones 2–10.*

Sabal palmetto

Salix babylonica
Weeping willow
Probably the most widely grown and recognized willow, this Chinese species grows to about 50 ft (15 m) high and wide. The narrow, bright green leaves, 3–6 in (8–15 cm) long, densely clothe flexible, arching branches that often droop right down to ground level. The catkins are insignificant. *Zones 5–10*.

Salix purpurea
Purple osier, Alaska blue willow
The tree-sized willows all grow to at least 25 ft (8 m) but there are some small species, of which *S. purpurea* is the best known. It grows to about 15 ft (5 m) high. In its darkest forms the catkins are an intense reddish purple. The leaves are silver-gray, often with a hint of purple on the undersides, and the stems are tinted purple. *Zones 3–10*.

Salix babylonica

Salix purpurea

SALVIA
Sage
The largest genus of the mint family, *Salvia* consists of some 900 species of annuals, perennials and soft-wooded shrubs, distributed through most parts of the world except very cold regions and tropical rainforests. Their distinguishing feature is the tubular, 2-lipped flower with the lower lip flat but the upper lip helmet- or boat-shaped; the calyx is also 2-lipped and may be colored. The flowers come in a wide range of colors. The genus derives from the Latin *salvus*, 'safe' or 'well', referring to the supposed healing properties of *Salvia officinalis*.

Cultivation
Sages prefer full sun, well drained, light-textured soil and adequate watering in summer. Propagate from seed in spring, cuttings in early summer, or division of rhizomatous species at almost any time.

Salvia clevelandii
Cleveland sage
This sage is a characteristic plant of the dry chaparral and scrublands of Califor-

Salvia clevelandii

Salvia greggii

Salvia leucantha

nia, where its aromatic foliage and flowers add a distinct fragrance to the air. A gray-green mound reaching 3–5 ft (1–1.5 m) tall and wide, its soft lavender-blue flowers are produced on stems rising 12–24 in (30–60 cm) above the foliage. 'Winifred Gilman' is more compact, with deeper blue flowers. *Zones 8–10.*

Salvia greggii
Fall sage, cherry sage, autumn sage
This shrub, which can reach 3–4 ft (1–1.2 m) in height, is native from Texas into Mexico and is a long-flowering addition to dryish gardens in California and southwestern USA. The leaves are small and aromatic; above the foliage rise slender stems with broad-lipped sage blossoms in red, orange, salmon, pink, pale yellow, white and blends. The flowers are produced from spring through autumn in coastal areas, and in fall and winter in the desert. Many hybrids and named selections are available. *Zones 9–10.*

Salvia leucantha
Mexican bush sage
This Mexican and tropical central American native is a woody subshrub

grown for its seemingly endless display of downy purple and white flowers on long, arching spikes. It will reach 3–4 ft (1–1.2 m) in height and spread, making it suitable for the middle of the border; it is often used as a flowering hedge in mild-winter regions. *Zones 8–10.*

SAMBUCUS
Caprifoliaceae
Elderberry
This genus includes about 25 species of perennial herbs, deciduous shrubs and soft-wooded trees. Although they have a tendency to be weedy and invasive, some species are useful and attractive. Most have pinnate leaves and, in late spring and early summer, large radiating sprays of tiny white flowers followed by clusters of purple-black, blue or red berries.

Cultivation
They thrive in any reasonably well-drained soil in sun or shade. Propagate from seed or cuttings.

Sambucus canadensis
American elder
An upright, deciduous shrub, this fast-growing species reaches about 12 ft (3.5 m)

tall with a similar spread, and has soft pithy stems. The compound leaves have 5 to 11 leaflets and the tiny, white, starry flowers appear in spring, borne in large sprays about 8 in (20 cm) across; they are followed by purple-black berries. *Zones 3–10.*

Sambucus nigra
European elder, elderberry

This deciduous shrub or small tree to 18 ft (6 m) high, sometimes regarded as a weed, has large, spring-borne sprays of tiny white flowers and clusters of purple-black berries. It has pinnate leaves made up of 5 to 9 deep green, serrated-edged leaflets. The berries are used in pies, the flowers and fruit to make wine or liqueurs. *Zones 4–10.*

SAPIUM

This is a genus of about 100 species of evergreen or semi-deciduous trees and shrubs found naturally in warm-climate areas from eastern Asia to tropical America. They have a milky sap that is poisonous to humans and animals which congeals on drying; some South American species have been tapped for rubber. The leaves are arranged alternately along the stems. The insignificant flowers are in spikes, while the fruits are hard-shelled capsules.

Cultivation

They thrive in full sun in well-drained soil enriched with organic matter. Propagate from freshly collected seed in spring or cuttings in summer.

Sapium sebiferum
Chinese tallow tree, vegetable tallow

From warm-climate areas of China and Japan and the only species commonly

Sambucus nigra

Sapium sebiferum

Sambucus canadensis

Sarcococca ruscifolia

Sassafras albidum

seen in cultivation, this fast-growing tree reaches 20–40 ft (6–12 m) with a spreading crown. It is semi-deciduous in hot climates, deciduous where winters are cooler. The bright green leaves, heart-shaped to oval with a pointed tip, color attractively to shades of yellow, orange, red and purple in autumn, even in a frost-free climate. In late spring spikes of tiny greenish yellow flowers are borne at the branch tips. The fall fruit contain 3 seeds that are covered with white wax. *Zones 8–11*.

SARCOCOCCA
Buxaceae
Sweet box, Christmas box

These wiry-stemmed evergreen shrubs from Asia have glossy, deep green, elliptical leaves and in late winter to spring produce small white to pink flowers that while not very showy are sweetly scented. The flowers are followed by conspicuous berries.

Cultivation
They prefer a relatively cool, moist climate with well-drained soil to match. They are largely trouble free. Propagate from seed, cuttings or layers.

Sarcococca ruscifolia
From Yunnan, Hubei and Sichuan in China, this species bears scented white flowers which are followed by red berries. It grows to about 5 ft (1.5 m) high and forms a densely foliaged clump. The leaves are oval, deep lustrous green above and paler beneath. *Zones 7–10*.

SASSAFRAS
This small genus of the laurel family contains 3 species of tall deciduous trees from China, North America and Taiwan. All parts of the trees have a spicy aroma that repels insects, and the wood has been used to make insect-proof cabinets and furniture. The alternate leaves of the trees can be entire or lobed, sometimes both on the same plant. The unisexual or bisexual flowers have no petals; usually greenish yellow, they are borne in clusters and appear with the leaves in spring. The inedible fruits are oval-shaped, blue-black drupes.

Cultivation
Plant in deep, fertile, well-drained, acid soil in full sun or light shade. Propagate from seed or suckers in autumn or from root cuttings in winter.

Schinus molle var. areira

Schinus terebinthifolius

Sassafras albidum
Common sassafras

This handsome tree occurs naturally in forests on the east coast of North America; it grows to 70 ft (21 m). The leaves are up to 4 in (10 cm) long, sometimes lobed, glossy dark green above and paler beneath; the foliage turns spectacular orange and scarlet shades in autumn. The insignificant spring flowers are small and greenish yellow. The inner bark yields the aromatic oil of sassafras, which was once used medicinally, as a food flavoring and in cosmetics but is now known to be poisonous. *Zones 4–10.*

SCHINUS
Anacardiaceae

These evergreen trees, from Central and South America, are drought resistant. Leaves usually consist of many leaflets but are sometimes simple. Flowers are tiny and arranged in clusters, male and female flowers on the same or separate trees. Female trees feature attractive round berries later in the season.

Cultivation

An open sunny location suits them, as well as well-drained, coarse soil. Propagate from fresh seed or cuttings.

Schinus molle var. areira
Pepper tree, peppercorn

This fast-growing tree has graceful drooping leaves and branchlets. The dark green, shiny leaves are composed of 10 to 18 pairs of small pointed leaflets. In late spring to early summer, pendulous open clusters of tiny cream flowers are borne at the branch tips. Long hanging bunches of poisonous peppercorn-like berries appear later in summer on female trees, and ripen to coral red. *Zones 9–11.*

Schinus terebinthifolius
Brazilian pepper tree

A round-headed tree up to about 30 ft (9 m) high, this species has bronze-green pinnate leaves usually composed of 7 leaflets. The drooping panicles of tiny cream flowers that appear in summer are followed by small green berries that redden as they ripen in winter. When trimmed it makes an excellent shade tree. In some warm, wet climates, such as in Hawaii, it has become a serious weed. *Zones 10–12.*

SEQUOIA
Taxodiaceae
California redwood, coast redwood

The sole species in this genus is *S. sempervirens*, renowned for being the tallest living trees, some measured at over 360 ft (110 m). It is a very long-lived, evergreen conifer indigenous to the west coast of the USA and is valued for its timber.

Cultivation

It does best in sun or partial shade with deep, well-drained soil. Propagate from seed or heeled cuttings.

Sequoia sempervirens

This single-trunked conical tree has bright green, flattened, leaf-like needles. The foliage is held horizontally on small side branches, with the main branches drooping slightly. The whole tree has a resinous aroma like pine wood, especially the red-brown, fibrous bark which is very thick and deeply fissured. A popular cultivar is 'Adpressa', which is very dwarf, for many years around 3 ft (1 m) high and 6 ft (2 m) wide, maturing to 10 ft (3 m) high. *Zones 8–10*.

SEQUOIADENDRON
Giant sequoia, big tree

From the Sierra Nevada area of California, the only species in this genus is a true giant of a tree. While not quite as tall as the California redwood (*Sequoia sempervirens*), it is far more heavily built and contains the largest timber volume of any tree. It is also very long-lived, and is an impressive tree for large parks and gardens. Its huge trunk is covered in rough, deeply fissured, reddish brown bark.

Cultivation

Trees of this size need a solid base, so plant in deep, well-drained soil in an open, sunny position and water well when young; it is frost-resistant, but dislikes dry conditions. Propagate from seed or cuttings.

Sequoiadendron giganteum
syns *Sequoia gigantea*, *Wellingtonia gigantea*

This conifer can grow up to 300 ft (90 m) tall, with a trunk up to 40 ft (12 m) in diameter at the base. It is an upright, single-trunked, conical tree with sprays of deep green, slightly prickly, cypress-like foliage. A specimen of this species in the Sequoia National Park in California is said to be 3,800 years old. 'Pendulum' has pendent side branches. *Zones 7–10*.

Sequoiadendron giganteum

Sequoia sempervirens

Shepherdia argentea

Skimmia japonica

SHEPHERDIA
Buffalo berry

There are 3 species of these North American evergreen or deciduous shrubs which are grown because they will tolerate dry, rocky conditions. They have minute, tubular flowers borne on spikes or racemes, followed by the simple, opposite leaves. The flowers are also followed by rounded red or yellowish red fruits on female plants.

Cultivation

These fully frost-hardy plants prefer full sun and moderately fertile, well-drained soil. The fruit will only be produced if both male and female plants are grown together. Propagate from seed or by division.

Shepherdia argentea
Silverberry, silver buffalo berry

This dense shrub grows to 12 ft (3.5 m) with thorny branches and intensely silver oblong leaves. The small yellow flowers are followed by single or clustered glossy bright red edible fruit, which can be made into a jelly. There is also a form with yellow fruit *(Shepherdia argentea* f. *xanthocarpa)*. It is sometimes used as a hedge because of its hardiness. *Zones 2–9.*

SKIMMIA
Rutaceae

These evergreen shrubs have deep glossy green oval leaves about 4–6 in (10–15 cm) long and about half as wide. The small starry flowers, which open from late winter, are white or cream and densely packed in conical clusters. They are followed by red or black berries depending on the species. At least one species is self-fertile, but others require male and female plants to be present for pollination.

Cultivation

They like shade or partial shade and moist, humus-rich, well-drained soil. Propagate from seed or semi-ripe cuttings.

Skimmia japonica

This hardy shrub from Japan, eastern Siberia and Taiwan grows to about 5 ft (1.5 m) high and wide. In spring terminal clusters of slightly fragrant, creamy white flowers are borne, followed by bright red berries that last well into winter. *Zones 7–10.*

SOLANUM
syn. *Lycianthes*

There are over 1,400 species in this genus including trees, shrubs, annuals, biennials, perennials and climbers from a range of habitats worldwide. Some are evergreen, others semi-evergreen or deciduous. The genus includes important food plants like the potato and eggplant (aubergine), though many species are poisonous. Ornamental species are grown for their flowers and fruits. The leaves are arranged alternately, while the showy flowers are solitary or in clusters, star-shaped to bell-shaped, ranging in color from white and yellow to blue and purple. The fruits are berries that contain many seeds.

Cultivation

These warm-climate plants have a wide range of requirements; most prefer full sun and rich, well-drained soil. Propagate from seed in spring or cuttings in summer.

Solanum rantonnetii
syn. *Lycianthes rantonnetii*
Paraguay nightshade, blue potato bush

This South American relative of the potato is a valuable long-blooming shrub or scrambling vine for warm-climate gardens. Simple green leaves cover the branches and provide a good foil for the summer-long profusion of deep violet-blue flowers. It can be used as 6–8 ft

(1.8–2.4 m) tall background shrub or trained on a trellis or arbor, where it may reach 12 ft (3.5 m) or more. 'Royal Robe' has deeper purple flowers. *Zones 9–11.*

SOLLYA

This Western Australian genus consists of 3 species of small evergreen climbers. They have narrow, thin, smooth-edged leaves and small 5-petaled, bell-shaped flowers borne in small loose clusters.

Cultivation

These frost-tender plants grow best in a sunny spot, but like some protection from midday sun, and fertile, humus-rich, moist but well-drained soil. Climbing stems need support. Propagate from seed in spring or cuttings in late spring or early summer.

Sollya heterophylla
Bluebell creeper, Australian bluebell creeper

The dainty bells of this species from Western Australia appear from spring to autumn. As well as the usual blue, there are white- and pink-flowered varieties available. The flowers are followed by decorative, navy blue fruit. It reaches a height of 6–10 ft (1.8–3 m) and has narrow, lance-shaped or oval leaves. *Zones 9–11.*

Solanum rantonnetii

Sollya heterophylla

Sophora japonica

Sophora tetraptera

SOPHORA
Leguminosae
Kowhai

This genus of some 50 species of deciduous or semi-evergreen trees and shrubs
is widespread in temperate regions of the
northern hemisphere, with a few species
from South America and New Zealand.
Most are open, many-branched trees
that grow to about 30 ft (10 m) high and
wide. They generally flower in spring
and produce pendulous racemes of pea-
flowers with cream or lavender blooms.
These are followed by bean-like pods.

Cultivation

Sophoras can adapt to a wide range of
conditions. Most prefer moist, well-
drained soil in sun or partial shade.
Propagate from seed, or semi-ripe or
hardwood cuttings. In Australia and
New Zealand caterpillars of the Kowhai
moth can defoliate plants in summer.

Sophora japonica
Pagoda tree

Despite its name, this deciduous tree
originates in central China. It grows to
around 40 ft (13 m) high. The light
green pinnate leaves are 8 in (20 cm)
long, and the cream, or occasionally pale

pink, flowers are borne in long panicles.
'Pendula' is often grafted on to 8 ft
(2.5 m) standards to produce a small
weeping tree. *Zones 4–10.*

Sophora tetraptera
Kowhai

This free-flowering, usually evergreen,
small tree from the North Island is New
Zealand's national flower. It may grow
to 30 ft (10 m) tall but is usually smaller.
Mature trees develop a semi-pendulous
habit with the branches somewhat
interlocked. The leaves consist of 20 to
30 pairs of small, gray-green leaflets.
The abundant spring pea-flowers, borne
in showy pendulous clusters, are pale to
golden yellow. *Zones 8–11.*

SORBUS
Rosaceae
Rowan, service tree, whitebalm

This genus is made up of deciduous trees
and shrubs from cool-climate regions of
the northern hemisphere, grown for
their foliage, timber and decorative fruit.
Most species have pinnate leaves and
terminal clusters of small creamy white
flowers in spring. Some species have
attractive autumn foliage but most show
little autumn coloration.

Sorbus hupehensis

Sorbus aucuparia

Sorbus cashmeriana

Cultivation

Rowans grow in any well-drained soil and do best in areas with distinct winters. Propagate species from stratified seed; graft selected forms.

Sorbus aucuparia
Mountain ash, rowan

The mountain ash grows to about 18 ft (6 m) high in gardens. The pinnate leaves, made up of 11 to 15 small, toothed leaflets, turn rich gold in autumn. The white spring flowers are followed by bright orange berries. There are several cultivars including 'Asplenifolia', with very finely cut leaves; and 'Edulis', a large-berried form whose fruit is used for jams and preserves. *Zones 3–7.*

Sorbus cashmeriana

This deciduous tree grows to around 33 ft (10 m) tall. Heads of small white flowers open in late spring from pink buds and develop into the main attraction of this relatively small tree — its stark white berries, which are borne in pendulous clusters. *Zones 5–9.*

Sorbus hupehensis
Chinese rowan

Indigenous to Hubei province in central China, this tall, vigorous tree has blue-green pinnate leaves made up of 9 to 17 leaflets. The foliage develops orange, red and purple autumn tones. Long-lasting berries are white, tinted pink, and are carried on red stems. *Zones 5–9.*

SPARTIUM
Fabaceae
Spanish broom

This genus contains one species of evergreen shrub which is indigenous to the Mediterranean area but has naturalized in a few areas with a similar climate. A yellow dye is derived from the flowers.

Cultivation

It is an adaptable plant but thrives in well-drained soils enriched with a little organic matter. Full sun is best. Pruning after flowering will maintain a compact well-shaped bush. Propagate from seed or soft-tip cuttings.

Spartium junceum

The shiny green leafless twigs give the Spanish broom a rush-like appearance (*junceum* is from the Latin for 'rush'). It bears masses of large, golden yellow, fragrant pea-flowers carried in loose spikes 10–12 in (25–30 cm) long at the shoot tips. It flowers profusely through spring into early summer. The bluish green, lance shaped leaves are only seen on the new growth, falling by mid-summer. It makes a bushy shrub 6–10 ft (2–3 m) tall and on older specimens the stems arch downwards. *Zones 6–11.*

SPIRAEA
Rosaceae

This genus consists of deciduous shrubs which form clumps of wiry stems that shoot up from the base. The plants are densely covered with narrow, toothed leaves. They are in the rose family, and under a magnifying glass the flowers do resemble tiny roses, but they are so small that the individual flower is lost among the mass of blooms carried on each flower cluster.

Cultivation

Spiraeas are adaptable plants that thrive under most conditions in temperate climates. They like moist, well-drained soil and a position sheltered from the hottest sun. Propagate from cuttings.

Spiraea japonica

This species from Japan and China grows to 5 ft (1.5 m), with many upright stems forming a dense clump. It blooms in summer with clusters of tiny pink flowers. It has many varieties and cultivars, like var. *fortunei*, up to 6 ft (2 m) with large flower heads; 'Little Princess', to 3 ft (1 m); and 'Anthony Waterer', with pale and deep pink flowers. *Zones 4–10.*

Spiraea nipponica

From Japan, this species reaches 6 ft (2 m) high and wide. Its rounded leaves

Spartium junceum

Spiraea japonica 'Anthony Waterer'

Stachyurus praecox

Spiraea nipponica

are finely serrated and its early summer flowers are pure white, in neat, round heads crowded along the branches. 'Snowmound' is a cultivar with white flowers. *Zones 5–10.*

STACHYURUS
Stachyuraceae

This genus includes some 10 species of deciduous shrubs and trees from the Himalayas and East Asia. It blooms in late winter or early spring before or just as the leaves are developing. It produces small cream to pale yellow flowers in drooping racemes at every leaf bud and has broadly lance-shaped leaves.

Cultivation

They prefer a humus-rich, well-drained, acidic soil in sun or light shade. Propagate from seed or semi-ripe cuttings.

Stachyurus praecox

A 7 ft (2 m) high and wide shrub indigenous to Japan, this species has gracefully drooping, 3 in (8 cm) long racemes of buds which appear on the bare branches in autumn, opening as small pale yellow flowers in late winter or early spring. The leaves that follow

are carried on somewhat tiered, reddish brown stems. *Zones 5–10.*

STEWARTIA
Theaceae

This East Asian and North American genus — sometimes spelled *Stuartia* — of deciduous small trees is closely allied to the camellias. The flowers are usually white with prominent golden anthers and resemble single camellia blooms. The leaves are elliptical and often develop bright orange and red autumn tones.

Cultivation

Stewartias grow best in moist, humus-rich, well-drained, slightly acidic soil in sun or partial shade. Propagate from seed or from semi-ripe cuttings.

Stewartia pseudocamellia
False camellia

This species can grow to 30 ft (10 m) high in the wild, but is more commonly about 18 ft (6 m) in cultivation. It blooms from late spring to early summer and the white flowers are followed by small, spherical, nut-like seed capsules that are a prominent feature from mid-summer. It also has attractive peeling bark and yellow, orange and red autumn foliage. *Zones 5–8.*

STREPTOSOLEN
Solanaceae
Marmalade bush

This genus consists of only one shrub species, occurring in parts of the northern Andes. The marmalade bush is grown outdoors in warm to hot climates, and as a greenhouse plant in cooler areas.

Cultivation

It does best in full sun with shelter from strong winds. A light well drained soil is ideal, preferably enriched with organic matter. Prune lightly after flowering. Propagate from soft-tip or semi-hardwood cuttings.

Streptosolen jamesonii

This handsome fast-growing evergreen shrub reaches 6 ft (2 m) high, with long flexible stems that arch slightly under the weight of the flower heads. Flowers are typically bright orange, but there is a yellow-flowered form. Flowering peaks in spring to summer but continues for much of the year. Individual flowers are tubular on a thin stalk and are strangely twisted. They form large dense clusters at the branch tips. Both foliage and flowers bear fine hairs. *Zones 9–11.*

STYRAX
Styracaceae
Snowbell

These small deciduous and evergreen trees occur naturally over a wide area of the Americas and eastern Asia, with one species native to Europe. Several cool-temperate deciduous species are cultivated for their neat growth habit and attractive spring display of slightly drooping sprays of small, bell-shaped, white flowers.

Stewartia pseudocamellia

Streptosolen jamesonii

Cultivation

They prefer cool, moist, well-drained soil and cool, moist summer climates. Propagate from stratified seed, or from hardwood or semi-ripe cuttings.

Styrax japonica
Japanese snowbell, Japanese snowdrop tree

This species is a native of Japan, Korea and China. It grows to around 25 ft (8 m) high and flowers from mid-spring. Its branches, which are clothed with rather narrow, deep green, shiny leaves, tend to be held horizontally which creates a somewhat tiered effect. It does best shaded from the hottest sun. *Zones 6–9.*

Styrax japonica

SYMPHORICARPOS
Caprifoliaceae

This genus is made up of 15 deciduous shrubs from North America, and one rare and obscure species from China. They have elliptical to nearly round leaves and very small, bell-shaped, pink or white flowers in spring. They are primarily grown for their large crops of distinctive berries that stand out clearly in winter when the branches are bare.

Cultivation

They like any moist, well-drained soil in sun or shade. Propagate from open-ground winter hardwood cuttings. Being resistant to shade, poor soil and pollution, they suit city gardens.

Symphoricarpos orbiculatus

Symphoricarpos orbiculatus
Indian currant

This tough, adaptable shrub from the USA and Mexico grows to about 6 ft (2 m) high and 10 ft (3 m) wide. It is very dense and twiggy and has oval leaves. The fruit is small, under ¼ in (10 mm) in diameter, but abundant and a conspicuous bright pink. The berries last long after the leaves have fallen. A hot summer will yield a heavier crop of berries. *Zones 2–9.*

SYRINGA
Oleaceae
Lilac

Lilacs have upright to arching panicles of small, highly fragrant spring flowers, which are massed in loose heads. They appear from mid-spring and range in color from white and pale yellow to all shades of pink, mauve and purple. The genus contains about 20 species, all deciduous shrubs and trees from Europe and northeastern Asia. Most reach about 8 ft (2.5 m) high and 6 ft (2 m) wide.

Cultivation

Lilacs prefer moist, humus-rich, well-drained soil in sun or light shade. They do best where winters are cold. Species may be raised from seed or cuttings. Established plants produce suckers that can be used for propagation.

Syringa × hyacinthiflora

This is a French hybrid between *S. oblata* and *S. vulgaris*. There are several cultivars and they closely resemble the common *S. vulgaris* cultivars in appearance but are generally not as fragrant. 'Blue Hyacinth' has rounded lavender-blue flower heads; 'Buffon' is pale lavender-pink; 'Clarke's Giant' is mauve to lavender-blue; and 'Esther Staley' is bright deep pink. *Zones 4–9.*

Syringa reticulata

Syringa reticulata

This Japanese lilac has comparatively small flowers but they produce a wonderful spring display of creamy white clusters at the ends of the branches. Sweetly fragrant, they stand out boldly against the dark green foliage, and also make excellent cut flowers. *S. reticulata* grows to 27 ft (9 m) and forms a squat, wide-crowned tree. Remove spent flowers regularly to prolong the display. *Zones 3–9.*

Syringa vulgaris

This is the species from which most of the garden cultivars were derived. It grows to around 12 ft (4 m) high, with pointed, oval or heart-shaped leaves and panicles of fragrant white to pale mauve flowers. The cultivar 'Katherine Havemeyer' has lavender-blue, very fragrant, semi-double flowers; 'Mme. F. Morel' has purplish pink flowers; 'Primrose' has pale yellow flowers and a compact growth-habit. *Zones 3–9.*

SYZYGIUM
Myrtaceae
Lillypilly, brush cherry

These evergreen trees and shrubs are from tropical and subtropical rainforests of Southeast Asia, Australia and Africa. The edible berries—white, pink, magenta or purple—ripen in late summer to autumn. Plants have a lush dense canopy of shiny green leaves; new growth in spring is often a contrasting red, pink or copper. Spring and summer flowers are mostly small with protruding white to mauve or crimson stamens giving a fluffy appearance.

Cultivation

They prefer full sun to semi-shade, and deep, moist, well-drained soil enriched with organic matter. Propagate from fresh seed or semi-hardwood cuttings.

Syzygium paniculatum
Magenta brush cherry
syn. Eugenia paniculata

This small to medium tree can grow up to 50–60 ft (15–18 m) tall with an irregular rounded and densely foliaged crown. Leaves are shiny green, variable in shape from oval to rounded, coppery brown when young, and held on reddish stalks. Fragrant flowers are creamy white, and are held in dense clusters. The large, decorative fruit is rose-purple, oval to rounded and appears in late summer and autumn. This lilly-pilly suits coastal gardens. *Zones 9–11.*

Syringa vulgaris 'Katherine Havemeyer'

Syzygium paniculatum

T

Tabebuia impetiginosa

Tabebuia chrysotricha

TABEBUIA
Trumpet tree

The 100 or so shrubs and trees of this genus occur naturally in tropical America and the West Indies, where some yield highly durable timber. Many are briefly deciduous during the tropical dry season; some are almost evergreen. The trumpet- to bell-shaped flowers, in shades of white, yellow, pink, red or purple, are clustered at the branch tips, usually when the leaves have fallen in late winter to spring. Fruits are bean-like capsules.

Cultivation

They need a hot to warm frost-free climate and deep, humus-rich soil with good drainage. A sunny position is best, with some shelter from wind. Propagate from seed or by layering in spring or from cuttings in summer; selected types are grafted.

Tabebuia chrysotricha
Golden trumpet tree

Native to Central America, this decidu-ous tree reaches 30–50 ft (9–15 m) high with a spread of 25 ft (8 m). It develops an open canopy and brownish hairs cover the branches, flower stalks, leaf stalks, lower leaf surfaces and fruit. The dark green leaves, mostly with 3 to 5 oval to oblong leaflets, are held on long stalks. Clusters of flowers almost smother the crown in late winter or early spring; each is trumpet-shaped, with bright yellow ruffled petals. Brownish lines and golden-brown hairs highlight the throat. *Zones 9–11.*

Tabebuia impetiginosa
syns *Tabebuia ipe, T. avellanedae, T. heptaphylla*
Pink trumpet tree, Argentine flame tree, pau d'arco

More upright than *T. chrysotricha*, this deciduous tree reaches 50 ft (15 m) or more high. Its rounded crown is formed by a network of branching stems sparsely clad with slender palmate leaves with 5 oval leaflets; these are shed briefly in spring. Clusters of rose-pink or purple-pink trumpet-shaped flowers are borne on the bare branches in spring. 'Pink Cloud' is a popular cultivar. *Zones 9–11.*

TAMARIX
Tamaricaceae

These tough shrubs and small trees occur naturally in southern Europe,

Taxodium distichum

Tamarix ramosissima

North Africa and temperate Asia in dry riverbeds, often in saline soils. Most are deciduous; a few are evergreen. They develop a short trunk and a graceful dense canopy of drooping branchlets. Leaves are minute and scale-like and have salt-secreting glands. Flowers are small and white or pink, in slender spikes.

Cultivation
They adapt to a wide range of soils, climates and conditions. They do best in deep sandy soil with good drainage. Propagate from seeds, or from semi-hardwood or hardwood cuttings.

Tamarix ramosissima
Late tamarisk
This open deciduous elegant shrub grows to about 15 ft (5 m) and carries tiny blue-green leaves on dark red-brown stems. Panicles up to 5 in (12 cm) long of profuse small pink flowers are borne in upright plumes during the late summer months. This is perhaps the most widely grown species. 'Pink Cascade' is a vigorous cultivar which bears rich rose-pink flowers. *Zones 2–10.*

TAXODIUM
Taxodiaceae
This genus of deciduous or evergreen conifers consists of 3 species. The genus name comes from the similarity of their foliage to that of the yews *(Taxus).*

Taxodium species shed their leaves in autumn, still attached to the branchlets. These are feather-like and turn coppery brown. Male (pollen) cones are tiny; female ones are globular.

Cultivation
These trees thrive in damp boggy soils. Propagate from seed or cuttings.

Taxodium distichum
Bald cypress, swamp cypress
This fast-growing tree has deeply fissured, fibrous, reddish brown bark and knobbly 'knees'. These are vertical woody growths sent up from the roots and are thought to allow the tree to breathe with its root system submerged. The crown spreads to 20 ft (7 m) or more, and bears tiny, slender, pointed leaves arranged in 2 rows. The wood is brittle, and trees are easily damaged by storms and strong winds. Its resinous, round, purple cones disintegrate when they fall to the ground. *Zones 4–10.*

Taxodium mucronatum
Mexican bald cypress, Montezuma cypress
Native to Mexico and southwest Texas, this conifer is only deciduous in cooler climates. It reaches a height of 100 ft (30 m) or more, with a massive trunk and widely spreading branches. The leaves are identical to those of *Taxodium distichum*; the cones are inconspicuous. There are some huge

Taxus baccata

Taxus cuspidata

Taxodium mucronatum

specimens in the Mexican highlands, notably the great tree of Tulé, which has a trunk more than 30 ft (9 m) in diameter. Although its age has been estimated at thousands of years, observations of its growth rate under good conditions suggest that it is no more than 1,000 years old. *Zones 9–10*.

TAXUS
Taxaceae

These slow growing, long lived, evergreen conifers are hardy and tolerate a wide range of conditions but do not enjoy warm winters or hot dry summers. As the trees age — over the centuries — they develop a domed crown and a

massive, thick trunk clothed in reddish brown or grayish brown bark which peels off in thin scales. Male and female flowers appear on separate trees in spring. The single, small brown seed is enclosed in a vivid red fleshy cup which is the only part of the plant that is not poisonous to humans and animals.

Cultivation
Propagate from seed or cuttings or by grafting.

Taxus baccata
English yew, common yew
This dense, dark tree grows best in a moist alkaline soil in an open position. The dark-colored trunk is erect and very thick in maturity; leaves are needle-like and dark green. The male tree bears scaly cones and the female cup-shaped, scarlet berries. Old trees may reach 45 ft (14 m) but cultivars rarely achieve this height. *Zones 5–10*.

Taxus cuspidata
Japanese yew
This conifer is popular in cold climates and tolerates dry, shady conditions. It forms a large shrub or small tree to 15 ft (4.5 m) or more in height and spread,

with an erect trunk covered in grayish brown bark. The dense foliage is composed of small, narrow leaves arranged in V-shaped rows on the stem. The leaves are dull green above and lighter below. Tolerant of pollution, it is one of the few conifers that performs well in difficult urban environments. *Zones 4–9.*

Taxus × media

These hybrids between the English and Japanese yews offer a range of sizes and shapes for the garden. 'Brownii', a male form, and 'Everlow' are low and rounded, eventually reaching 8 ft (2.4 m) tall and wide; they are easily kept smaller by pruning. 'Hatfield' is the broad, upright male form, while 'Hicksii' is narrow, upright and female; both are good for hedging. *Zones 4–9.*

TECOMARIA

Bignoniaceae

These upright to semi-climbing evergreen shrubs grow naturally in tropical and subtropical southern Africa. They bear trumpet-shaped flowers in shades of yellow, orange or scarlet, in clusters at the ends of shoots. Leaves are arranged opposite each other or in groups of 3, with an odd number of leaflets. The fruit is an oblong narrow capsule.

Cultivation

They like full sun; soil should be well drained with added organic matter. Propagate from seed or cuttings.

Tecomaria capensis
Cape honeysuckle

The Cape honeysuckle is a scrambling shrub with orange-red to scarlet curved trumpet-shaped flowers borne in short spikes from late summer to late autumn. Branches are slender and sprawling, forming roots where they touch the ground and able to climb to a height of 15 ft (5 m). The glossy green leaves are divided into 5 to 9 rounded to oval leaflets with a serrated edge. It can be grown as a hedge. *Zones 10–11.*

TERNSTROEMIA

Most of the 85 species of shrubs and small trees in this genus are native to tropical America, but one occurs in eastern Asia and two in tropical Africa. Their evergreen foliage resembles that of camellias, to which they are closely related. The small flowers are usually solitary, though sometimes appear in small clusters; they are followed by fleshy fruits.

Cultivation

Well-drained, slightly acidic soil suits them best, with plenty of moisture

Taxus × media 'Everlow'

Tecomaria capensis

during dry spells. They benefit from an annual dressing of organic mulch spread thickly over the roots. Young plants can be trained to form a dense hedge. Propagate from ripe seed or from cuttings in fall.

Ternstroemia gymnanthcra
syn. *Ternstroemia japonica*
Japanese ternstroemia
This attractive shrub or small tree is one of the few species in cultivation. Occurring naturally from Japan to southwestern China, it reaches a height of 15 ft (4.5 m) with a rounded crown about 8 ft (2.4 m) wide. The oval, glossy green, pointed leaves are thick and are arranged in spirals; young foliage is coppery red. Borne in late spring and early summer, the small white flowers hang in clusters of 3 and are delicately perfumed. These are followed by berries that ripen to scarlet. *Zones 7–10.*

TETRAPANAX
Araliaceae
Rice-paper plant
This evergreen, suckering shrub or small tree is grown for its large, fan-like leaves where an exotic, tropical effect is

Ternstroemia gymnanthera

required and space is available for its often rampant growth.

Cultivation
Propagate from seed or cuttings.

Tetrapanax papyrifera
This freely suckering shrub grows vigorously to 20 ft (7 m). The individual flowers are creamy white fluffy balls, held in large, loose, showy clusters. *Zones 8–11.*

THEVETIA
All 8 species of this genus of evergreen trees and shrubs have a poisonous milky sap; in fact, all parts of the plants are poisonous. Relatives of the oleander (*Nerium*), they are indigenous to tropical America. They feature clusters of showy, mostly yellow, funnel-shaped flowers at the shoot tips; flowering peaks in summer. The fruits are berry-like. The leaves are arranged spirally on the branchlets.

Cultivation
These frost-tender plants grow best in a sandy, well-drained soil enriched with organic matter. They need plenty of water while in flower. The ideal location provides shelter from wind, plus full sun to part-shade. Prune after flowering to maintain dense growth. Propagate from seed in spring or from cuttings in summer.

Tetrapanax papyrifera

Thevetia peruviana

Thuja occidentalis

Thuja plicata 'Zebrina'

Thevetia peruviana
syn. *Thevetia neriifolia*
Yellow oleander, lucky nut

This domed tree grows to 25 ft (8 m) tall. The long, shiny, rich green leaves are hard and strap-like to narrowly lance-shaped, with barely any stalk. The yellow to soft orange, slightly perfumed flowers, each 2 in (5 cm) across, are held on long stalks. They bloom on and off for most of the year in their native habitat; in cooler climates, they bloom in summer. The fruit are oddly shaped, fleshy drupes, rounded and with prominent ridges. *Zones 10–11.*

THUJA
Cupressaceae
Arbor-vitae

These evergreen conifers have erect, straight trunks covered in deeply fissured, fibrous bark, and are columnar to pyramidal. The aromatic foliage consists of sprays of scale-like leaves. The small, egg-shaped cones are covered with overlapping scales. Dwarf cultivars suit rock gardens or containers.

Cultivation

Propagate from seed or cuttings.

Thuja occidentalis

This tree reaches 50 ft (15 m). The dense foliage is composed of yellow-green glandular leaves with bluish undersides held on spreading branchlets. There are many cultivars ranging from dwarf shrubs to large trees. *Zones 3–8.*

Thuja plicata
Western red cedar

This fast-growing conifer reaches about 80 ft (25 m). It has long been harvested for its durable and versatile softwood timber. Of conical habit, it becomes columnar in maturity, with branches sweeping the ground. Compact 'Zebrina' has glossy bright green foliage striped with yellow. *Zones 5–8.*

THUJOPSIS
Mock thuja, hiba, false arbor-vitae

This genus from Japan contains only a single species, *Thujopsis dolabrata*. It resembles *Thuja*, but is distinguished by several important features, namely round, woody cones, winged seeds and larger leaves. It is the parent of several cultivars, which vary in habit and foliage color.

Cultivation

Tolerant of cold, it thrives in moist, well-drained, acidic or alkaline soil and an open, sunny position. Propagation is from seed, or cuttings for selected forms.

Thujopsis dolabrata

This evergreen conifer is variable in growth habit, from upright and pyramidal to spreading and bushy. It reaches a height of 30–50 ft (9–15 m) with a spread of 10–20 ft (3–6 m). Its foliage is composed of flattened, scale-like leaves which are dark green above with frosted white undersides. Its small cones are bluish gray, round and scaly. The dwarf

Tibouchina urvilleana

cultivar 'Nana' forms a spreading, bun shape 24 in (60 cm) high by 5 ft (1.5 m) wide. *Zones 5–10.*

TIBOUCHINA
Melastomataceae
Lasiandra, glory bush

There are over 300 species of these evergreen shrubs, small trees and climbers. Flowers are large and vivid, commonly purple, pink or white, with 5 satiny petals. They are borne either singly or in clusters at the shoot tips.

Cultivation

Propagate from tip cuttings.

Tibouchina urvilleana

syns *Lasiandra semidecandra*, *Tibouchina semidecandra*
Princess flower, glory bush

This slender-branched species develops a short trunk topped by a bushy rounded crown and reaches 15 ft (4.5 m)

Thujopsis dolabrata

Tilia cordata

Tilia americana

in height. The young stems are reddish and slightly hairy, turning brown later. The oval to slightly oblong leaves are 2–4 in (5–10 cm) long, shiny dark green above and slightly hairy below. The rich purple to violet, satiny flowers are borne singly or in small groups. The flower buds are large, reddish and hairy. *Zones 9–11*.

TILIA
Tiliaceae
Lime tree, linden
These deciduous trees have thick, buttressed trunks. The small, fragrant, cup-shaped cream flowers are borne in clusters. Both flowers and bracts are dried to make linden tea.

Cultivation
Propagate from seed, cuttings or layering.

Tilia americana
Basswood, American linden
This attractive, sturdy tree from eastern-central USA and Canada grows to 110 ft (36 m) tall. It has an erect trunk with smooth gray bark which becomes fissured with age. Its young branches are green and form a compact, narrow crown. The heart-shaped, dull green leaves are up to 6 in (15 cm) long and have toothed edges. Yellowish white fragrant flowers in pendent clusters appear in summer, followed by small, hairy fruit. 'Redmond', a selected form raised in Nebraska in about 1926, has a dense conical habit. *Zones 3–8*.

Tilia cordata
This species grows to 100 ft (30 m) with a dome-shaped crown. Its leathery round leaves are bright green on top with pale undersides. Its small flowers are pale yellow and sweetly scented and its fruit is gray. *Zones 3–9*.

Trachycarpus fortunei

Tristaniopsis laurina

Tsuga canadensis 'Pendula'

TRACHYCARPUS
Arecaceae

These ornamental palms tolerate cooler climates better than most palms. The fan-like, dark green leaves are divided into narrow, pointed blades and can be as much as 5 ft (1.5 m) across. Small yellowish flowers are followed by dark berries.

Cultivation
Propagate from seed.

Trachycarpus fortunei
This palm reaches 30 ft (10 m) tall. The leaves are dark green above, blue-green below; dead leaves persist as a 'skirt' on the tree. Dense, showy clusters of small yellow flowers precede the marble-sized, dark blue berries which have a coating of whitish wax. It is slow growing. *Zones 8–11.*

TRISTANIOPSIS
Myrtaceae

This genus of evergreen trees contains several species indigenous to high-rainfall coastal forests of eastern Australia.

Cultivation
Propagate from seed.

Tristaniopsis laurina
An evergreen conical tree reaching a height of 30–50 ft (10–15 m), the water gum is a good shade or specimen tree. Leaves are oblong to lance shaped, the upper surface dark green and the undersides paler. New leaves are pinkish. Clusters of small, deep yellow flowers appear in summer. *Zones 10–11.*

TSUGA
Pinaceae
Hemlock

These 10 or so species of evergreen conifers range from tall trees to small shrubs. Conical to pyramidal in growth-habit, the spreading branches droop gracefully. They do not enjoy urban environments or exposed positions. Male cones are small, female cones are scaly and contain winged seeds. The common name has no connection to the poisonous herb—the trees are not poisonous.

Cultivation
Propagate from seed or cuttings.

Tsuga canadensis
This tree reaches 80 ft (25 m) and forms a broad pyramidal crown with thin branches and pendulous tips. 'Pendula', a weeping conifer, forms a semi-prostrate mound, to 6 ft (2 m) high and wide. *Zones 3–9.*

U, V

UGNI
Myrtaceae

Members of this genus of evergreen shrubs from temperate regions of Central and South America have attractive, edible fruit. Most species form a clump of slender branches clothed in deep green, glossy leaves. They can be pruned in winter to keep the plant compact and bushy.

Cultivation

They need well-drained, moist, acid soil and prefer full sun. Propagate from seed or cuttings.

Ugni molinae
Chilean guava, Chilean cranberry

This species has interestingly shaped, fragrant, purplish red, berry-like fruit. These are edible, though tart, and are often made into jam. The small, bell-shaped flowers are pink or white, with prominent stamens, and are borne in leaf axils. Its dense growth, to about 15 ft (5 m), makes the Chilean guava suitable for hedges, and it tolerates light shade. *Zones 8–10.*

ULMUS
Ulmaceae

Elms are hardy, deciduous trees, recognized by a combination of leaf and fruit features. The leaves are usually very one-sided at the base, with many prominent, parallel, lateral veins, and the margins are regularly toothed; the small fruit are disc-like and dry with a membranous wing, and are carried in clusters near the branch tips usually in late spring or early summer. They have furrowed gray bark and high, domed crowns.

Cultivation

Elms require cool to cold winters. They prefer deep, moist soil and tolerate waterlogging for short periods. Propagate from semi-ripe cuttings, or by grafting the suckers. Many fine specimens have been destroyed by the fungus, Dutch elm disease.

Ulmus americana
American elm, white elm

The largest North American elm, this species occurs naturally over eastern and central USA, and southern Canada. It can reach a height of 120 ft (36 m) in the wild—about half that in cultivation—and has high-arching limbs. Mature trees develop a broad crown and may become strongly buttressed at the base; the ash-gray bark is deeply fissured. The leaves, 4–6 in (10–15 cm) long, have smooth upper sides with slightly downy undersides, and unforked lateral veins. 'Delaware' is broadly vase-shaped, fast

Ugni molinae

Ulmus americana

growing and claimed to be resistant to Dutch elm disease. 'Princeton' is also vase-shaped, and vigorous with some resistance to elm leaf beetle. *Zones 3–9.*

Ulmus parvifolia
Chinese elm, lacebark elm

Native to China and Japan, this elm grows to 60 ft (18 m) tall and has a spreading, sinuous habit and bark mottled with dark gray, reddish brown and cream. It is semi-evergreen in mild climates. The small, leathery, dark green leaves, smooth and shiny on top, have small, blunt teeth. The fruit mature in autumn, much later than those of most other elms. It is relatively resistant to Dutch elm disease. 'Frosty' is a shrubby, slow-growing form with small, neatly arranged leaves bearing white teeth. *Zones 4–9.*

VACCINIUM
Ericaceae
Blueberry, cranberry

Some species of these deciduous shrubs have edible berries, known according to the species as bilberry, blueberry, cranberry, huckleberry or whortleberry, which are red or blue-black and often covered with a bloom when ripe. They are grown commercially for fresh fruit, as well as for juicing and canning. Small bell-shaped flowers, pale pink, white, purple or red, appear in late spring or early summer.

Cultivation

They are generally cold tolerant and shade loving, and need acid, well-drained soil with plenty of humus and regular water. Propagate by division or from cuttings.

Vaccinium corymbosum
Highbush blueberry

Also known as the swamp blueberry because of its preference for boggy soils, this deciduous species is mainly grown for its edible blue-black berries. It also has fine scarlet autumn foliage. It forms a dense thicket with upright stems with a height and spread of 6 ft (2 m). 'Blue Ray' has delicious, sweet, juicy fruit. *Zones 3–9.*

Vaccinium ovatum
Evergreen huckleberry

Occurring naturally from Oregon through to southern California, this is a dense, compact shrub. Its dark green, glossy foliage is prized by florists as it lasts well in water; in fact, this demand has driven the wild plants very nearly to extinction. The plant forms a spreading clump 3 ft (1 m) high and 5 ft (1.5 m) wide and can reach 8–10 ft (2.4 –3 m) in

Ulmus parvifolia

Vaccinium corymbosum 'Blue Ray'

Viburnum × bodnantense

Vaccinium ovatum

Viburnum × burkwoodii

shady spots. The white or pink flowers appear in early summer. Its tangy, edible berries are red when young, maturing to blue-black. *Zones 7–10.*

VIBURNUM
Caprifoliaceae

This genus is made up of some 150 species of evergreen and deciduous cool-climate shrubs, primarily of Asian origin with a few species from North America,

Europe and northern Africa. Many of the cultivated species and forms have fragrant, showy flowers and may also produce colorful berries or bright autumn foliage. The evergreen species are often used for hedging.

Cultivation

They grow in any well-drained soil in sun or light shade. They can be trimmed after flowering, though this will prevent fruit forming. Propagate from cuttings.

Viburnum × bodnantense

A hybrid between *V. farreri* and *V. grandiflorum,* this 9 ft (3 m) high decidu-ous shrub has slightly glossy, deep green, oval leaves that are pale green on the undersides. Before they fall in autumn they develop intense orange, red and purple tones. The flowers are bright pink in the bud, open pale pink and fade to white. They are heavily scented. *Zones 7–10.*

Viburnum dentatum

Viburnum × *carlcephalum*

Viburnum × burkwoodii

A hybrid between *V. carlesii* and *V. utile,* this 10 ft (3 m) high semi-evergreen plant has glossy, deep green, pointed, oval leaves. They are pale sage green on the undersides and those that are to fall in autumn develop bright yellow and red tones. From early to late spring ball-shaped clusters of small starry, fragrant flowers open; they are pink in the bud, opening white. *Zones 5–10.*

Viburnum × carlcephalum
Fragrant viburnum

This is a deciduous, spring-flowering hybrid with large, rounded heads of fragrant, creamy white flowers that are pink when in bud. The dark green foliage often turns red in autumn. It has a rounded, bushy habit and grows to a height and spread of about 8 ft (2.4 m). *Zones 5–9.*

Viburnum carlesii
Korean viburnum

This densely foliaged deciduous shrub grows to about 5 ft (1.5 m) high with a similar spread. The Korean viburnum has pointed oval leaves with finely serrated edges. The starry flowers open from mid- to late spring; they are pale pink aging to white and sweetly scented. The flowers are carried in rounded clusters. The fruit ripens to black and is sporadic in cultivation. Several cultivars are available, including 'Aurora', with deep pink buds. *Zones 5–8.*

Viburnum dentatum
Southern arrow-wood

The Native Americans used the stems of this shrub from eastern USA for the shafts of arrows. Today, its uses are purely decorative, as it makes an attractive deciduous shrub which reaches 8–15 ft (2.4–4.5 m) high and has a spread of about 6 ft (1.8 m). Its rounded, prominently veined, toothed leaves are occasionally tufted beneath. Glossy green when young, they turn rich red in autumn. Flowering in early summer, its white blooms are borne in clusters on the ends of long stalks. The egg-shaped fruit are bluish black. *Zones 2–9.*

Viburnum opulus
Guelder rose, snowball tree

This deciduous shrub produces clusters of snowy white, lacy flowers in summer. It grows to 12 ft (4 m), and has gray bark and a spreading habit with long, pale green shoots. Its paired leaves are lobed and turn deep crimson in autumn. The fruit is shiny, translucent and orange-red. 'Compactum' is a dense, compact shrub bearing large quantities of flowers and fruit. 'Xanthocarpum' has clear yellow fruit. *Zones 2–10.*

Viburnum plicatum

This deciduous shrub grows to about 15 ft (5 m) high and wide. It has hazel-like, mid-green, pointed, oval leaves with serrated edges and a somewhat tiered growth-habit, a feature emphasized in the cultivar 'Mariesii'. Large creamy white flower clusters with a mass of tiny fertile flowers in the center, surrounded by large sterile flowers open in spring, followed by small red berries that ripen to black. 'Pink Beauty' has a pale pink tinge to the flowers. *Zones 5–9.*

Viburnum prunifolium
Black-haw

This shrub from eastern USA features deciduous leaves that turn orange and red in autumn; broadly oval to round with a finely toothed edge, each is 3 in (8 cm) long on a reddish stalk. It grows to about 15 ft (4.5 m) tall. In spring the small white flowers are borne in flat-topped clusters 4 in (10 cm) across. The

Viburnum carlesii 'Aurora'

Viburnum plicatum 'Pink Beauty'

Viburnum opulus 'Compactum'

Viburnum prunifolium

berries are bluish black in flattened clusters, each one measuring just over ½ in (12 mm) long. The root of this plant is used for medicinal purposes. *Zones 3–9.*

Viburnum tinus
Laurustinus

This very densely foliaged evergreen shrub may eventually grow to 15 ft (5 m) high and 18 ft (6 m) wide, though it is usually kept smaller by trimming. It is an excellent hedging plant and tolerates heavy shade. The dark green, pointed, elliptical leaves develop purplish tones in cold weather. Cream and yellow variegated foliage forms are available. Clusters of white flowers open from pink buds from late winter, followed by blue-black berries. *Zones 7–10.*

VITEX
Verbenaceae

This genus is made up of about 100 mainly tropical and subtropical trees and shrubs; some evergreen, some deciduous. Highlights are sprays of tubular flowers in shades of white, yellow, red, blue or purple, and fleshy drupes. In some species both the leaves and the flowers are aromatic.

Cultivation

They do best in fertile soil with good drainage, and a sheltered spot in full sun. Propagate from seed or cuttings.

Vitex agnus-castus
Chaste tree

This moderately frost-hardy shrub, indigenous to southern Europe and western Asia, has aromatic leaves; these are 6–8 in (15–20 cm) long with 5 to 7 lance-shaped to rounded leaflets, deep green on top and felty gray underneath. This deciduous, rounded shrub or small tree reaches 10–20 ft (3–6 m) tall with an upright, branching, woody stem.

From early summer to autumn it bears dense, erect sprays of faintly perfumed, lavender flowers up to 12 in (30 cm) long. Small purple fruit follow. White-flowered and variegated-leaf forms are also available. *Vitex agnus-castus* var. *latifolia* has shorter, broader leaves. *Zones 7–9.*

Vitex lucens
Puriri

This fine evergreen tree from New Zealand reaches a height of 30–50 ft (10–15 m) and features a rounded crown and a smooth pale trunk. Sprays of bright red or pink flowers are a winter bonus. Large, bright red drupes mature in spring. The leaves consist of 3 to 5

Viburnum tinus

Vitex agnus-castus

Vitex negundo

large, oval to round leaflets, smooth and shiny rich green, with a wavy edge. *Zones 9–11.*

Vitex negundo

This useful shrub or small tree, native to warm-climate areas from southern and eastern Asia, is grown for its pleasantly aromatic foliage and fragrant flowers. It grows to 15 ft (4.5 m) tall and produces long leaves composed of deeply cut leaflets which are dark green above with pale, furry undersides. The fragrant flowers are mauve and appear in loose sprays in spring. *Zones 6–11.*

Vitex lucens

W, X, Y, Z

WEIGELA
Caprifoliaceae

This genus includes about 10 species of deciduous shrubs from Japan, Korea and northeastern China. Most grow to 6–10 ft (2–3 m) high and wide, and have pointed, elliptical, deep green leaves. The foliage often develops orange, red and purple tones in autumn before falling. In spring, weigelas bear masses of white, pink or crimson, sometimes yellowish, bell- or trumpet-shaped flowers.

Cultivation
Most species do best in full sun or light shade in moist, well-drained soil. Propagate from summer cuttings.

Weigela florida
This arching deciduous shrub grows up to 10 ft (3 m) or so. It has a lavish spring display of flowers, white, pink or crimson according to cultivar (the wild plant is usually rose-pink). 'Variegata' has bright green leaves edged with cream and in spring bears masses of bright pink, trumpet-shaped flowers. *Zones 4–10.*

Weigela florida 'Variegata'

Westringia fruticosa

WESTRINGIA
Lamiaceae

These Australian evergreen shrubs have square woody stems which are clothed in small stiff leaves arranged in whorls of 3 or 4. The tubular flowers consist of 2 lips, the upper one with 2 lobes, the lower with 3. They appear for many months in the leaf axils, flowering peaking in spring.

Cultivation
Westringias thrive in mild-winter climates. Many grow naturally near the sea and relish these conditions. They prefer an open sunny spot and adapt to most well-drained soils. Propagate from soft-tip or semi-hardwood cuttings.

Westringia fruticosa
Coast rosemary, Australian rosemary
This species makes a compact rounded shrub 6 ft (2 m) high and about as wide, but can be kept more compact. Slender spreading branches bear narrow leaves arranged in fours; they are gray-green on top, white and felty underneath. Small flowers, white with purple blotches in the throat, are present much of the year. It can be grown as a clipped or informal hedge. *Zones 9–11.*

XANTHOCERAS
Yellow horn

Native to China, this genus consists of only one species. Although related to *Koelreuteria*, it is very different in general appearance. Except for its vulnerability to occasional injury by late spring frosts, this deciduous shrub or small tree is easily grown. The fragrant, erect flower spikes recall those of the horse chestnut.

Cultivation

While it tolerates low winter temperatures, it should be protected from late frosts and needs long, hot summers to flower well. It prefers well-drained, good loamy soil and tolerates mild alkalinity. It requires plenty of sunshine but does well in cooler areas if sited in a warm, sheltered position. Propagate from stratified seed in spring or root cuttings or suckers in late winter. It is susceptible to coral spot fungus.

Xanthoceras sorbifolium

This deciduous upright shrub or small tree to about 20 ft (6 m) is native to China. The bright green leaves are composed of many sharply toothed leaflets. The white flowers are borne in erect sprays from the leaf axils in late spring and summer; each flower has a

Xanthoceras sorbifolium

carmine red blotch at the base of the petals. The large fruiting capsules are pear-shaped and contain small seeds like chestnuts. It has thick, fleshy yellow roots. *Zones 4–10.*

YUCCA
Agavaceae

These unusual evergreen plants are usually slow growing, forming rosettes of stiff, sword-like leaves usually tipped with a formidable spine; as the plant matures some species develop an upright woody trunk, often branched. Yuccas bear showy tall panicles of drooping, white or off-white, bell- to cup-shaped flowers. The fruit can be fleshy or a dry capsule, but is rarely seen away from the plants' native lands as the flowers must be pollinated by the yucca moth.

Cultivation

Yuccas do best in areas of low humidity; they prefer full sun and sandy soil with good drainage. Propagate from seed (if available), cuttings or suckers.

Yucca baccata
Blue yucca, banana yucca, datil yucca

Yucca baccata comes from southwestern USA and northern Mexico and grows to

Yucca baccata

5 ft (1.5 m) in height. Its twisted leaves are flexible near the base and are dark green tinged with yellow or blue. The pendent flowers are bell-shaped, white or cream and often tinged with purple. *Zones 9–11.*

Yucca elephantipes

This yucca grows naturally in Mexico. There it develops a rough thick trunk that often branches and reaches a height of 30 ft (10 m), but under cultivation it grows slowly and is usually smaller. Leaves are 4 ft (1.2 m) long, shiny dark green with rough serrated edges. They are held in rosettes at the tips of the branches and droop downwards. White to off-white bell-shaped flowers are clustered along spikes through summer. *Zones 10–11.*

Yucca elephantipes

Yucca filamentosa
Adam's needle

The long green leaves, edged with white threads, on this evergreen plant form a basal rosette. The flowers that bloom in terminal spikes from the middle to the end of summer are white and bell-shaped. It grows to about 6 ft (2 m) high. It is fully hardy. *Zones 4–10.*

Yucca gloriosa
Spanish dagger, mound lily

The stout erect stem on this evergreen plant has a tufted crown of stiff, spear-

Yucca gloriosa

Yucca filamentosa

like leaves, which start out with a grayish cast, but as they mature, turn a deeper green. White, bell-shaped flowers appear in very long terminal spikes in summer. It reaches a height and spread of about 3 ft (1 m). *Zones 7–10.*

Yucca recurvifolia
syn. *Yucca pendula*
Weeping yucca
This striking plant from southeastern USA reaches 6–10 ft (1.8–3 m) in height, with several short trunks and long, dark blue-green leaves that often bend and droop at the tips. The 3 ft (1 m) tall flower spike bears creamy white blooms in summer. *Zones 8–11.*

ZELKOVA
Ulmaceae
Occurring from Asia Minor across cool-climate areas of western Asia, these fine

Yucca recurvifolia

deciduous trees are important timber trees in China and Japan. The leaves resemble but are smaller than the English or American elms. Though related to the elms, they are not plagued by the same diseases and are becoming popular as elm substitutes.

Cultivation
They need well-drained soil and plenty of water in summer. Propagate from seed or cuttings, or by grafting.

Zelkova serrata
Japanese elm
This ornamental tree grows to 80 ft (25 m) or more with a wide-spreading crown. It has smooth bark dappled gray and brown and the new shoots are tinged purple. The pointed, oblong, sharply serrated leaves are light green and slightly hairy above, with shiny under-

sides. Foliage turns golden yellow to rusty brown in autumn. *Zones 4–10*.

ZIZIPHUS

This genus of about 80 or so species of deciduous or evergreen trees and shrubs occurs naturally in warm- to hot-climate areas of both the northern and southern hemispheres. Some have spiny branches. Their leaves are usually marked with 3 veins and there are spines at the base of each leaf stalk. The insignificant flowers are small, greenish, whitish or yellow, arranged in clusters in the leaf axils.

Cultivation

Frost tender, grow them in open, loamy, well-drained soil in full sun, and water well. Tip prune to maintain compact growth. Propagate from seed or root cuttings in late winter, or by grafting.

Ziziphus jujuba
Jujube, Chinese date

This deciduous tree, distributed from western Asia to China, grows to 40 ft (12 m) tall. The oval to lance-shaped leaves are 1–2 in (2.5–5 cm) long and green in color, with 2 spines at the base of the leaf stalk, one of which is usually bent backwards. Small greenish flowers are borne in spring. The reddish, oblong to rounded fruit ripen from autumn to winter on the bare branches. Apple-like in taste, the fruit may be stewed, dried or used in confections. *Zones 7–10*.

Ziziphus jujuba

Zelkova serrata

Reference
Table

The following table provides information about the shrubs and trees described in this book. It covers some of the various uses you can make of the shrubs and trees you choose. The table also provides information on how tall the plants may grow after 5 years and 20 years, so you can make informed decisions about where to place your shrubs and trees. However, variations in geographic locations and climate will mean differences in growth habits, especially size. Ask at your local garden center if you have any doubts about particular plants.

Reference Table

NAME	KIND	ZONE	HEIGHT AT 5 & 20 YEARS	DECIDUOUS/ EVERGREEN	USES
Abelia × *grandiflora*	shrub	6–10	6 ft 8 ft (2 m 2.5 m)	evergreen	shrub border, hedge, courtyards
Abies balsamea	tree	3–7	6 ft 25 ft (2 m 8 m)	evergreen	windbreaks, rock gardens, Christmas trees
Abies pinsapo	tree	5–9	8 ft 25 ft (2.5 m 8 m)	evergreen	lawn specimen, parks
Abutilon × *hybridum*	shrub	9–11	6 ft 8 ft (2 m 2.5 m)	evergreen	lawn specimen, parks
Acacia baileyana	tree	8–10	12 ft 20 ft (4 m 6 m)	evergreen	shrub border, streets, parks
Acalypha wilkesiana	shrub	10–11	4 ft 8 ft (1.2 m 2.5 m)	evergreen	shrub border, courtyards, plazas, indoor
Acer griseum	tree	5–8	8 ft 25 ft (2.5 m 8 m)	deciduous	lawn specimen, parks
Acer negundo	tree	3–10	8 ft 35 ft (2.5 m 8 m)	deciduous	lawn specimen, parks, streets
Acer palmatum	tree	5–10	6 ft 20 ft (2 m 6 m)	deciduous	lawn specimen, parks
Acer platanoides	tree	4–7	8 ft 40 ft (2.5 m 12 m)	deciduous	lawn specimen, parks, streets
Acer rubrum	tree	3–9	8 ft 30 ft (2.5 m 9 m)	deciduous	✓ shade tree, lawn specimen, parks
Acer saccharum	tree	4–9	40 ft 50 ft (12 m 15 m)	deciduous	timber, maple syrup, lawn specimen
Aesculus × *carnea*	tree	5–9	6 ft 30 ft (2 m 9 m)	deciduous	lawn specimen, parks, streets
Aesculus hippocastanum	tree	4–9	6 ft 25 ft (2 m 8 m)	deciduous	parks, avenues
Agave americana	shrub	9–11	4 ft 6 ft (1.2 m 2 m)	evergreen	large rock gardens, embankments
Agonis flexuosa	tree	9–10	8 ft 20 ft (2.5 m 6 m)	evergreen	parks, streets, coastal planting
Albizia julibrissin	tree	6–10	6 ft 20 ft (2 m 6 m)	deciduous	lawn specimen, shrub border, container
Alnus glutinosa	tree	4–9	8 ft 40 ft (2.5 m 12 m)	deciduous	boggy lawn, woodland garden, edge of stream or pond
Aloysia triphylla	shrub	8–11	4 ft 6 ft (1.2 m 2 m)	evergreen	shrub border, herb garden, espalier
Alyogyne huegeli	shrub	10–11	6 ft 8 ft (2 m 2.5 m)	evergreen	shrub border
Amelanchier arborea	tree	4–9	6 ft 25 ft (2 m 8 m)	deciduous	lawn specimen
Andromeda polifolia	shrub	2–9	2 ft 2 ft (0.6 m 0.6 m)	evergreen	shrub border, rock garden, woodland garden
Anisodontea × *hypomadarum*	shrub	9–11	3 ft 6 ft (1 m 2 m)	evergreen	lawn specimen, woodland garden
Aralia chinensis	tree	7–10	4 ft 15 ft (1.2 m 5 m)	deciduous	shrub border, lawn specimen
Araucaria araucana	tree	8–9	4 ft 20 ft (1.2 m 6 m)	evergreen	lawn specimen
Araucaria heterophylla	tree	10–11	5 ft 25 ft (1.5 m 8 m)	evergreen	lawn specimen, parks, coastal planting, indoor
Arbutus 'Marina'	tree	9–10	6 ft 20 ft (2 m 6 m)	evergreen	lawn specimen, parks
Arbutus menziesii	tree	7–9	8 ft 20 ft (2.5 m 6 m)	evergreen	lawn specimen, parks, streets
Arbutus unedo	tree	7–10	8 ft 20 ft (2.5 m 6 m)	evergreen	parks, informal hedges
Archontophoenix alexandrae	palm	10–11	6 ft 25 ft (2 m 8 m)	evergreen	courtyards, swimming pools, plazas, container
Archontophoenix cunninghamiana	palm	9–11	4 ft 20 ft (1.2 m 6 m)	evergreen	lawn grouping, courtyard, swimming pools, plazas, container
Arctostaphylos 'Emerald Carpet'	shrub	8–10	12 in 12 in (0.3 m 0.3 m)	evergreen	ground cover, container
Arctostaphylos manzanita	shrub	7–10	4 ft 8 ft (1.2 m 2.5 m)	evergreen	lawn specimen, shrub border, coastal planting

NAME	KIND	ZONE	HEIGHT AT 5 & 20 YEARS	DECIDUOUS/ EVERGREEN	USES
Arctostaphylos uva-ursi	shrub	2–9	1 ft 2 ft (0.3 m 0.6 m)	evergreen	ground cover, rock gardens
Ardisia crenata	shrub	8–11	3 ft 6 ft (1 m 2 m)	evergreen	shrub border, courtyards, container
Aucuba japonica	shrub	7–10	4 ft 8 ft (1.2 m 2.5 m)	evergreen	shrub border, woodland garden, container
Azara microphylla	tree	7–9	6 ft 20 ft (2 m 6 m)	evergreen	shrub border, screen, hedge, woodland garden
Bambusa multiplex	shrub	9–11	10 ft 30 ft (3 m 9 m)	evergreen	informal hedge, parks
Bauera sessiliflora	shrub	9–10	3 ft 6 ft (1m 2m)	evergreen	woodland garden, courtyard
Bauhinia × blakeana	tree	10–11	8 ft 20 ft (2.5 m 6 m)	evergreen	lawn specimen, cut flowers
Bauhinia variegata	tree	9–11	8 ft 20 ft (2.5 m 6 m)	deciduous	shrub border, lawn specimen, parks
Beaucarnea recurvata	tree	9–11	3 ft 12 ft (1 m 4 m)	evergreen	courtyard, plaza, swimming pool, container
Berberis darwinii	shrub	7–10	4 ft 6 ft (1.2 m 2 m)	evergreen	shrub border, informal hedge, courtyard
Berberis thunbergii	shrub	4 9	3 ft 5 ft (1 m 1.5 m)	deciduous	✓ formal hedge, courtyard, rock garden, shrub border
Berberis wilsoniae	shrub	5–10	3 ft 5 ft (1 m 1.5 m)	deciduous	informal hedge, shrub border, ground cover
Betula papyrifera	tree	2–7	10 ft 40 ft (3 m 12 m)	deciduous	lawn specimen, parks, streets
Betula pendula	tree	2–9	10 ft 40 ft (3 m 12 m)	deciduous	lawn specimen, parks
Betula utilis	tree	7–9	12 ft 50 ft (4 m 15 m)	deciduous	lawn specimen, parks, streets
Boronia heterophylla	shrub	9–10	4 ft - (1.2 m -)	evergreen	rock garden, courtyard, cut flowers
Boronia megastigma	shrub	9–10	5 ft - (1.5 m -)	evergreen	woodland garden, courtyard, cut flowers
Bouvardia longiflora	shrub	10–11	3 ft - (1 m -)	evergreen	courtyard, balcony, indoor, cut flowers
Brachychiton acerifolius	tree	9–11	6 ft 25 ft (2 m 8 m)	deciduous	lawn specimen, parks
Brachychiton populneus	tree	8–11	6 ft 20 ft (2 m 6 m)	evergreen	streets, parks, shade
Brahea armata	palm	9–11	3 ft 10 ft (1 m 3 m)	evergreen	lawn specimen, plaza
Brugmansia × candida	tree	10–11	6 ft 15 ft (2 m 5 m)	evergreen	courtyard, shrub border, conservatory
Brugmansia suaveolens	shrub	10–11	6 ft 15 ft (2 m 5 m)	evergreen	courtyard, shrub border, conservatory
Brunfelsia pauciflora	shrub	10–11	3 ft 5 ft (1 m 1.5 m)	evergreen	shrub border, courtyard, woodland garden
Buddleia alternifolia	shrub	5–9	6 ft 12 ft (2 m 4 m)	deciduous	lawn specimen, shrub border
Buddleia davidii	shrub	5–10	8 ft 15 ft (2.5 m 5 m)	deciduous	shrub border
Buddleia globosa	shrub	7–10	8 ft 15 ft (2.5 m 5 m)	evergreen	lawn specimen, shrub border
Butia capitata	palm	8–11	4 ft 12 ft (1.2 m 4 m)	evergreen	park, lawn specimen, courtyard, plaza
Buxus microphylla	shrub	6–10	3 ft 5 ft (1 m 1.5 m)	evergreen	✓ formal hedge, topiary
Buxus sempervirens	shrub	5–10	3 ft 15 ft (1 m 5 m)	evergreen	✓ formal hedge, topiary, formal bed edging
Caesalpinia gilliesii	shrub	9–11	6 ft 10 ft (2 m 3 m)	deciduous	shrub border, courtyard
Caesalpinia pulcherrima	shrub	10–11	6 ft 15 ft (2 m 5 m)	evergreen	shrub border, plaza
Calceolaria integrifolia	shrub	8–10	2 ft 4 ft (0.6 m 1.2 m)	evergreen	shrub border, courtyard, container
Calliandra haematocepala	shrub	10–11	5 ft 12 ft (1.5 m 4 m)	evergreen	shrub border, informal hedge, swimming pool
Calliandra tweedii	shrub	9–11	4 ft 6 ft (1.2 m 2 m)	evergreen	shrub border, informal hedge
Callistemon citrinus	shrub	8–11	4 ft 15 ft (1.2 m 5 m)	evergreen	informal hedge, shrub border, courtyard

NAME	KIND	ZONE	HEIGHT AT 5 & 20 YEARS	DECIDUOUS/ EVERGREEN	USES
Callistemon salignus	tree	9–11	8 ft 25 ft (2.5 m 8 m)	evergreen	lawn specimen, streets, parks, hedge, boggy areas
Callistemon viminalis	tree	9–11	8 ft 20 ft (2.5 m 6 m)	evergreen	lawn specimen, streets, parks, shrub border
Calluna vulgaris	shrub	4–9	1 ft 2 ft (0.3 m 0.6 m)	evergreen	rock garden, embankment, heather garden
Calocedrus decurrens	tree	5–9	5 ft 25 ft (1.5 m 8 m)	evergreen	lawn specimen, informal hedge, parks
Calycanthus floridus	shrub	4–10	5 ft 8 ft (1.5 m 2.5 m)	deciduous	shrub border
Calycanthus occidentalis	shrub	6–10	5 ft 8 ft (1.5 m 2.5 m)	deciduous	shrub border
Camellia japonica	shrub	7–10	4 ft 15 ft (1.2 m 5 m)	evergreen	shrub border, woodland garden, cut flowers, container
Camellia reticulata	shrub	8–10	8 ft 15 ft (2.5 m 5 m)	evergreen	shrub border, woodland garden, cut flowers
Camellia sasanqua	shrub	9–11	8 ft 20 ft (2.5. m 6 m)	evergreen	informal or formal hedge, lawn specimen, street, espalier, container
Camellia sinensis	shrub	9–11	4 ft 8 ft (1.2 m 2.5 m)	evergreen	hedge, espalier, tea plantation
Camellia × williamsii	shrub	7–10	5 ft 15 ft (1.5 m 5 m)	evergreen	shrub border, woodland garden, cut flowers, container
Carissa macrocarpa	shrub	9–11	4 ft 10 ft (1.2 m 3 m)	evergreen	shrub border, courtyard, container, thorny hedge
Carpentaria californica	shrub	7–9	4 ft 8 ft (1.2 m 2.5 m)	evergreen	shrub border, courtyard
Carpinus betulus	tree	5–9	8 ft 40 ft (2.5 m 12 m)	deciduous	lawn specimen, hedge, shade
Carpinus caroliniana	tree	3–9	8 ft 40 ft (2.5 m 12 m)	deciduous	lawn specimen, shade
Carya illinoinensis	tree	5–11	10 ft 40 ft (3 m 12 m)	deciduous	orchards, parks, avenues
Caryopteris × clandonensis	shrub	5–9	2 ft 3 ft (0.6 m 1 m)	deciduous	shrub border, container
Caryopteris incana	shrub	7–10	3 ft 5 ft (1 m 1.5 m)	deciduous	shrub border, container
Castanea sativa	tree	5–9	8 ft 40 ft (2.5 m 12 m)	deciduous	orchard, timber, lawn specimen
Castanospermum australe	tree	10–11	8 ft 30 ft (2.5 m 9 m)	evergreen	lawn specimen, shade, parks, timber
Casuarina cunninghamiana	tree	8–11	15 ft 50 ft (5 m 15 m)	evergreen	✓ shade, screens, windbreaks, parks, streets, farms
Catalpa bignonioides	tree	5–10	8 ft 35 ft (2.5 m 10.5 m)	deciduous	lawn specimen, parks, streets
Catalpa speciosa	tree	4–10	8 ft 40 ft (2.5 m 12 m)	deciduous	parks, streets, timber, shade
Ceanothus griseus	shrub	8–10	5 ft 10 ft (1.5 m 3 m)	evergreen	coastal planting, rock garden, swimming pool
Ceanothus impressus	shrub	8–10	3 ft 6 ft (1 m 2 m)	evergreen	coastal planting, rock garden embankment, swimming pool
Cedrus atlantica	tree	6–9	6 ft 35 ft (2 m 10.5 m)	evergreen	lawn specimen, parks, avenues
Cedrus deodara	tree	7–10	8 ft 40 ft (2.5 m 12 m)	evergreen	lawn specimen, windbreaks, parks, streets
Cedrus libani	tree	5–8	6 ft 40 ft (2 m 12 m)	evergreen	lawn specimen, parks
Celtis australis	tree	8–10	10 ft 30 ft (3 m 9 m)	deciduous	parks, shade
Celtis occidentalis	tree	2–10	10 ft 30 ft (3 m 9 m)	deciduous	parks, shade
Cephalotaxus fortunei	tree	6–10	4 ft 15 ft (1.2 m 5 m)	evergreen	shrub border, courtyard
Cephalotaxus harringtonia	shrub	6–10	3 ft 10 ft (1 m 3 m)	evergreen	shrub border, lawn specimen, courtyard, container
Ceratonia siliqua	tree	9–11	6 ft 25 ft (2 m 8 m)	evergreen	lawn specimen, parks, streets, farms, fodder, chocolate substitute

NAME	KIND	ZONE	HEIGHT AT 5 & 20 YEARS	DECIDUOUS/ EVERGREEN	USES
Ceratostigma willottianum	shrub	6–10	2 ft 3 ft (0.6 m 1 m)	deciduous	rock garden, shrub border, herbaceous border, courtyard, swimming pool
Cercis canadensis	tree	4–9	4 ft 25 ft (1.2 m 8 m)	deciduous	lawn specimen, shrub border, courtyard
Cercis siliquastrum	tree	7–9	4 ft 15 ft (1.2 m 5 m)	deciduous	lawn specimen, parks, streets
Cestrum nocturnum	shrub	10–11	6 ft 10 ft (2 m 3 m)	evergreen	shrub border, courtyard
Chaenomeles speciosa	shrub	6–10	5 ft 10 ft (1.5 m 3 m)	deciduous	shrub border, courtyard, cut flowers, espalier
Chaenomeles × superba	shrub	6–10	3 ft 6 ft (1 m 2 m)	deciduous	cut flowers
Chamaecyparis lawsonia	tree	4–9	8 ft 40 ft (2.5 m 12 m)	evergreen	lawn specimen, parks, group plantings, windbreaks
Chamaecyparis obtusa	tree	5–9	6 ft 25 ft (2 m 8 m)	evergreen	lawn specimen, parks, courtyards, rock gardens (dwarf cultivars), timber
Chamaecyparis pisifera	tree	5–10	6 ft 25 ft (2 m 8 m)	evergreen	lawn specimen, courtyard, rock garden (dwarf cultivars)
Chamelaucium uncinatum	shrub	10–11	8 ft 10 ft (2.5 m 3 m)	evergreen	cut flowers, shrub border, courtyard
Chimonanthus praecox	shrub	6–10	4 ft 15 ft (1.2 m 5 m)	deciduous	shrub border, courtyard
Chionanthus retusus	tree	6–10	5 ft 20 ft (1.5 m 6 m)	deciduous	lawn specimen, parks
Choisya ternata	shrub	7–9	4 ft 8 ft (1.2 m 2.5 m)	evergreen	shrub border, hedge
Cinnamomum camphora	tree	9–11	8 ft 30 ft (2.5 m 9 m)	evergreen	parks, avenues, timber
Cistus ladanifer	shrub	8–10	4 ft 6 ft (1.2 m 2 m)	evergreen	shrub border, coastal planting, courtyard
Cistus × purpureus	shrub	7–9	2 ft 3 ft (0.6 m 1 m)	evergreen	shrub border, coastal planting, courtyard, rock garden
Clerodendrum trichotomum	shrub	7–10	6 ft 20 ft (2 m 6 m)	deciduous	shrub border, lawn specimen, courtyard
Coleonema pulchellum	shrub	9–10	3 ft 5 ft (1 m 1.5 m)	evergreen	shrub border, courtyard, rock garden, cut flowers
Convolvulus cneorum	shrub	8–10	1 ft 2 ft (0.3 m 0.6 m)	evergreen	rock garden, courtyard, herbaceous border, container
Coprosma repens	shrub	9–11	3 ft 8 ft (1 m 2.5 m)	evergreen	coastal planting, hedge, courtyard, container
Cordyline australis	tree	8–11	4 ft 15 ft (1.2 m 5 m)	evergreen	shrub border, courtyard, swimming pool, container, indoor
Cornus alba	shrub	3–8	4 ft 10 ft (1.2 m 3 m)	deciduous	shrub border, hedge, edge of pond or lake
Cornus florida	tree	5–9	6 ft 20 ft (2 m 6 m)	deciduous	lawn specimen, woodland garden
Cornus nuttallii	tree	7–9	5 ft 15 ft (1.5 m 5 m)	deciduous	lawn specimen, woodland garden
Correa pulchella	shrub	9–10	2 ft 3 ft (0.6 m 1 m)	evergreen	shrub border, courtyard, container
Corylus avellana	shrub	4–9	6 ft 15 ft (2 m 5 m)	deciduous	orchard, lawn specimen, hedge, cut stems ('Contorta')
Cotinus coggygria	shrub	5–9	5 ft 15 ft (1.5 m 5 m)	deciduous	lawn specimen, shrub border, hedge
Cotoneaster dammeri	shrub	5–8	1 ft 2 ft (0.3 m 0.6 m)	evergreen	rock garden, retaining wall, courtyard, ground cover
Cotoneaster horizontalis	shrub	5–7	2 ft 3 ft (0.6 m 1 m)	deciduous	ground cover, courtyard, rock garden, espalier
Crataegus laevigata	tree	4–9	8 ft 20 ft (2.5 m 6 m)	deciduous	lawn specimen, parks, streets
Crataegus phaenopyrum	tree	4–10	8 ft 15 ft (2.5 m 5 m)	deciduous	lawn specimen, hedge, cut foliage
Cryptomeria japonica	tree	6–10	10 ft 40 ft (3 m 12 m)	evergreen	lawn specimen, screen, windbreak, timber, parks

NAME	KIND	ZONE	HEIGHT AT 5 & 20 YEARS	DECIDUOUS/ EVERGREEN	USES
Cuphea micropetala	shrub	9–11	2 ft 3 ft (0.6 m 1 m)	evergreen	courtyard, container, shrub border
× *Cupressocyparis leylandii*	tree	5–10	12 ft 50 ft (4 m 15 m)	evergreen	windbreak, hedge
Cupressus arizonica	tree	7–10	15 ft 40 ft (5 m 12 m)	evergreen	lawn specimen, windbreak
Cupressus lusitanica	tree	8–11	10 ft 40 ft (3 m 12 m)	evergreen	lawn specimen, screen, windbreak
Cupressus macrocarpa	tree	7–10	12 ft 50 ft (4 m 15 m)	evergreen	parks, windbreaks, shade, hedges, timber, coastal planting
Cupressus sempervirens	tree	7–10	8 ft 30 ft (2.5 m 9 m)	evergreen	courtyards, screens, parks, hedge, topiary, coastal planting
Cycas revoluta	cycad	9–11	2 ft 5 ft (0.6 m 1.5 m)	evergreen	courtyard, plaza, container, bonsai
Cytisus × *praecox*	shrub	5–9	3 ft 4 ft (1 m 1.2 m)	evergreen	shrub border, courtyard, rock garden
Daboecia cantabrica	shrub	7–9	1 ft 2 ft (0.3 m 0.6 m)	evergreen	rock garden, shrub border, heather garden, coastal planting
Daphne × *burkwoodii*	shrub	5–9	2 ft 3 ft (0.6 m 1 m)	evergreen	rock garden, woodland garden, shrub border
Daphne cneorum	shrub	4–9	1 ft 1 ft (0.3 m 0.3 m)	evergreen	rock garden, embankment
Daphne odora	shrub	8–10	1 ft 3 ft (0.3 m 1 m)	evergreen	rock garden, courtyard, cut flowers
Davidia involucrata	tree	7–9	8 ft 25 ft (2.5 m 8 m)	deciduous	lawn specimen, parks
Deutzia × *elegantissima*	shrub	5–9	4 ft 6 ft (1.2 m 2 m)	deciduous	shrub border, woodland garden
Deutzia × *rosea*	shrub	5–9	2 ft 3 ft (0.6 m 1 m)	deciduous	shrub border, woodland garden
Deutzia scabra	shrub	5–10	4 ft 10 ft (1.2 m 3 m)	deciduous	shrub border
Dodonaea viscosa	tree	9–11	8 ft 12 ft (2.5 m 4 m)	evergreen	shrub border, informal hedge, coastal planting
Dracaena draco	tree	10–11	2 ft 8 ft (0.6 m 2.5 m)	evergreen	courtyard, plaza, swimming pool, conservatory, container
Duranta erecta	shrub	10–11	8 ft 15 ft (2.5 m 5 m)	evergreen	shrub border, informal hedge, courtyard
Elaeagnus pungens	shrub	6–10	3 ft 15 ft (1 m 5 m)	evergreen	shrub border, informal hedge
Enkianthus campanulatus	shrub	5–9	4 ft 10 ft (1.2 m 3 m)	deciduous	shrub border, woodland garden
Enkianthus perulatus	shrub	5–9	3 ft 6 ft (1 m 2 m)	deciduous	shrub border, woodland garden
Erica carnea	shrub	5–9	1 ft 1 ft (0.3 m 0.3 m)	evergreen	ground cover, rock garden, shrub border, embankment
Erica × *darleyensis*	shrub	6–9	2 ft 2 ft (0.6 m 0.6 m)	evergreen	rock garden, ground cover, embankment
Eriobotrya japonica	tree	8–10	6 ft 20 ft (2 m 6 m)	evergreen	home orchard, lawn specimen
Erythrina caffra	tree	9–11	8 ft 30 ft (2.5 m 9 m)	deciduous	lawn specimen, parks, shade
Erythrina crista-galli	tree	8–11	6 ft 15 ft (2 m 5 m)	deciduous	lawn specimen, shrub border
Escallonia 'Appleblossom'	shrub	7–10	6 ft 12 ft (2 m 4 m)	evergreen	hedge, shrub border
Eucalyptus citriodora	tree	9–11	10 ft 40 ft (3 m 12 m)	evergreen	lawn specimen, parks, streets, lemon oil
Eucalyptus ficifolia	tree	9–10	8 ft 20 ft (2.5 m 6 m)	evergreen	lawn specimen, parks, streets
Eucalyptus pauciflora	tree	7–9	12 ft 30 ft (4 m 9 m)	evergreen	lawn specimen, parks, windbreaks
Euonymus europaeus	shrub	6–9	5 ft 12 ft (1.5 m 4 m)	deciduous	shrub border, lawn specimen
Euonymus japonicus	shrub	8–10	3 ft 8 ft (1 m 2.5 m)	evergreen	hedge, seaside planting, shrub border, rock garden, topiary, container

NAME	KIND	ZONE	HEIGHT AT 5 & 20 YEARS	DECIDUOUS/ EVERGREEN	USES
Euphorbia pulcherrima	shrub	10–11	4 ft 12 ft (1.2 m 4 m)	deciduous	shrub border, courtyard, container
Euryops pectinatus	shrub	9–11	2 ft 3 ft (0.6 m 1 m)	evergreen	courtyard, conservatory, rock garden
Exochorda × macrantha	shrub	6–9	4 ft 8 ft (1.2 m 2.5 m)	deciduous	shrub border
Fagus sylvatica	tree	5–9	8 ft 30 ft (2.5 m 9 m)	deciduous	parks, streets, woodland garden, timber
Fatsia japonica	shrub	8–11	3 ft 6 ft (1 m 2 m)	deciduous	courtyard, swimming pool, woodland garden
Ficus elastica	tree	10–11	10 ft 30 ft (3 m 9 m)	evergreen	parks, indoors, plazas
Ficus macrophylla	tree	10–11	8 ft 30 ft (2.5 m 9 m)	evergreen	parks, streets
Forsythia × intermedia	shrub	5–9	4 ft 10 ft (1.2 m 3 m)	deciduous	shrub border, courtyard, lawn grouping
Forsythia suspensa	shrub	4–9	6 ft 12 ft (2 m 4 m)	deciduous	shrub border, courtyard, lawn grouping, espalier
Fraxinus americana	tree	4–10	10 ft 40 ft (3 m 12 m)	deciduous	parks, streets, timber
Fraxinus angustifolia	tree	6–10	10 ft 30 ft (3 m 9 m)	deciduous	parks, streets
Fraxinus ornus	tree	6–10	8 ft 25 ft (2.5 m 8 m)	deciduous	lawn specimen, parks, streets
Fremontodendron californicum	shrub	8–10	8 ft 15 ft (2.5 m 5 m)	evergreen	shrub border, courtyard, espalier
Fuchsia denticulata	shrub	9–11	3 ft 8 ft (1 m 2.5 m)	evergreen	shrub border, courtyard, woodland garden
Fuchsia fulgens	shrub	9–11	5 ft 10 ft (1.5 m 3 m)	evergreen	shrub border, courtyard, woodland garden
Fuchsia magellanica	shrub	7–10	4 ft 8 ft (1.2 m 2.5 m)	evergreen	shrub border, courtyard, espalier, container, informal hedge, conservatory
Gardenia augusta	shrub	10–11	4 ft 6ft (1.2 m 2 m)	evergreen	courtyard, container, informal hedge, conservatory, cut flowers
Genista lydia	shrub	6–9	1 ft 2 ft (0.3 m 0.6 m)	deciduous	rock garden, retaining wall
Genista × spachiana	shrub	9–11	3 ft 8 ft (1 m 2.5 m)	evergreen	container, courtyard, rock garden, embankment
Ginkgo biloba	tree	3–10	6 ft 25 ft (2 m 8 m)	deciduous	lawn specimen, courtyard, parks, streets
Gleditsia triacanthos	tree	4–9	10 ft 40 ft (3 m 12 m)	deciduous	parks, lawn specimen, farms, boggy areas
Grevillea lanigera	shrub	7–9	2 ft 3 ft (0.6 m 1 m)	evergreen	shrub border, rock garden
Grevillea 'Robin Gordon'	shrub	9–11	3 ft 3 ft (1 m 1m)	evergreen	informal hedge, shrub border, courtyard, embankment
Grevillea rosmarinifolia	shrub	8–10	5 ft 8 ft (1.5 m 2.5 m)	evergreen	formal hedge, shrub border, screen
Grewia occidentalis	shrub	9–11	8 ft 10 ft (2.5 m 3 m)	evergreen	informal hedge, shrub border, espalier
Griselinia littoralis	shrub	8–10	6 ft 20 ft (2 m 6 m)	evergreen	informal hedge, shrub border, seashores
Hakea laurina	shrub	9–11	5 ft 12 ft (1.5 m 4 m)	evergreen	shrub border, screen, informal hedge
Hamamelis × intermedia	shrub	4–9	5 ft 12 ft (1.5 m 4 m)	deciduous	shrub border, lawn specimen, cut flowers
Hamamelis mollis	shrub	5–8	5 ft 15 ft (1.5 m 5 m)	deciduous	shrub border, lawn specimen
Hebe speciosa	shrub	8–9	2 ft 3 ft (0.6 m 1 m)	evergreen	seashores, shrub border, courtyard
Hebe 'Wiri' hybrids	shrub	8–10	18 in (45 cm)	evergreen	container, shrub border
Hibiscus rosa-sinensis	shrub	10–11	5 ft 12 ft (1.5 m 4 m)	evergreen	shrub border, courtyard, swimming pool
Hibiscus syriacus	shrub	5–9	6 ft 12 ft (2 m 4 m)	evergreen	shrub border, screen, informal hedge
Hovenia dulcis	tree	8–10	8 ft 25 ft (2.5 m 8 m)	deciduous	lawn specimen
Howea forsteriana	tree	10–11	3 ft 10 ft (1 m 3 m)	evergreen	indoors, courtyard, container, swimming pool

NAME	KIND	ZONE	HEIGHT AT 5 & 20 YEARS	DECIDUOUS/ EVERGREEN	USES
Hydrangea macrophylla	shrub	6–10	4 ft 6 ft (1.2 m 2 m)	deciduous	shrub border, courtyard, conservatory, cut flowers
Hydrangea quercifolia	shrub	5–9	4 ft 6 ft (1.2 m 2 m)	deciduous	shrub border, courtyard
Hymenosporum flavum	tree	9–11	8 ft 25 ft (2.5 m 8 m)	evergreen	shrub border, lawn specimen, streets
Hypericum calycinum	shrub	5–9	1 ft 1.5 ft (0.3 m 0.3 m)	evergreen	ground cover, woodland garden, embankment
Ilex × altaclarensis	tree	6–10	8 ft 25 ft (2.5 m 8 m)	evergreen	shrub border, lawn specimen, screen, cut foliage & berries
Ilex aquifolium	tree	6–10	6 ft 20 ft (2 m 6 m)	evergreen	shrub border, lawn specimen, screen, cut foliage & berries
Ilex crenata	shrub	6–10	4 ft 10 ft (1.2 m 3 m)	evergreen	formal hedge, topiary, courtyard, rock garden, container
Ilex opaca	tree	5–10	5 ft 40 ft (1.5 m 12 m)	evergreen	lawn specimen, screen, cut foliage & berries
Ilex verticillata	shrub	3–9	5 ft 10 ft (1.5 m 3 m)	deciduous	shrub border, cut foliage & berries
Ilex vomitora	tree	7–10	6 ft 15 ft (2 m 2.5 m)	evergreen	shrub border, cut foliage & berries
Iochroma cyaneum	shrub	9–11	5 ft 8 ft (1.5 m 2.5 m)	evergreen	shrub border, courtyard, container
Iochroma grandiflorum	shrub	9–11	6 ft 12 ft (2 m 4 m)	evergreen	shrub border, courtyard
Itea virginica	shrub	5–9	4 ft 6 ft (1.2 m 2 m)	deciduous	shrub border, woodland garden, boggy areas
Jacaranda mimosifolia	tree	9–11	10 ft 30 ft (3 m 9 m)	deciduous	lawn specimen, parks, streets
Jubaea chilensis	palm	9–11	5 ft 20 ft (1.5 m 6 m)	evergreen	lawn specimen, parks, shrub border
Juniperus chinensis	tree	3–9	8 ft 25 ft (2.5 m 8 m)	evergreen	lawn specimen, parks, shrub border
Juniperus communis	tree	2–9	4 ft 15 ft (1.2 m 5 m)	evergreen	shrub border, hedges, berries used for flavoring
Juniperus conferta	tree	5–10	1 ft 1 ft (0.3 m 0.3 m)	evergreen	ground cover, coastal planting, rock garden
Juniperus horizontalis	tree	4–10	1 ft 2 ft (0.3 m 0.6 m)	evergreen	ground cover, rock garden, embankments
Juniperus × media	tree	4–10	5 ft 10 ft (1.5 m 3 m)	evergreen	lawn specimen, shrub border
Juniperus virginiana	tree	2–9	6 ft 25 ft (2 m 8 m)	evergreen	shrub border, lawn specimen, timber
Justicia brandegeana	shrub	9–11	3 ft 5 ft (1 m 1.5 m)	evergreen	shrub border, container, courtyard
Kalmia latifolia	shrub	3–9	3 ft 10 ft (1 m 3 m)	evergreen	shrub border, courtyard, woodland garden
Kalopanax septemlobus	tree	4–9	8 ft 30 ft (2.5 m 9 m)	deciduous	lawn specimen, parks, shade
Kerria japonica	shrub	5–10	4 ft 6 ft (1.2 m 2 m)	deciduous	shrub border, courtyard
Keolreuteria bipinnata	tree	8–11	10 ft 30 ft (3 m 9 m)	deciduous	lawn specimen, parks
Koelreuteria paniculata	tree	4–10	8 ft 25 ft (2.5 m 8 m)	deciduous	lawn specimen, parks, streets
Kolkwitzia amabilis	shrub	4–9	6 ft 10 ft (2 m 3 m)	deciduous	shrub border, informal hedge
Laburnum × watereri	tree	3–9	8 ft 20 ft (2.5 m 6 m)	deciduous	lawn specimen, espalier
Lagerstroemia indica	tree	6–11	6 ft 20 ft (2 m 6 m)	deciduous	lawn specimen, streets
Lagunaria patersonia	tree	10–11	6 ft 20 ft (2 m 6 m)	evergreen	lawn specimen, parks, coastal planting
Lantana carnarva	shrub	9–11	2 ft 6 ft (0.6 m 2 m)	evergreen	shrub border, informal hedge, espalier
Lantana montevidensis	shrub	9–11	18 in 3 ft (45 cm 1 m)	evergreen	shrub border, informal hedge, espalier
Larix decidua	tree	3–8	10 ft 40 ft (3 m 12 m)	deciduous	timber, lawn specimen, parks, shelter
Larix kaempferi	tree	4–7	10 ft 40 ft (3 m 12 m)	deciduous	timber, lawn specimen, parks, shelter

NAME	KIND	CLIMATE	HEIGHT AT 5 & 20 YEARS	DECIDUOUS/ EVERGREEN	USES
Laurus nobilis	tree	7–10	6 ft 20 ft (2 m 6 m)	evergreen	lawn specimen, hedge, screen, container, culinary herb
Lavandula angustifolia	shrub	5–9	2 ft 2 ft (0.6 m 0.6 m)	evergreen	herbaceous border, rock garden, container
Lavandula dentata	shrub	8–10	2 ft 3 ft (0.6 m 1 m)	evergreen	shrub border, low hedge, container, cut flowers, coastal planting
Lavandula × intermedia	shrub	6–10	2 ft 3 ft (0.6 m 1 m)	evergreen	informal hedge, container, cut flowers
Lavandula stoechas	shrub	7–10	2 ft 2 ft (0.6 m 0.6 m)	evergreen	herbaceous border, rock garden, container, coastal planting
Lavatera thuringiaca	shrub	6–10	3 ft 5 ft (1 m 1.5 m)	evergreen	shrub border, informal hedge, cut flowers
Leptospermum laevigatum	shrub	9–11	8 ft 20 ft (2.5 m 6 m)	evergreen	coastal planting, informal hedge, screen, windbreak
Leptospermum scoparium	shrub	8–10	6 ft 10 ft (2 m 3 m)	evergreen	shrub border, informal hedge, courtyard, container
Lespedeza thunbergii	shrub	5–8	3 ft 6 ft (1 m 2 m)	deciduous	shrub border, courtyard
Leucophyllum frutescens	shrub	8–11	6 ft 8 ft (2 m 2.5 m)	evergreen	lawn specimen, group planting
Leucothoë fontanesiana	shrub	4–8	3 ft 5 ft (1 m 1.5 m)	evergreen	shrub border, courtyard, woodland garden
Leycesteria formosa	shrub	7–10	5 ft 8 ft (1.5 m 2.5 m)	deciduous	shrub border, courtyard
Ligustrum japonicum	shrub	7–11	5 ft 10 ft (1.5 m 3 m)	evergreen	shrub border, lawn specimen, hedge
Ligustrum lucidum	tree	7–11	12 ft 30 ft (4 m 9 m)	evergreen	shrub border, lawn specimen, streets, hedge
Lindera obtusiloba	shrub	6–10	5 ft 20 ft (1.5 m 6 m)	deciduous	shrub border, lawn specimen, woodland garden
Liquidambar styraciflua	tree	5–11	10 ft 50 ft (3 m 15 m)	deciduous	lawn specimen, parks, streets, shade, timber
Liriodendron tulipifera	tree	4–10	12 ft 50 ft (4 m 15 m)	deciduous	lawn specimen, parks, streets, timber
Livistonia chinensis	palm	8–11	4 ft 15 ft (1.2 m 5 m)	evergreen	lawn grouping, courtyard, container, plaza
Lonicera fragrantissima	shrub	4–9	6 ft 10 ft (2 m 3 m)	deciduous	shrub border, courtyard
Lonicerna × heckrottii	shrub	4–9	10 ft 20 ft (3 m 6 m)	deciduous	shrub border
Lonicera nitida	shrub	7–9	3 ft 5 ft (1 m 1.5 m)	evergreen	courtyard, hedge, topiary
Luma apiculata	shrub	9–11	5 ft 15 ft (1.5 m 5 m)	evergreen	shrub border, courtyard
Maclura pomifera	tree	4–9	8 ft 35 ft (2.5 m 10.5 m)	deciduous	hedge, timber
Magnolia campbelii	tree	7–10	5 ft 20 ft (1.5 m 6 m)	deciduous	lawn specimen, woodland garden
Magnolia denudata	tree	5–8	6 ft 30 ft (2 m 9 m)	deciduous	lawn specimen, shrub border, courtyard
Magnolia grandiflora	tree	6–11	6 ft 30 ft (2 m 9 m)	evergreen	lawn specimen, parks, streets
Magnolia liliiflora	shrub	5–8	5 ft 12 ft (1.5 m 4 m)	deciduous	shrub border
Magnolia × soulangiana	tree	5–10	6 ft 20 ft (2 m 6 m)	deciduous	shrub border, lawn specimen, courtyard
Magnolia stellata	shrub	4–9	4 ft 15 ft (1.2 m 5 m)	deciduous	shrub border, courtyard, container
Mahonia aquifolium	shrub	5–8	2 ft 6 ft (0.6 m 2 m)	evergreen	shrub border, rock garden, courtyard, informal hedge
Mahonia lomariifolia	shrub	7–10	6 ft 12 ft (2 m 4 m)	evergreen	shrub border, screen, courtyard
Malus × domestica	tree	3–9	8 ft 20 ft (2.5 m 6 m)	deciduous	orchard, screen
Malus floribunda	tree	4–9	8 ft 20 ft (2.5 m 6 m)	deciduous	lawn specimen
Malus ioensis	tree	2–9	6 ft 25 ft (2 m 8 m)	deciduous	lawn specimen, shrub border

NAME	KIND	ZONE	HEIGHT AT 5 & 20 YEARS	DECIDUOUS/ EVERGREEN	USES
Malus sargentii	shrub	4–9	4 ft 10 ft (h2 m 3 m)	deciduous	shrub border, courtyard, lawn specimen
Malus sylvestris	tree	3–9	8 ft 25 ft (2.5 m 8 m)	deciduous	lawn specimen
Malvaviscus arboreus	shrub	9–11	6 ft 10 ft (2 m 3 m)	evergreen	shrub border, courtyard, swimming pool
Melaleuca fulgens	shrub	9–11	4 ft 5 ft (1.2 m 1.5 m)	evergreen	shrub border, courtyard
Melaleuca linarifolia	tree	9–11	10 ft 25 ft (3 m 8 m)	evergreen	lawn specimen, windbreak, parks, boggy areas
Melaleuca nesophila	shrub	9–11	5 ft 10 ft (1.5 m 3 m)	evergreen	lawn specimen, shrub border
Melaleuca thymifolia	shrub	9–11	2 ft 3 ft (0.6 m 1 m)	evergreen	shrub border, rock garden, boggy areas
Melaleuca viridiflora	shrub	10–11	8 ft 25 ft (2.5 m 8 m)	evergreen	lawn specimen, parks, streets, boggy areas
Melia azedarach	tree	8–11	10 ft 30 ft (3 m 9 m)	deciduous	lawn specimen, shade, streets
Metasequoia glyptostroboides	tree	5–8	15 ft 60 ft (5 m 18 m)	deciduous	lawn specimen, parks, streets
Metrosideros excelsa	tree	10–11	6 ft 20 ft (2 m 6 m)	evergreen	coastal planting, screen, lawn specimen, hedge, streets
Metrosideros kermadecensis	tree	10–11	6 ft 15 ft (2 m 5 m)	evergreen	coastal planting, screen, lawn specimen, hedge, streets
Michelia doltsopa	tree	9–11	6 ft 20 ft (2 m 6 m)	evergreen	lawn specimen, courtyard
Michelia figo	shrub	9–11	3 ft 10 ft (1 m 3 m)	evergreen	courtyard, shrub border, container, hedge
Microbiota decussata	shrub	3–9	1 ft 2 ft (0.3 m 0.6 m)	evergreen	ground cover, rock garden
Morus alba	tree	5–9	12 ft 30 ft (4 m 9 m)	deciduous	lawn specimen, home orchard, shade, silkworms
Morus nigra	tree	6–10	6 ft 15 ft (2 m 5 m)	deciduous	home orchard
Murraya paniculata	shrub	10–11	3 ft 10 ft (1 m 3 m)	evergreen	courtyard, container, hedge, shrub border
Myrica californica	tree	7–10	10 ft 25 ft (3 m 8 m)	evergreen	shrub border
Myrsine africana	tree	9–11	4 ft 8 ft (1.2 m 2.5 m)	evergreen	lawn specimen, cut foliage
Myrtus communis	shrub	8–11	3 ft 8 ft (1 m 2.5 m)	evergreen	courtyard, container, hedge, topiary
Nandina domestica	shrub	6–9	4 ft 6 ft (1.2 m 2 m)	evergreen	courtyard, swimming pool, shrub border
Nerium oleander	shrub	8–11	8 ft 10 ft (2.5 m 3 m)	evergreen	shrub border, screen, streets, container
Nothofagus cunninghamii	tree	8–9	8 ft 30 ft (2.5 m 9 m)	evergreen	lawn specimen, screen, timber
Nothofagus fusca	tree	7–10	5 ft 23 ft (1.5 m 7 m)	evergreen	lawn specimen, screen, timber
Nyssa sylvatica	tree	4–9	10 ft 30 ft (3 m 9 m)	deciduous	lawn specimen, parks, streets
Olea europaea	tree	8–11	8 ft 25 ft (2.5 m 8 m)	evergreen	preserved fruit, edible oil, timber, lawn specimen, streets
Olearia macrodonta	shrub	8–10	4 ft 6 ft (1.2 m 2 m)	evergreen	shrub border
Olearia phlogopappa	shrub	8–10	3 ft 6 ft (1 m 2 m)	evergreen	shrub border, rock garden, coastal planting
Osmanthus × burkwoodii	shrub	6–9	5 ft 8 ft (1.5 m 2.5 m)	evergreen	shrub border, courtyard
Osmanthus delavayi	shrub	7–9	3 ft 6 ft (1 m 2 m)	evergreen	shrub border, courtyard
Osmanthus fragrans	shrub	7–11	3 ft 15 ft (1 m 5 m)	evergreen	shrub border, courtyard, container
Oxydendrum arboreum	tree	4–9	8 ft 25 ft (2.5 m 8 m)	deciduous	shrub border, lawn specimen, woodland garden
Pachystegia insignis	shrub	8–11	1 ft 3 ft (0.3 m 1 m)	evergreen	rock garden, courtyard, seaside planting

NAME	KIND	ZONE	HEIGHT AT 5 & 20 YEARS	DECIDUOUS/ EVERGREEN	USES
Paeonia lutea	shrub	6–9	3 ft 6 ft (1 m 2 m)	deciduous	shrub border, courtyard
Paeonia suffruticosa	shrub	4–9	2 ft 4 ft (0.6 m 1.2 m)	deciduous	shrub border, perennial border, courtyard
Parrotia persica	tree	5–9	8 ft 20 ft (2.5 m 6 m)	deciduous	lawn specimen, parks
Paulownia tomentosa	tree	5–9	10 ft 30 ft (3 m 9 m)	deciduous	lawn specimen
Persea americana	tree	10–11	10 ft 60 ft (3 m 18 m)	evergreen	orchard, lawn specimen, courtyard
Persoonia pinifolia	shrub	10–11	6 ft 12 ft (2 m 4 m)	evergreen	shrub border, courtyard, cut foliage
Philadelphus coronarius	shrub	4–9	4 ft 12 ft (1.2 m 4 m)	deciduous	shrub border, woodland garden, courtyard
Philadelphus 'Lemoinei'	shrub	5–9	5 ft 8 ft (1.5 m 2.5 m)	deciduous	shrub border, woodland garden, courtyard
Philadelphus 'Virginal'	shrub	5–9	5 ft 10 ft (1.5 m 3 m)	deciduous	shrub border, courtyard
Philodendron bipinnatifidum	shrub	10–11	5 ft 10 ft (1.5 m 3 m)	evergreen	courtyard, plazas, swimming pool, indoors
Phlomis fruticosa	shrub	7–10	30 in 30 in (75 cm 75 cm)	evergreen	shrub border, coastal planting, cut flowers
Phoenix canariensis	palm	9–11	4 ft 15 ft (1.2 m 5 m)	evergreen	parks, avenues, plazas
Phoenix roebeleni	palm	9–11	2 ft 8 ft (0.6 m 2.5 m)	evergreen	courtyard, swimming pool, indoors
Photinia × fraseri	shrub	7–10	6 ft 15 ft (2 m 5 m)	evergreen	formal and informal hedge, windbreak
Photinia serrulata	tree	7–10	6 ft 15 ft (2 m 5 m)	evergreen	lawn specimen, streets, windbreak
Physocarpus monogynus	shrub	5–7	3 ft 4 ft (1 m 1.2 m)	deciduous	shrub border, courtyard, cut flowers & foliage
Picea abies	tree	3–8	8 ft 30 ft (2.5 m 9 m)	evergreen	timber, lawn specimen, Christmas tree
Picea glauca	tree	2–6	6 ft 25 ft (2 m 8 m)	evergreen	timber, paper pulp
Picea pungens	tree	3–8	6 ft 25 ft (2 m 8 m)	evergreen	lawn specimen, parks
Pieris formosa	shrub	6–9	5 ft 10 ft (1.5 m 3 m)	evergreen	shrub border, lawn specimen, courtyard
Pieris japonica	shrub	4–10	4 ft 6 ft (1.2 m 2 m)	evergreen	shrub border, woodland garden, container, bonsai
Pinus canariensis	tree	8–11	10 ft 40 ft (3 m 12 m)	evergreen	timber, windbreak, parks
Pinus contorta	tree	6–9	8 ft 30 ft (2.5 m 9 m)	evergreen	timber, windbreak
Pinus densiflora	tree	4–9	6 ft 30 ft (2 m 9 m)	evergreen	lawn specimen, courtyard, bonsai
Pinus halepensis	tree	7–10	8 ft 30 ft (2.5 m 9 m)	evergreen	windbreak, lawn specimen, parks, Christmas tree
Pinus mugo	shrub	3–8	5 ft 15 ft (1.5 m 5 m)	evergreen	rock garden, bonsai, container, hedge
Pinus nigra	tree	4–8	10 ft 35 ft (3 m 10.5 m)	evergreen	timber, lawn specimen, windbreak
Pinus parviflora	tree	3–9	5 ft 20 ft (1.5 m 6 m)	evergreen	lawn specimen, courtyard, bonsai
Pinus patula	tree	9–11	10 ft 40 ft (3 m 12 m)	evergreen	lawn specimen, shade, parks, timber, wood pulp
Pinus pinea	tree	8–10	8 ft 25 ft (2.5 m 8 m)	evergreen	edible seeds, lawn specimen, avenues, coastal planting
Pinus strobus	tree	3–8	10 ft 50 ft (3 m 15 m)	evergreen	lawn specimen, parks, timber
Pinus sylvestris	tree	3–7	8 ft 30 ft (2.5 m 9 m)	evergreen	lawn specimen, parks, timber
Pinus thunbergii	tree	5–8	8 ft 30 ft (2.5 m 9 m)	evergreen	courtyard, lawn specimen, container, bonsai
Pistacia chinensis	tree	6–9	8 ft 35 ft (2.5 m 10.5 m)	deciduous	lawn specimen, parks
Pittosporum crassifolium	tree	8–10	8 ft 20 ft (2.5 m 6 m)	evergreen	seaside planting, hedge, lawn specimen, screen
Pittosporum eugenioides	tree	9–11	8 ft 25 ft (2.5 m 8 m)	evergreen	seaside planting, hedge, lawn specimen, screen

NAME	KIND	CLIMATE	HEIGHT AT 5 & 20 YEARS	DECIDUOUS/ EVERGREEN	USES
Pittosporum tenuifolium	tree	9–11	6 ft 20 ft (2 m 6 m)	evergreen	shrub border, hedge, windbreak, cut foliage
Pittosporum tobira	tree	9–11	3 ft 12 ft (1 m 4 m)	evergreen	hedge, shrub border, courtyard, container
Platanus × acerifolia	tree	4–9	8 ft 35 ft (2.5 m 10.5 m)	deciduous	parks, avenues, shade
Platycladus orientalis	tree	6–11	6 ft 20 ft (2 m 6 m)	evergreen	lawn specimen, courtyard, container
Plumbago auriculata	shrub	9–11	4 ft 6 ft (1.2 m 2 m)	evergreen	informal hedge, courtyard, shrub border, espalier
Plumeria rubra	tree	10–11	6 ft 15 ft (2 m 5 m)	deciduous	lawn specimen, courtyard, parks, plazas
Podocarpus elatus	tree	9–11	8 ft 30 ft (2.5 m 9 m)	evergreen	lawn specimen, parks, streets, hedges
Podocarpus macrophyllus	tree	8–11	4 ft 20 ft (1.2 m 6 m)	evergreen	lawn specimen, courtyards, container, plazas
Populus nigra	tree	3–9	15 ft 50 ft (5 m 15 m)	deciduous	avenues, windbreak, farms, parks
Populus tremula	tree	1–7	12 ft 40 ft (4 m 12 m)	deciduous	lawn specimen, parks
Potentilla fruticosa	shrub	2–7	3 ft 4 ft (1 m 1.2 m)	deciduous	shrub border, container
Prosopis glandulosa	tree	8–11	15 ft 30 ft (5 m 9 m)	deciduous	shade, hedge
Prunus × blireiana	tree	5–10	6 ft 15 ft (2 m 5 m)	deciduous	lawn specimen
Prunus campanulata	tree	7–11	10 ft 30 ft (3 m 9 m)	deciduous	lawn specimen
Prunus cerasifera	tree	4–8	8 ft 30 ft (2.5 m 9 m)	deciduous	lawn specimen, parks, streets
Prunus laurocerasus	tree	6–8	8 ft 18 ft (2.5 m 5.5 m)	evergreen	hedge, screen, windbreak, cut foliage (funeral wreaths)
Prunus mume	tree	6–9	8 ft 20 ft (2.5 m 6 m)	evergreen	lawn specimen, cut flowers, parks
Prunus persica	tree	5–9	5 ft 15 ft (1.5 m 5 m)	deciduous	lawn specimen, orchard, cut flowers
Prunus sargentii	tree	4–7	8 ft 25 ft (2.5 m 8 m)	deciduous	lawn specimen, parks, streets
Prunus serrula	tree	5–9	8 ft 25 ft (2.5 m 8 m)	deciduous	lawn specimen, parks
Prunus serrulata	tree	5–9	10 ft 30 ft (3 m 9 m)	deciduous	lawn specimen, courtyard
Prunus subhirtella	tree	5–8	8 ft 20 ft (2.5 m 6 m)	deciduous	lawn specimen, courtyard, woodland garden
Prunus × yedoensis	tree	5–8	8 ft 25 ft (2.5 m 8 m)	deciduous	lawn specimen, streets
Pseudopanax lessonii	tree	9–10	6 ft 20 ft (2 m 6 m)	evergreen	courtyard, shrub border, container, swimming pool
Psidium cattleianum	shrub	9–11	5 ft 15 ft (1.5 m 5 m)	evergreen	home orchard, shrub border, courtyard
Ptelea trifoliata	tree	3–9	6 ft 20 ft (2 m 6 m)	deciduous	shrub border, lawn specimen
Pterocarya stenoptera	tree	6–8	25 ft 50 ft (8 m 15 m)	deciduous	lawn specimen, parks, shade
Pterostyrax hispida	tree	4–8	6 ft 25 ft (2 m 8 m)	deciduous	lawn specimen, parks, woodland garden
Punica granatum	shrub	8–11	5 ft 15 ft (1.5 m 5 m)	evergreen	shrub border, courtyard, home orchard, container
Pyracantha angustifolia	shrub	5–11	4 ft 10 ft (1.2 m 3 m)	evergreen	hedge, shrub border
Pyracantha coccinea	shrub	5–9	4 ft 15 ft (1.2 m 5 m)	evergreen	shrub border, courtyard, hedge
Pyrus calleryana	tree	5–9	10 ft 35 ft (3 m 10.5 m)	deciduous	lawn specimen, parks, streets, graft stock
Pyrus communis	tree	4–9	6 ft 25 ft (2 m 8 m)	deciduous	orchard, lawn specimen
Pyrus kawakamii	tree	8–10	10 ft 25 ft (3 m 8 m)	deciduous	orchard, lawn specimen
Pyrus salicifolia	tree	4–7	6 ft 20 ft (2 m 6 m)	deciduous	lawn specimen
Quercus alba	tree	3–9	10 ft 40 ft (3 m 12 m)	deciduous	timber, parks, wine casks

NAME	KIND	CLIMATE	HEIGHT AT 5 & 20 YEARS	DECIDUOUS/ EVERGREEN	USES
Quercus coccinea	tree	4–9	10 ft 40 ft (3 m 12 m)	deciduous	lawn specimen, parks, streets
Quercus ilex	tree	7–10	8 ft 30 ft (2.5 m 9 m)	evergreen	parks, streets, hedge, coastal planting, topiary
Quercus palustris	tree	4–8	15 ft 50 ft (5 m 15 m)	deciduous	lawn specimen, parks, streets
Quercus robur	tree	4–8	12 ft 40 ft (4 m 12 m)	deciduous	lawn specimen, parks, streets, timber, tan bark, wine casks
Quercus virginiana	tree	7–11	10 ft 30 ft (3 m 9 m)	evergreen	parks, streets, woodland garden, coastal planting
Radermachera sinica	tree	10–11	12 ft 30 ft (4 m 9 m)	evergreen	indoor, courtyard, swimming pool, lawn specimen
Rhamnus alaternus	shrub	8–10	6 ft 12 ft (2 m 4 m)	evergreen	hedge, shrub border, courtyard, container
Rhaphiolepis indica	shrub	8–11	4 ft 8 ft (1.2 m 2.5 m)	evergreen	shrub border, courtyard, hedge
Rhaphiolepis umbellata	shrub	8–11	2 ft 6 ft (0.6 m 2 m)	evergreen	coastal planting, hedge, rock garden, courtyard, swimming pool
Rhododendron arboreum	tree	7–11	4 ft 12 ft (1.2 m 4 m)	evergreen	shrub border, woodland garden
Rhododendron augustinii	shrub	6–9	2 ft 5 ft (0.6 m 1.5 m)	evergreen	shrub border, woodland garden, rock garden
Rhododendron degronianum	shrub	7–9	2 ft 3 ft (0.6 m 1 m)	evergreen	shrub border, woodland garden, rock garden
Rhododendron fastigiatum	shrub	6–9	18 in 4 ft (45 cm 1.2 m)	evergreen	rock garden, conservatory, shrub border
Rhododendron griffithianum	shrub	8–9	4 ft 12 ft (1.2 m 4 m)	evergreen	shrub border, woodland garden
Rhododendron kiusianum	shrub	6–10	2 ft 3 ft (0.6 m 1 m)	evergreen	shrub border, rock garden, woodland garden, bonsai
Rhododendron nuttallii	shrub	9–10	4 ft 8 ft (1.2 m 2.5 m)	evergreen	woodland garden, conservatory
Rhododendron occidentale	shrub	6–9	4 ft 8 ft (1.2 m 2.5 m)	deciduous	shrub border, woodland garden
Rhododendron 'Patty Bee'	shrub	6–9	12 in 19 in (30 cm 50 cm)	evergreen	container, rock garden
Rhododendron sinogrande	shrub	8–10	2 ft 10 ft (0.6 m 3 m)	evergreen	woodland garden
Rhododendron Azaleas	shrub	7–11	variable to 10 ft (3 m)	evergreen	shrub border, woodland garden, cut flowers
Rhus aromatica	shrub	3–9	2 ft 5 ft (0.6 m 1.5 m)	deciduous	shrub border, courtyard, embankment, ground cover
Rhus ovata	shrub	9–11	10 ft 12 ft (3 m 4 m)	evergreen	edible fruit, screen
Rhus typhina	shrub	4–9	6 ft 15 ft (2 m 5 m)	deciduous	shrub border, lawn specimen
Ribes odoratum	shrub	4–7	3 ft 8 ft (1 m 2.5 m)	deciduous	shrub border, courtyard
Ribes sanguineum	shrub	5–10	5 ft 10 ft (1.5 m 3 m)	deciduous	shrub border, hedge, lawn specimen, courtyard
Robinia pseudoacacia	tree	4–10	10 ft 30 ft (3 m 9 m)	deciduous	lawn specimen, streets, farms, timber, boggy areas
Rosa banksiae	shrub	7–10	15 ft 50 ft (5 m 15 m)	deciduous	shrub border, rock garden, courtyard
Rosa chinensis	shrub	7–10	5 ft 12 ft (1.5 m 4 m)	deciduous	shrub border, formal garden, courtyard
Rosa foetida	shrub	4–9	4 ft 10 ft (1.2 m 3 m)	deciduous	shrub border, courtyard
Rosa gallica	shrub	5–9	3 ft 3 ft (1 m 1 m)	deciduous	shrub border, woodland garden
Rosa moyesii	shrub	5–9	4 ft 6 ft (1.2 m 2 m)	deciduous	shrub border, woodland garden, cut fruiting stems
Rosa rugosa	shrub	2–10	3 ft 5 ft (1 m 1.5 m)	deciduous	coastal planting, embankment, hedge
Rosa sericea var. *pteracantha*	shrub	6–10	3 ft 6 ft (1 m 2 m)	deciduous	shrub border, woodland garden
Rosmarinus officinalis	shrub	6–11	2 ft 4 ft (0.6 m 1.2 m)	evergreen	herb garden, rock garden, hedge, courtyard, container

NAME	KIND	ZONE	HEIGHT AT 5, 10, 20 YEARS	DECIDUOUS/ EVERGREEN	USES
Rubus 'Benenden'	shrub	5–9	10 ft 10 ft (3 m 3 m)	deciduous	edible fruit
Sabal palmetto	palm	8–11	2 ft 10 ft (0.6 m 3 m)	evergreen	lawn grouping, parks, streets
Salix alba	tree	2–10	12 ft 60 ft (4 m 18 m)	deciduous	stream & lake edges, boggy areas, timber
Salix babylonica	tree	5–10	12 ft 40 ft (4 m 12 m)	deciduous	lawn specimen, boggy areas, stream edges
Salix purpurea	shrub	3–10	6 ft 12 ft (2 m 4 m)	deciduous	shrub border, pond edge
Salvia clevelandii	shrub	8–10	3 ft 5 ft (1 m 1.5 m)	evergreen	rock garden, shrub border, container
Salvia greggii	shrub	9–10	3 ft 4 ft (1 m 1.2 m)	evergreen	rock garden, shrub border, container
Salvia leucantha	shrub	8–10	3 ft 4 ft (1 m 1.2 m)	evergreen	rock garden, shrub border, container
Sambucus canadensis	shrub	3–10	8 ft 12 ft (2.5 m 4 m)	deciduous	shrub border, lawn specimen
Sambucus nigra	shrub	4–10	6 ft 15 ft (2 m 5 m)	deciduous	shrub border, lawn specimen
Sapium sebiferum	tree	8–11	10 ft 40 ft (3 m 12 m)	deciduous	lawn specimen, parks, streets
Sarcococca ruscifolia	shrub	7–10	3 ft 5 ft (1 m 1.5 m)	evergreen	shrub border, courtyard, hedge, woodland garden
Sassafras albidum	tree	4–10	10 ft 70 ft (3 m 21 m)	deciduous	lawn specimen, parks, streets, aromatic oil from leaves
Schinus molle var. *areira*	tree	9–11	10 ft 30 ft (3 m 9 m)	evergreen	lawn specimen, parks, streets, plazas
Schinus terebinthifolius	tree	10–12	8 ft 30 ft (2.5 m 9 m)	evergreen	lawn specimen, shade
Sequoia sempervirens	tree	8–10	8 ft 40 ft (2.5 m 12 m)	evergreen	parks, avenues
Sequoiadendron giganteum	tree	7–10	6 ft 40 ft (2 m 12 m)	evergreen	parks, streets
Shepherdia argentea	shrub	2–9	4 ft 12 ft (1.2 m 4 m)	evergreen	hedge, rock garden
Skimmia japonica	shrub	7–10	2 ft 5 ft (0.6 m 1.5 m)	evergreen	rock garden, shrub border, courtyard
Solanum rantonnetii	shrub	9–11	4 ft 8 ft (1.2 m 2.5 m)	evergreen	shrub border, cut stems, trellis
Sollya heterophylla	shrub	9–11	6 ft 10 ft (2 m 3 m)	evergreen	courtyard, trellis
Sophora japonica	tree	4–10	6 ft 25 ft (2 m 8 m)	deciduous	lawn specimen
Sophora tetraptera	tree	8–11	5 ft 15 ft (1.5 m 5 m)	deciduous	shrub border, lawn specimen
Sorbus aucuparia	tree	3–7	6 ft 20 ft (2 m 6 m)	deciduous	lawn specimen, parks, streets
Sorbus cashmeriana	tree	5–9	6 ft 30 ft (1.8 m 9 m)	deciduous	lawn specimen, parks
Sorbus hupehensis	tree	5–9	8 ft 25 ft (2.5 m 8 m)	deciduous	lawn specimen, parks, streets
Spartium junceum	shrub	6–11	4 ft 10 ft (1.2 m 3 m)	evergreen	shrub border, screen, courtyard
Spiraea japonica	shrub	3–10	3 ft 5 ft (1 m 1.5 m)	deciduous	shrub border, courtyard, rock garden, container
Spiraea nipponica	shrub	4–10	3 ft 6 ft (1 m 2 m)	deciduous	shrub border, courtyard, rock garden
Stachyurus praecox	shrub	5–10	4 ft 8 ft (1.2 m 2.5 m)	deciduous	shrub border, woodland garden, courtyard
Stewartia pseudocamellia	tree	5–8	4 ft 15 ft (1.2 m 5 m)	deciduous	lawn specimen, woodland garden
Streptosolen jamesonii	shrub	9–11	3 ft 6 ft (1 m 2 m)	evergreen	shrub border, courtyard, conservatory, swimming pool
Styrax japonica	tree	6–9	6 ft 20 ft (2 m 6 m)	deciduous	lawn specimen, woodland garden
Symphoricarpos orbiculatus	shrub	2–9	3 ft 6 ft (1 m 2 m)	deciduous	shrub border, courtyard, woodland garden

NAME	KIND	ZONE	HEIGHT AT 5 & 20 YEARS	DECIDUOUS/ EVERGREEN	USES
Syringa × hyacinthiflora	shrub	4–9	3 ft 8 ft (1 m 2.5 m)	deciduous	shrub border, courtyard, lawn specimen
Syringa reticulata	tree	3–9	5 ft 20 ft (1.5 m 6 m)	deciduous	lawn specimen, shrub border, cut flowers
Syringa vulgaris	shrub	3–9	3 ft 8 ft (1 m 2.5 m)	deciduous	lawn specimen, shrub border, cut flowers, courtyard
Syzygium paniculatum	tree	9–11	8 ft 30 ft (2.5 m 9 m)	evergreen	lawn specimen, coastal planting, parks, streets
Tabebuia chrysotricha	tree	9–11	10 ft 50 ft (3 m 15 m)	deciduous	lawn specimen, parks
Tabebuia impetiginosa	tree	9–11	15 ft 50 ft (5 m 15 m)	deciduous	lawn specimen, parks, streets
Tamarix ramosissima	shrub	2–10	6 ft 15 ft (2 m 5 m)	deciduous	shrub border, hedge, screen
Taxodium distichum	tree	4–10	8 ft 30 ft (2.5 m 9 m)	deciduous	lawn specimen, parks, streets, boggy areas
Taxodium mucronatum	tree	9–10	8 ft 40 ft (2.5 m 12 m)	evergreen	parks, streets
Taxus baccata	tree	5–10	3 ft 20 ft (1 m 6 m)	evergreen	lawn specimen, hedge, topiary, container
Taxus cuspidata	tree	4–9	3 ft 20 ft (1 m 6 m)	evergreen	lawn specimen, hedge, topiary
Taxus × media	shrub	4–9	5 ft 8 ft (1.5 m 2.5 m)	evergreen	hedge, container
Tecomaria capensis	shrub	10–11	4 ft 15 ft (1.2 m 5 m)	evergreen	shrub border, courtyard, hedge
Ternstroemia gymnanthera	shrub	7–10	4 ft 15 ft (1.2 m 5 m)	evergreen	shrub border, courtyard, lawn specimen
Tetrapanax papyrifera	shrub	8–11	6 ft 15 ft (2 m 5 m)	evergreen	shrub border, plaza
Thevetia peruviana	shrub	10–11	4 ft 25 ft (1.2 m 8 m)	evergreen	shrub border, courtyard, lawn specimen
Thuja occidentalis	tree	3–8	5 ft 25 ft (1.5 m 8 m)	evergren	lawn specimen, parks
Thuja plicata	tree	5–8	6 ft 25 ft (2 m 8 m)	evergreen	timber (western red cedar), lawn specimen, parks
Thujopsis dolabrata	tree	5–10	3 ft 50 ft (1 m 15 m)	evergreen	lawn specimen, screen
Tibouchina urvilleana	tree	9–11	5 ft 15 ft (1.5 m 5 m)	evergreen	shrub border, courtyard, conservatory, espalier
Tilia americana	tree	3–8	10 ft 40 ft (3 m 12 m)	deciduous	parks, streets, timber
Tilia cordata	tree	3–9	8 ft 30 ft (2.5 m 9 m)	deciduous	lawn specimen, parks, streets, timber
Trachycarpus fortunei	palm	8–11	3 ft 12 ft (1 m 4 m)	evergreen	lawn grouping, shrub border, courtyard, parks
Tristaniopsis laurina	tree	10–11	8 ft 25 ft (2.5 m 8 m)	evergreen	lawn specimen, parks, streets, stream banks
Tsuga canadensis	tree	3–9	6 ft 20 ft (2 m 6 m)	evergreen	lawn specimen, parks, topiary, Christmas tree
Ugni molinae	shrub	8–10	5 ft 12 ft (1.5 m 4 m)	evergreen	shrub border, lawn specimen, hedge, screen
Ulmus americana	tree	3–9	10 ft 40 ft (3 m 12 m)	deciduous	parks, streets, timber
Ulmus parvifolia	tree	4–9	8 ft 60 ft (2.5 m 18 m)	deciduous	lawn specimen, park, courtyard
Vaccinium corymbosum	shrub	3–9	4 ft 6 ft (1.2 m 2 m)	deciduous	shrub border, woodland garden
Vaccinium ovatum	shrub	7–10	2 ft 8 ft (0.6 m 2.5 m)	evergreen	shrub border, cut foliage
Viburnum × bodnantense	shrub	7–10	3 ft 10 ft (1 m 3 m)	deciduous	shrub border, courtyard, woodland garden
Viburnum × burkwoodii	shrub	5–10	3 ft 10 ft (1 m 3 m)	evergreen	shrub border, courtyard, woodland garden
Viburnum × carlcephalum	shrub	5–9	3 ft 8 ft (1 m 2.5 m)	evergreen	shrub border, courtyard, woodland garden
Viburnum carlesii	shrub	5–8	2 ft 5 ft (0.6 m 1.5 m)	deciduous	shrub border, courtyard, woodland garden
Viburnum dentatum	shrub	2–9	6 ft 15 ft (2 m 5 m)	deciduous	shrub border, informal hedge
Viburnum opulus	shrub	2–10	6 ft 12 ft (2 m 4 m)	deciduous	shrub border, woodland garden

NAME	KIND	ZONE	HEIGHT AT 5 & 20 YEARS	DECIDUOUS/ EVERGREEN	USES
Viburnum plicatum	shrub	5–9	3 ft 10 ft (1 m 3 m)	deciduous	shrub border, courtyard, woodland garden
Viburnum prunifolium	shrub	3–9	5 ft 15 ft (1.5 m 5 m)	deciduous	shrub border, hedge, screen
Viburnum tinus	shrub	7–10	4 ft 12 ft (1.2 m 4 m)	evergreen	hedge, shrub border, coastal planting, courtyard
Vitex agnus-castus	shrub	7–9	6 ft 20 ft (2 m 6 m)	evergreen	shrub border, courtyard
Vitex lucens	tree	9–11	6 ft 25 ft (2 m 8 m)	evergreen	lawn specimen, parks, streets
Vitex negundo	shrub	6–11	6 ft 15 ft (2 m 5 m)	evergreen	shrub border, courtyard
Weigela florida	shrub	4–10	6 ft 10 ft (2 m 3 m)	deciduous	shrub border, courtyard
Westringia fruticosa	shrub	9–11	4 ft 6 ft (1.2 m 2 m)	evergreen	coastal planting, courtyard, hedge, plaza
Xanthoceras sorbifolium	shrub	4–10	6 ft 20 ft (2 m 6 m)	deciduous	courtyard, lawn specimen
Yucca baccata	shrub	9–11	3 ft 5 ft (1 m 1.5 m)	evergreen	courtyard, container
Yucca elephantipes	tree	10–11	3 ft 12 ft (1 m 4 m)	evergreen	courtyard, plaza, lawn specimen
Yucca filamentosa	tree	4–10	3 ft 6 ft (1 m 2 m)	evergreen	lawn specimen, courtyard
Yucca gloriosa	shrub	7–10	30 in 10 ft (75 cm 3 m)	evergreen	container, courtyard
Yucca recurvifolia	shrub	8–11	6 ft 10 ft (2 m 3 m)	evergreen	lawn specimen, parks, streets
Zelkova serrata	tree	4–10	6 ft 40 ft (2 m 12 m)	deciduous	lawn specimen, parks, streets
Ziziphus jujuba	tree	7–10	8 ft 40 ft (2.5 m 12 m)	deciduous	lawn specimen, courtyard, orchard

INDEX